God's People on the Move

God's People on the Move

Biblical and Global Perspectives
on Migration and Mission

edited by
VanTHANH NGUYEN
and JOHN M. PRIOR

PICKWICK *Publications* · Eugene, Oregon

GOD'S PEOPLE ON THE MOVE
Biblical and Global Perspectives on Migration and Mission

Pickwick Publications
An Imprint of Wipf and Stock Publishers
199 W. 8th Ave., Suite 3
Eugene, OR 97401

www.wipfandstock.com

ISBN 13: 978–1-62564–079-6

Cataloging-in-Publication data:

God's people on the move : biblical and global perspectives on migration and mission / edited by vanThanh Nguyen and John M. Prior.

xviii + 186 p. ; 23 cm. —Includes bibliographical references and index.

ISBN 13: 978–1-62564–079-6

1. Emigration and immigration—Religious aspects—Christianity. 2. Globalization—Religious aspects—Christianity. 3. Missions—History—21st century. I. Title.

BR115.G59 G67 2014

Manufactured in the U.S.A.

Dedicated to
Strangers, Migrants, and Refugees!

Contents

Contributors

Philemon Gibungula Beghela, Ph.D., holds a doctorate in missiology from the University of South Africa (UNISA). He is a researcher at UNISA and a Mennonite pastor.

Robert L. Gallagher, Ph.D., is an associate professor of Intercultural Studies, Chair of the Intercultural Studies department, and Director of the M.A. (Intercultural Studies) Program at Wheaton College Graduate School in Wheaton, Illinois. He co-edited two books with Paul Hertig: *Mission in Acts: Ancient Narratives in Contemporary Context* (Orbis, 2004) and *Landmark Essays in Mission and World Christianity* (Orbis, 2009).

Sarita D. Gallagher, Ph.D., is an assistant professor of religion at George Fox University in Newberg, Oregon. She served as a missionary with the CRC Churches International in Papua New Guinea and Australia. She is the author of *Abrahamic Blessing: A Missiological Narrative of Revival in Papua New Guinea* (Pickwick, 2014).

Craig Steven Hendrickson, Ph.D., is an adjunct instructor in Intercultural Studies at Fuller Theological Seminary in Pasadena, California, and a trainer and leadership partner with the Arrow Leadership Program. He is also the Athletic Chaplain and College Life Coordinator at North Park University in Chicago, IL.

Paul Hertig, Ph.D., is a Global Studies Professor at Azusa Pacific University (APU), Azusa, California. He co-edited two books with Robert Gallagher: *Mission in Acts: Ancient Narratives in Contemporary Context* and *Landmark Essays in Mission and World Christianity*.

Timothy A. Lenchak, S.V.D., S.Th.D., holds a Licentiate from the Pontifical Biblical Institute and a Doctorate from the Pontifical Gregorian University in Rome. He is the author of *"Choose Life!": A Rhetorical-Critical Investigation of Deuteronomy 28, 69–30*; *The Spirituality of the Psalms* (co-edited with Carroll Stuhlmueller); and a regular contributor to *The Bible Today*. He is currently the president of Divine Word College in Epworth, Iowa.

vanThanh Nguyen, S.V.D., S.Th.D., is an associate professor of New Testament Studies and the Director of the Master of Divinity Program at Catholic Theological Union in Chicago, Illinois. He is the author of *Peter and Cornelius: A Story of Conversion and Mission* (Pickwick, 2012) and *Stories of Early Christianity* (Ligouri, 2013). Since 2013 he has been the convenor of the Bible Studies and Mission (BISAM) study group of the International Association for Mission Studies (IAMS).

John M. Prior, Ph.D., lectures in the contextual theology post-graduate programme at St. Paul's Institute of Philosophy Ledalero, Indonesia. He is a board member of the Intercultural Bible Collective (Vrije Universiteit, Amsterdam). From 2004–2012 he was convenor of the Bible Studies and Mission (BISAM) study group of the International Association for Mission Studies (IAMS). John is also an Honorary Researcher at MCD University of Divinity, Melbourne.

Amy C. West, Ph.D., is a Senior Scripture Engagement Consultant with SIL International. She facilitates workshops and seminars that focus on helping people use God's Word to speak to the challenges of their culture.

George M. Wieland, Ph.D., is the Director of Mission Research and Training at Carey Baptist College, Auckland, New Zealand, where he also taught New Testament Studies for several years. He has worked in cross-cultural mission in Brazil and in pastoral and community ministry in the United Kingdom. He is the author of *The Significance of Salvation: A Study of Salvation Language in the Pastoral Epistles* (Paternoster, 2006).

Introduction

—vanThanh Nguyen and John M. Prior

On the highways and byways of every continent, hundreds of millions of immigrants are constantly on the move.[1] Because of growing inequalities of wealth caused by unregulated economic globalization, political and ethnic conflicts, environmental degradation, instant communication, and viable means of transportation, more and more people are migrating than ever before. Crossing international borders, whether compelled or voluntarily, is a major characteristic of our present epoch. No countries or regions are immune from this reality. Facing the growing scope, complexity and impact of the current worldwide phenomenon, *God's People on the Move* seeks to develop appropriate biblical and missiological responses to the issue of human migration and dislocation.

Migration is by no means a recent happening. The Bible is filled with stories written by, for, and about strangers, migrants and refugees. It begins with the first human parents being exiled from Paradise and ends with the prophet John in exile on the island of Patmos envisioning all peoples migrating to the New Jerusalem. Encapsulated between these two bookends, namely Genesis and Revelation, are stories of God's people constantly being purified and transformed as they struggled to find their way home to be with their creator. Thus, one scholar correctly noted that the Bible is essentially "a literary tapestry woven from the stories of migrants."[2] Since the Bible is the

---

1. The United Nations Statistics Division collects statistics on international migration flows and on the stock of migrant population through the *Demographic Yearbook* data collection system. See, *International Migration Report 2013* at http://www.un.org/en/development/desa/population/publications/migration/migration-report-2013.shtml (accessed January 3, 2014).

2. Hoppe, "Israel and Egypt," 209.

word of God and the ultimate authority of faith and practice, contributors to this volume will turn to the Judeo-Christian Scriptures to search for guidance and attend responsibly to the issues of human dislocation. The purpose of this selection of articles is to offer fresh perspectives on these historic global realities and provide a biblical spirituality for immigrants as well as a missional theology of migration. Since every migrant is a potential missionary, migrants are not simply objects, but also agents of mission.

The book is divided into two major sections. Part one, "Biblical Perspectives on Migration and Mission," contains six articles that focus on various biblical themes or texts that deal with migration and mission. In chapter one, *Sarita Gallagher* explores the relationship between the mission of God and Abraham's life as a foreign migrant. In the narrative of Genesis, Abraham enters as a nomadic foreigner called by God as a representative of the nations for the nations. Of unknown ethnic heritage, the biblical text is remarkably silent on Abraham's prior history, listing no personal achievements, no remarkable character traits, and no religious background. Yet it is through this unknown migrant that God chose to proclaim his greatest blessing, declaring that "in [Abraham] all the nations of the earth will be blessed" (Gen 12:3). The missiological exploration of the person of Abraham usually ends with this divine proclamation, however this is simply the beginning of the outworking of God's missional promise during Abraham's lifetime. In analyzing Abraham's cross-cultural encounters as a migrant the full importance of the fulfillment of Genesis 12:3 emerges in addition to God's strategic implementation of mission from the periphery.

Chapter two, written by *Timothy Lenchak*, examines the lives of Israel's ancestors Abraham and Sarah in order to discover what attitudes the Bible has toward strangers, migrants, and refugees. Genesis pictures Abraham and Sarah as *gerim* (a Hebrew term for "resident aliens" or "immigrants") and *Habiru* (an Akkadian term for social outsiders who had neither citizenship nor legal rights). They lived lives of insecurity in a land that was promised to them but which they did not own. In their wanderings they sometimes sought hospitality from others. However, despite their outsider status, Genesis 18:1–15 reveals that Abraham and Sarah were models in *offering* hospitality. Their nephew Lot also knew how to offer hospitality in Gen 19:1–11. Hospitality is an important virtue in the Bible, and it was even incorporated into Israelite law. The God of Israel identified with the poor and the outsider and expected the Israelite to welcome even the stranger. The Book of Genesis challenges modern Christians to be hospitable toward others. If migration is characteristic of our modern age, then hospitality should be characteristic of today's Christians.

In chapter three, *Robert Gallagher* investigates the relationship between the resident alien and the mission of God. This essay claims that migration served an important function of the mission of God in the Old Testament in two major aspects. First, as detailed in the Mosaic covenant, God's people were to love the stranger in their midst, and in doing so offer an invitation to participate in the community. Second, God's people in migration were potential agents of transformation in developing faith in the LORD within those nations they came into contact. The case study of David's migrations to Gath shows the intersection of migration and mission. Because of the political turmoil within Israel, David was forced to immigrate to the city of Gath, which provided him an ongoing opportunity to intermingle with these Philistines. As a result, it would appear that King Achish was brought to some awareness of the Hebrew God, which influenced the evolving destiny of the inhabitants of that city. Whether deliberate or accidental, David showed that migration played a role in the mission of God, and should be considered as a strategy of the church today. Migratory movements of God's people continue to serve as an important facet in the spread of the Christian faith to bring about the mission of God.

In chapter four, *Paul Hertig* examines Jesus' migration in Matthew. According to Hertig, Jesus engages in the multicultural and migratory context of "Galilee of the Gentiles," rooted in a history of invasion, migration, exile, and return. He eradicates boundaries, barriers, and borders in his childhood and adulthood journeys. This study explores the nuances and contexts of the verb "withdraw" in key turning points of Matthew's gospel, depicting Jesus' movement from the center to the margin as a place of refuge and transformation. The "withdrawal" represents a redirection of Jesus' mission into uncharted territory, a rite of passage that detaches from fixed, religious paradigms and an entrance into new paradigms of mission. Of the six uses of "withdrawal," five indicate Gentile presence and activity. Jesus' "withdrawals" that separate from the old and prepare for the new, have parallels with what anthropologists call "liminality," which detaches from fixed, religious paradigms and leads to unrestricted possibilities of spirituality, transformation, and mission.

In chapter five, *vanThanh Nguyen* argues that the early Christian migration movement, whether stimulated by mission or caused by persecution, was historically a prime factor in the expansion of the Good News of Jesus Christ and the church. The case of Priscilla and Aquila will demonstrate that migration and mission were closely connected. This Judean Christ-believing-couple was constantly on the move for the cause of the Gospel. They first settled in Rome then, forced to migrate to Corinth because of the Edict of Claudius in 49 CE, relocated in Ephesus for the purpose of evangelization, and finally returned to Rome after Claudius' death in 54 CE. Having experienced the trauma and travail of displacement, up-rootedness, and migration, they knew the importance of being welcomed and providing hospitality to strangers. Consequently, the examination of this model immigrant couple can inspire every Christian who is on the move to become a potential missionary.

In chapter six, *Amy West* examines the story of Paul and Barnabas in Lystra. Ministering in cross-cultural contexts, God's people are often faced with beliefs, relational structures and ritual practices that are very unfamiliar to them. When the underlying reasons and purposes of these practices are verbalized, people have the opportunity to grapple with them. This chapter draws lessons from Paul and Barnabas' response to the Lycaonians in Acts 14. It considers the factors involved in decision-making with a special focus on Paul's plea for them to turn to the living God. It then suggests present-day applications for those in cross-cultural ministry. Two lessons are drawn from this event: the necessity of understanding the new context's rituals with their underlying relationships and beliefs and the necessity of addressing each of those elements from Scripture.

Part two, "Contemporary Issues of Migration and Mission," contains six articles that address different immigration issues around the world. In chapter seven, *Timothy Lenchak* examines the situation of undocumented workers in the United States of America. This chapter argues that the Parable of the Good Samaritan can challenge our attitudes toward unauthorized workers. Every society must decide how to deal with those who do not belong – especially those who have entered a country illegally. The temptation is to reject their presence and deny their needs. In the United States undocumented workers are designated as "illegal aliens," a term which tends to dehumanize them. Criminalizing unauthorized immigrants helps us to reject their humanity and ignore their suffering. But can Christians accept such an attitude? Jesus challenges the view that we must necessarily exclude strangers, foreigners, and outsiders, even if they are undocumented. His Parable of the Good Samaritan narrates the story of an outsider who cares for a complete stranger. It costs the outsider both time and money. The lawyer from the dominant culture who challenged Jesus reluctantly admits that the Samaritan acted as a neighbor to the victim. The question is whether or not we can learn the same lesson.

In chapter eight, *Craig Hendrickson* explores the urban culture of displacement in the North American church. He states that the culture of displacement characteristic of Western society, which is also shaping the social imagination of the church, has created significant challenges for congregations located in North America's urban centers. The chapter seeks to develop a missional theology of place for churches located in these urban environments by first briefly exploring how Americans got here; that is, highlighting how place has been deconstructed and de-valued in the North American urban context through the influence of various forces characteristic of modernity and late capitalism. He then proposes a pathway forward for churches located in North American urban environments by examining the themes of placement (land), displacement (exile), and re-placement (homecoming) in the biblical narrative. He suggests that God's desire is for local congregations to participate in his mission as a placed people in the current urban culture of displacement. The author concludes by recommending that both leaders and congregants of local churches are required to dwell with neighbors in humanized relationships, a presence characterized by reciprocal hospitality, mutuality, and interdependence, which can ultimately lead us towards embodying God's *shalom* in our communities together.

In chapter nine, *Philemon Beghela* examines the situation of francophone migrant churches in Pretoria, South Africa. There are more than 30 francophone churches in Pretoria that minister to migrants from other African countries. This chapter explores how francophone migrant Christians interpret exilic passages like Jeremiah 29 and Psalm 137 to shape their Christian identity and sense of mission in a situation of displacement. Do they play a constructive missional role by singing the Lord's song in the strange land of Pretoria? The chapter is based on interviews and focus groups conducted with members of these migrant churches. The interviews invited them to explore passages of scripture in relation to their everyday experiences and the role of the church in their lives. Complex questions of identity, faith and mission are explored, tracing the reflections of migrants on their vulnerable and uprooted existence but also on the opportunities they have for witness and service in a fast-changing urban environment. What emerges from the study is the resilient and creative witness of migrant Christian communities.

In chapter ten, *John Prior* examines the heartbreaking situation of failed migrants returning to Indonesia. The chapter details how an "intuitive reading" of the Book of Ruth by a group of HIV carriers from Flores island, Indonesia, renewed their faith. The men caught the virus as economic migrants and then proceeded to give it to their wives on returning home sick. Rejected by family and by many members of the clergy, they have formed their own support group. Coming from the interior, most were not regular churchgoers before contracting the virus. A few years ago they began reading the Scriptures regularly once a month. They easily identified with Naomi and Ruth, with their failed migration, and with the tactics they were forced to use in order to survive on returning to Bethlehem. Members of the HIV support group, originally unsupported by the institutional Church or by their extended families, have discovered in reading the Bible together a liberating Word that has rekindled a deep personal faith in the God of compassion.

In chapter eleven, *George Wieland* looks at the situation of migrants in Auckland, New Zealand. In a context of increasing demographic and cultural diversity the Christian community needs fresh direction and re-sourcing for mission. The book of Acts narrates a story of mission in which the themes of movement and migration are prominent. A missional herme-neutic that reads the biblical text within the larger story of the mission of God approaches the text in self-conscious locatedness in a contemporary mission context. As it adopts the posture of a participant in the continu-ing story of mission, it might have the potential to bring readers into an effective engagement with the biblical text that might in turn orient them towards mission in their context that is coherent with that discovered in the text. Some results of such readings in Auckland are illustrated.

Finally, in chapter twelve, *vanThanh Nguyen* examines the various cur-rent trends of migration in Asia, for example, temporary labor migrants, feminization, and highly qualified migrants and students. While the con-temporary trends of labor migration have brought "a breath of fresh air" to the region's economic landscape, the situation raises serious concerns about the inhumane treatment of the vulnerable migrant workers and their psy-chological marginalization and alienation while living away from home. It is even more heartbreaking to see the many host countries in Asia treating their very own Asian brothers and sisters as aliens and strangers without much dignity or rights. How should Christians therefore react and respond more appropriately to the migration issue today? The author turns to the Bible for guidance and inspiration. The author insists that hospitality, for example welcoming of the stranger, is the most appropriate response to migration demanded by the Judeo-Christian tradition as well as by other religions. This chapter will serve as a conclusion to the book.

The contributors of this volume are women and men from different ethnic backgrounds, working and living on all five continents. The interna-tionality of the contributors gives this volume a unique global perspective on migration and mission. Many of the contributors are either immigrants themselves or working with immigrants or migrants. Most of these papers were first presented at the 13th Quadrennial Assembly of the International Association for Mission Studies (IAMS) in Toronto, Canada (15–20 Au-gust 2012) at sessions of the Biblical Studies and Mission (BISAM) study group. Five BISAM papers that were presented in Toronto were published in *Mission Studies* 30.2 (2013), the journal of IAMS. Two of these articles reappear in this edited collection: Sarita D. Gallagher, "Abraham on the Move: The Outpouring of God's Blessing through a Migrant"; and vanThanh Nguyen, "Migrants as Missionaries: The Case of Priscilla and Aquila." We thank Brill Publishers for allowing us to reprint these two articles.

PART I

Biblical Perspectives
on Migration and Mission

1

Abraham on the Move

The Outpouring of God's Blessing through a Migrant

—Sarita D. Gallagher

"Where are you from?" This is a question that I have been asked for the past twenty-three years. Having immigrated to the United States in 1990, my still-strong Australian accent has garnered attention wherever I go. Conversations regularly begin in this way:

Stranger: "What a lovely accent. Where are you from?"

Me: "I'm originally from Australia."

Stranger: "How wonderful. How long have you lived in the United States?"

Me: "Twenty-three years."

Stranger: "But your accent is so strong!"

Me: "Yes, it is . . . ."

Immigration has long been a part of my family tradition. It originated with the forced immigration of my convict ancestors to Australia, followed by my maternal grandparents' immigration from Spain, and my immediate family's transfer to the United States. The challenges associated with immigration have also been a constant in my family history. In particular, the struggle to adapt to new cultural traditions and values, language and communication barriers, the ache of family members left behind, and the reality of always being an outsider have marked my family's journey. These challenges are familiar threads in the story of immigration.

In the narratives of Genesis, Abraham[1] was also identified as an immigrant and a stranger in the land. Like all immigrants, Abraham would have faced many of the same challenges: culture shock, social displacement, cultural confusion, and language barriers. In Genesis Abraham's status as a nomadic foreigner is significant in the overarching narrative. In fact, it is Abraham's identity as an immigrant that directly facilitates the outworking of God's blessing given to Abraham in Genesis 12:3. In this essay, I explore this integral relationship between Abraham's life as an immigrant and the fulfillment of God's promise to Abraham. It is in examining God's original declaration to Abraham—"I will bless those who bless you, and whoever curses you I will curse, and all peoples on earth will be blessed through you"[2] (Gen 12:3)—that the true missional nature and purpose of God's universal blessing is revealed.

In order to fully comprehend the missional significance of migration in Genesis, the life of the most prominent immigrant in biblical history, Abraham of Ur, must be considered. In the following section I thus examine Abraham's life as an immigrant in addition to what we know of his familial, cultural, and religious background before his encounter with God. In the second section, I examine three cross-cultural narratives in which Abraham conveys the blessing or curse of God upon his foreign neighbors. Finally, I highlight the missional implications of God's blessing being first distributed to the nations through the migratory journeys of Abraham, the wandering Aramean.

ABRAHAM THE IMMIGRANT

Through archeological evidence and ancient literary archives, biblical scholars have pieced together most of what we know about Abraham. Originally said to be from a community of nomadic tribes called the "Apiru," Abraham appears to have been a member of a group of traveling merchants who moved throughout Babylonia during the late third and early second millennium BCE.[3] Although some scholars point to the term "Hebrew," which later

---

1. For reasons of consistency the use of Abram's name "Abraham" will be used throughout this essay to refer to the patriarch both before and after his name change in Genesis 17:5.

2. The New International Version (NIV) is adopted throughout this essay unless otherwise indicated.

3. Albright, "From the Patriarchs to Moses," 7–15.

was connected with Abraham and his descendants (Gen 14:13; 39:14, 17; 40:15; 41:12; 43:32), as generating from the clan name "Apiru"[4], it was most likely not a "national designation, but rather a frequent designation. . .for a lower class of society."[5] Gerhard Von Rad explains that in "the Old Testament the expression is used by non–Israelites or Israelites for foreigners."[6] Thus, Abraham the Hebrew[7] in his very name is marked from his entrance into the land of Canaan to his dying day in Mamre, as a foreigner living in a foreign land.

Few details are given about Abraham in his literary introduction in Genesis 11:26–32. The audience is informed of the following particulars about Abraham: the patriarch was from the line of Shem, son of Noah (Gen 11:10); was the son of Terah (Gen 11:26); was the brother of Nahor and Haran (Gen 11:26); was the husband of Sarah,[8] who was barren (Gen 11:28–30); and was originally from Ur of the Chaldeans, but was now living in Hārān (Gen 11:31). Additional information is given regarding Abraham's relatives: Abraham's brother Haran had a son, Lot (Gen 11:31); Haran died in Ur (Gen 11:28); Terah died in Hārān (Gen 11:32); and Lot accompanied his grandfather to Hārān (Gen 11:31). But, the information given remains general and distant.

Although there is no indication in the text of Genesis 11:26–32 as to Abraham's religious history, there are later scriptural hints suggesting an idolatrous past. Joshua probably gives the most straightforward interpretation of Abraham's history: "Long ago your forefathers, including Terah the father of Abraham and Nahor, lived beyond the River and worshipped other gods. But I took your father Abraham from the land beyond the River and led him throughout Canaan" (24:2–3). The mention of Abraham "worship[ing] other gods" is further enforced by Abraham's continued use of some of the common religious forms of surrounding religions although he now followed YHWH. David Burnett writes:

> The conversion of Abram from his traditional religion to that of worshipping Yahweh did not mean a distinct break with his culture. In the majority of his ways Abram still lived according to the customs of his people. He set up shrines in a similar way to those erected by the people of Canaan. He established "sacred

4. Ibid.

5. Von Rad, *Genesis*, 174.

6. Ibid.

7. Abraham is identified as "Abram the Hebrew" in Genesis 14:13.

8. For reasons of consistency the use of Sarai's name "Sarah" will be used throughout to refer to Abraham's wife both before and after her name change in Genesis 17:15.

places" at Shechem (Gen 12:6), Bethel (Gen 12:8), Hebron (Gen
13:18) and Beersheba (Gen 21:33).[9]

Despite this adherence to the religious forms of his time, Abraham made a
clean break from his idolatrous past upon deciding to obey God in Genesis
12:4–9. The covenant relationship of Genesis 12:1–3 appears to dissolve any
previous religious affiliations as worshiping idols was no longer mentioned
in connection with Abraham in the biblical text.

Although Abraham was chosen by God in Genesis 11:26—12:5 the
text gives no indication as to why God would single out Abraham from all
the peoples of the world. For a person who later rose to religious acclaim
within the Jewish community, it is curious that no redeeming characteristic
is mentioned, that no note of special talents is recorded, and particularly
that no indication of Abraham's previous relationship with God is told. A
clear contrast to this literary silence can be seen in God's choosing of Noah
in Genesis 6:8–9. In this narrative, the author(s) notably describe Noah as
finding "favor in the eyes of the Lord" (Gen 6:8). Noah is moreover described as "walk[ing] with God" of being "a righteous man, blameless in
his generation" (Gen 6:9).[10] While there is still no indication as to whether
these qualities determined Noah's election, there exists imbedded in the
narrative a possible rationale for God's choice. This additional commentary,
however, is not evident in the Abrahamic narrative. Abraham, unlike Noah,
is simply presented as a man without distinction or mark. It is thus that
Abraham begins his entrance into literary fame as an unknown with no
recorded personal achievements, no remarkable character traits, and no
glorious religious past.

The sparse historical account of Abraham reinforces his role as a universal figure within the biblical text. Richard DeRidder describes it this way:
"In choosing Abraham, God created a new people from the very bosom of
the peoples of the world."[11] In God's selection of Abraham, God chooses one
of the nation's own to be a vehicle of his blessing to the nations. Charles E.
Van Engen states "All Israel knew that their forefather Abraham was chosen
by God because he wanted to do something in Abraham's life—but more
profoundly, because YHWH wanted to do something in the lives of all the
families of the earth. Israel's ancestor was not only to be an example of blessing, but a channel, means, and cause of blessing."[12]

---

9. Burnett, *God's Mission*, 57.

10. NRSV.

11. De Ridder, *Discipling the Nations*, 32.

12. Van Engen, *Growth of the True Church*, 142.

Abraham's identity as an immigrant also highlights the universal intentions of God. It was through Abraham's presence as a stranger in the land that God's mission to the nations was fulfilled. Van Engen elaborates:

> The People of Israel recognized that an important aspect of their self-understanding, their identity as a special people, derived from being strangers, sojourners, aliens, immigrants. (See, for example, Job 19:15; Ps 69:8; Eph 2:12; and Col 1:21.) God himself says to Abram, 'Know for certain that your descendants will be strangers in a country not their own, and they will be enslaved and mistreated four hundred years...' (Gen 15:13–14; see also Gen 23:4; 28:4; Exod 3:13–15; 6:2–4.). Thus an integral aspect of Abraham's missionary call to be an instrument of God's mission to the nations implied that he and his family would be strangers, aliens, sojourners, immigrants.[13]

As the Abrahamic narrative unfolds, it becomes apparent that "God would bless the nations through Abram precisely through his being a stranger, pilgrim, foreigner and immigrant."[14] In a very literal way Abraham encounters the peoples of the world as an immigrant, traveling through their land. During Abraham's lifetime, he lives among the Canaanites (Gen 12:6–8), Egyptians (Gen 12:10), Hittites and Amorites (Gen 14:13), and the Philistines (Gen 21:32–34). God in essence takes Abraham and his family to the nations. This intentionality on God's part emphasizes the importance of the fulfillment of God's promise to Abraham in Genesis 12:3. As such, Abraham and his family's very status as foreigners in the land serves as one of the primary means by which God's missional purpose comes to pass.

Abraham's decision to leave his father's household and follow God was a bold move. In leaving Hārān, Abraham transferred the wellbeing and survival of his entire household to his new God. Hermann Gunkel notes the enormity of this decision: "the ancient lives at home in the secure protection of large and small units . . . . Abroad, he is free as a bird. Expulsion is like death."[15] Recognizing the potential stress of this situation, Jonathan Magonet writes:

> When God first calls Abraham, He says, 'lekh l'kha', go away from your land, your kinsfolk and your father's house. A moment's thought will make us realize that these instructions are not a matter of geography—you cannot leave your land without first leaving behind your kinsfolk and without leaving your father's

13. Van Engen, "Biblical Perspectives," 33–34.
14. Ibid., 35.
15. Gunkel, *Genesis*, 163.

house prior to that. The sequence has to do with increasingly harder emotional decisions—from your land, from the family in which you grew up, your culture and society, to the house of your father, the strongest, most emotional tie that a person has. All of these he is asked to give up to follow a mysterious God.[16]

In obedience's to God's call, Abraham left behind all the social, emotional, and economic security that he had ever known. Von Rad explains that Abraham was called to "radically [abandon] all natural roots," systematically dismissing his general connection with the "land," his clan, his distant relatives, until finally his own immediate family is highlighted.[17] While following God proved to be a wise decision, the opening passages of Abraham's story present a man newly disconnected from all he had known and on the cusp of a world that he has yet to know.

Once in the promised land, Abraham's migratory wanderings continued. Although God declared to Abraham: "To your offspring I will give this land [Canaan]" (Gen 12:7). Soon after entering the land, a severe famine forced Abraham and his entire household down to Egypt (Gen 12:10). As a traveler, Abraham's personal decisions and circumstances led the patriarch to continually migrate across the Negev. While the covenantal promise of land was repeated throughout Abraham's lifetime (Gen 12:7; 13:14–18; 15:7–8, 17–21; 17:8), the only land that Abraham owned at the end of his lifetime was a Hittite field and cave facing Mamre (Hebron) where he buried his wife Sarah (Gen 23:19–20) and was himself later buried (Gen 25:9–10). This migratory pattern continued throughout the lives of all of Abraham's descendants, and the book of Genesis ends with the placement of Abraham's family in yet another foreign land, Egypt (Gen 45–50).

As Abraham wandered through the land of Canaan, Egypt, and Philistia, he engaged continually with the people of the land. He made alliances with them (Gen 14:15), fought alongside them in battle (Gen 14:14–24), cut covenants with them (Gen 21:22–32), bought land from them (Gen 23:3–20), and developed life-long friendships with them (Gen 14:13). In was in the midst of Abraham living among his multicultural neighbors that the fulfillment of God's covenantal promise came to pass. As an immigrant in a foreign land, Abraham walked the fine line between dependence upon God and reliance on his neighbors. In the semi-arid land, it was culturally appropriate and necessary to forge alliances with local community leaders to guarantee access to water, land, and military assistance. For Abraham, the social vulnerability of his status created a natural need for protection

16. Magonet, "Abraham and God," 162–63.

17. Von Rad, Genesis, 154.

and strategic relationships during his lifetime. "As an immigrant. . . [Abraham] would lack the support and protection afforded by the wider family network,"[18] and would constantly face the possibility of exploitation. While it took a lot of faith for Abraham to leave Hārān and follow God into the land of Canaan, it also took a lot of faith for the patriarch to depend upon God's provision in the face of the harsh realities of his nomadic lifestyle.

FULFILLMENT OF GOD'S BLESSING

It was amidst the complex interplay between Abraham's divine and human relationships that Abraham imparted the blessing and curse of God upon his international neighbors. As Abraham engaged with the peoples around him, his dependency and faith in God became key elements in determining the outcome of his cross-cultural encounters. While numerous incidents reflect this interrelationship, in this section I highlight three specific narratives which exhibit this connection between Abraham's nomadic journeys and his role as a blessing to the nations: 1) Abraham's victory over the kings of Shinar, Ellasar, Elam, and Goyim (Gen 14:1–24); 2) Abraham's deception of the Egyptian Pharaoh (Gen 12:10–20) and Abimelech the King of Gerar (Gen 20:1–18); and 3) Abraham's covenant with Abimelech of Gerar (Gen 21:22–34).

God's promise to bless the nations through Abraham is fulfilled in numerous encounters in Genesis including Abraham's victory over the kings of Shinar, Ellasar, Elam, and Goyim in Genesis 14:1–24. While living among the Amorites and Hittites outside of Hebron, Abraham the Hebrew is told of the capture of his nephew Lot from the city of Sodom (Gen 14:13). The kings of Sodom, Gomorrah, Zeboyim and Zoar had recently suffered an incredible military defeat at the hand of rival monarchs who "seized all the goods of Sodom and Gomorrah and all their food" (Gen 14:12). Upon hearing that Lot and his household were among the captured population, Abraham called upon three Amorite brothers, Mamre, Eshkol and Aner, "all of whom were allied with Abram" (Gen 14:13). While the relationship between Abraham and the Amorite brothers is not expanded upon in the text, it is implied that their allegiance bound them together in a treaty of mutual protection. Traveling with Abraham in attack, the brothers joined the patriarch's "Three hundred and eighteen trained men born in his household and went in pursuit [of the kings] as far as Dan" (Gen 14:14). Recovering all the materials and individuals captured from Sodom and Gomorrah in addition

18. Wenham, *Genesis 1–15*, 287.

to his nephew Lot and all his possessions, Abraham and his allies returned with all the plundered goods.

In the text, the success of Abraham and his allies is juxtaposed with the defeat of the four kings of Sodom, Gomorrah, Zeboyim and Zoar (Gen 14:8–12). The blessing of God is evident in this swift victory as Abraham with fewer than four hundred men defeated the five formidable kings and their armies (Gen 14:1–11). When the King of Sodom came out to meet the victorious Abraham, he offered to give Abraham all the requisitioned goods (Gen 14:21). The patriarch's response is curious as he declared:

> With raised hand I have sworn an oath to the Lord, God Most High, Creator of heaven and earth, that I will accept nothing belonging to you, not even a thread or the strap of a sandal, so that you will never be able to say, 'I made Abram rich.' I will accept nothing but what my men have eaten and the share that belongs to the men who went with me—to Aner, Eshkol and Mamre. Let them have their share. (Gen 14:22–24)

Taking "only what is absolutely necessary for the needs of his troops,"[19] Abraham indicated that his victory and current wealth were a testimony of his God's greatness alone. In this action, Abraham enforced that it is through his God that this military victory and the recovery of all the captured goods and population was possible.

In this vignette, God's blessing directly impacted the cross-cultural neighbors of Abraham. The Hebrew term "to bless," *brk*, is complex in both its original meaning and application. Used more frequently within Genesis and Deuteronomy than anywhere else in the Old Testament, the act of blessing within Genesis refers to a divine act wherein God imparts "vital power" to creation or human beings.[20] The tangible results of blessing impacted both the material and spiritual realms leading to prosperity in life and health, and in the fertility of the people, their animals, and their land.[21] Derek Kidner refers to divine blessing as "God turning full–face to the recipient . . . in self–giving."[22] This supernatural essence of blessing has also been described as the imparting of one's soul into another.[23] It is this act of imparting power and life that so distinguishes the pronouncement of blessing from that of speaking mere words.

19. Westermann, *Genesis 12–36*, 203.
20. Westermann, *Blessing in the Bible*, 18, 29.
21. Mowinckel, *Religion*, 66.
22. Kidner, *Genesis*, 52.
23. Westermann, *Blessing*, 18.

In the Genesis 14 narrative, there are several key recipients of God's blessing. First, the military victory given to Abraham by God brought tangible rewards to the kings of Sodom, Gomorrah, Zeboyim, and Zoar (Gen 14:16). Second, Abraham's allies, the Amorites Aner, Eshkol, and Mamre, experienced God's blessing as they shared in the spoils of war (Gen 14:24). Similarly, the catalyst of the entire narrative, Abraham's nephew Lot, regained his freedom and that of his entire household (Gen 14:16), again benefiting from the blessing of God upon Abraham. Finally, in addition to the blessing received by those around him, Abraham himself was blessed by Melchizedek king of Salem (Gen 14:18–20). Returning from battle, the author notes that Melchizedek, priest of the Most High God, "brought out bread and wine . . . and . . . blessed Abram saying, 'Blessed be Abram by God Most High, Creator of heaven and earth. And praise be to God Most High, who delivered your enemies into your hand'" (Gen 14:17–20). Within this narrative there are thus multiple layers of blessing that result from Abraham's covenant relationship with God and the cross-cultural alliances he developed while "living near the great trees of Mamre the Amorite" (Gen 14:13).

Although Abraham served as a vehicle of God's blessing, he also attracted the curse of God upon his cross-cultural neighbors. Judith Plaskow notes that "[the] Torah . . . makes clear that our ancestors are by no means always models of ethical behavior that edify and inspire us. On the contrary, often the Torah holds up a mirror to the ugliest aspects of human nature and human society."[24] In the account of Abraham's life, this evaluation is very much true. While there are high points in Abraham's interaction with his neighbors (e.g. Abraham's intercession for Sodom and Gomorrah [Gen 18:16–33] and interaction with King Melchizedek of Salem [Gen 14:17–24]), Abraham's cross-cultural encounters often tend to be relational miscalculations fueled by fear and a lack of faith. In fact, the unfolding events of Abraham's life often highlight God's faithfulness despite Abraham and his wife Sarah's recurring doubt, and God's justice and mercy in contrast to Abraham's deception and unethical behavior. It is within these accounts of miscalculations and error that God's declaration to Abraham that "whoever curses you I will curse" (Gen 12:3) comes into play.

These words of affliction are appropriated in the stories of Abraham's deception of the Egyptian Pharaoh (Gen 12:10–20) and of Abimelech the King of Gerar (Gen 20:1–18). In each case, God cursed the foreigners independently for acquiring Abraham's wife Sarah. In analyzing this misappropriation of Abraham's wife Sarah, Walter Brueggemann explained:

---

24. Plaskow, "Contemporary Reflection," 107.

Abraham has been told, "By you all families will be blessed."
The narrative makes clear that Abraham may indeed have the
power to cause a blessing for an outsider. But Abraham also has
the power to curse others (also in 12:3) . . . . Both Abimelech
and Pharaoh are on notice: It is dangerous business to deal with
Abraham. Something powerful is at work here, more powerful
than the father or the empire. When Abraham acts faithlessly, as
he has obviously done, curse is released in the world.[25]

This potential to release curse upon the world is the direct result of God
entering into covenant relationship with Abraham (Gen 12:3; 15:1–21). In
this treaty, God bound himself to Abraham as his protector, and source of
peace, prosperity, and victory. The repercussions of this relationship continue to be evident throughout the lifetime of the patriarchs and the nation
of Israel. Brueggemann, noting this continuation of curse and blessing in
the nation of Israel, explained: "The faith and/or faithlessness of Israel matters not only to Israel. It is decisive for the nations. In this strange way, Israel
has the capacity to impact the affairs of nations. That is anticipated in the
programmatic promise of 12:3b and now demonstrated in this narrative."[26]
It is therefore in Abraham and later Israel's covenant relationship with God
that the patriarch and the nation of Israel's actions directly impacted the
surrounding nations for good or ill.

While the potential curses of Genesis 12:3 are not listed in the text,
those witnessed in the Abimelech and Egyptian Pharaoh narratives are
decidedly destructive. Where God's blessing brings life, God's curse brings
disease (Gen 12:17) and the absence of life and fruitfulness (20:18). In the
case of the Egyptian Pharaoh, "the Lord inflicted serious diseases on Pharaoh and his household because of Abram's wife Sarai" (Gen 12:17), and in
Abimelech's household "the Lord had kept all the women in Abimelech's
household from conceiving because of Abraham's wife Sarah" (Gen 20:18).
Therefore just as the blessings of God effect real and tangible change in the
lives of its recipients, so the curse of God also results in visible suffering,
pain, and infertility. With the curse of God, as with the blessing of God,
the sovereignty of God is once again extended beyond the boundaries of
Abraham's clan.

The complexity of these deception narratives is established in the fact
that Abraham, not the recipients of the curse, wrongfully crossed ethical
boundaries. Nevertheless, God cursed the blameless targets of Abraham's
deception not Abraham himself. As Brueggemann explained, "The strange

25. Brueggemann, *Genesis*, 129.
26. Ibid.

calculus of the narrative is that Abraham's shabby action does bring curse. However, the curse is not on himself (as we might expect in a good moral lesson), but on innocent others."[27] The severity of Abraham's dishonesty is also evident from a cultural perspective as "the taking of a wife from someone was a serious crime in the ancient world, for she was not only property, she was a sexual partner who would bear children and give future to her husband."[28] Thus, by lying to both the Egyptian Pharaoh and Abimelech, Abraham directly placed them in a situation of unwitting wrongdoing. Even in the monarchs' reactions to Abraham's deception, they showed a higher sense of morality and respect for God than Abraham.[29] Yet, despite Abraham's faithless actions, God's covenantal promise to Abraham stood strong. In the face of Abraham's wrongdoing, lack of faith, and doubt, God reaffirmed the binding nature of the covenant between them. Even in the midst of Abraham's faithlessness, God's faithfulness and covenant relationship remained firm.

The great narrative twist in both accounts is that the vehicle of God's curse, Abraham, also became the means of God's restoration and blessing. In the story of Abimelech, it is Abraham who prayed to God on behalf of the cursed sovereign causing God's healing to come upon Abimelech and the females in his household (Gen 20:17). It is likewise implied in the story of the Egyptian Pharaoh that the restoration of Sarah to her husband Abraham also released his kingdom from the curse of God (Gen 12:18–20). In addition to Abraham bringing blessing upon those he cursed, Abraham himself also experienced the blessing of God in the midst of his wrongdoing. In the middle of his deception of the Egyptian Pharaoh, the biblical author wrote that "[Pharaoh] treated Abram well for her sake, and Abram acquired sheep and cattle, male and female donkeys, male and female servants, and camels" (Gen 12:16). Abimelech also showered Abraham with physical wealth in the form of sheep, cattle, male and female servants, silver, and free access to his land upon learning of God's curse upon him (Gen 20:14–16). In both cases, God's blessing fell upon the Pharaoh, Abimelech, and Abraham, through and despite the patriarch.

The Abrahamic blessing of God in the book of Genesis was also passed on through the establishment of covenantal relationships. Ironically, Abimelech King of Gerar, who was deceived by both Abraham (Gen 20:1–18) and Isaac (Gen 26:7–16), sought to establish covenant treaties with both patriarchs. Even though in later years the nation of Israel did not always

27. Ibid.
28. Holgren, "Looking Back on Abraham's Encounter with a Canaanite King," 371.
29. Wenham, *Genesis 1–15*, 291.

maintain amiable relations with non–Israelites, "during the patriarchal period we sense a very cordial relationship with the Gentiles."[30] Abraham, for
example, not only settled among the nations as a resident alien but also married "two secondary wives, Hagar (Gen 16:1–4) and Keturah (Gen 25:1),
from the local people."[31] Thus, when Abimelech approached Abraham (Gen
21:22) to establish a covenant, it would have been an accepted and usual
occurrence to receive such a request.

Abimelech's act of cutting a covenant with Abraham not only provided
him with personal security but it also gave him a powerful ally in the form
of the patriarch and his God.[32] Having been on the side of one cursed by the
patriarch's God (Gen 20:17–18), it was no surprise that Abimelech desired
to be on the side of the patriarch the next time around. In line with this understanding, Abimelech's foremost request to Abraham was that he brought
no harm upon his family or his descendents: "swear to me here by God *that
you will not deal falsely with me* or with my offspring or with my posterity"
(Gen 21:23).[33] This request made sense in light of the recent curses placed
upon Abimelech that devastated his family. With an attitude of self–preser-
vation Abimelech approached Abraham to establish a covenant.

A further insight into the rationale of Abimelech's desire to cut a covenant with Abraham comes as he professed his observation of God's blessing upon the patriarch. In explaining his request to Abraham, Abimelech
stated: "*God is with you in all that you do; now therefore* swear to me here by
God that you will not deal falsely with me or with my offspring or with my
posterity. . .and the two men made a covenant" (Gen 21:22–27).[34] As proclaimed in this statement, one of the major reasons that Abimelech sought
after a covenant relationship with the patriarch was the powerful evidence
of God's blessing upon Abraham and his descendents. Not only was this
blessing evident to Abimelech but his advisors and military leaders also saw
the clear hand of God upon Abraham's family (Gen 21:22).

As Abimelech set forth his request, he introduced the cultural practice
of hospitality to cement the deal: "Show to me and the country where you
now reside as a foreigner the same kindness I have shown to you" (Gen
20:23). By appealing to Abraham's nomadic roots where hospitality and

30. Senior and Stuhlmueller, *Biblical Foundations*, 90.

31. Ibid.

32. "Covenants in the Near East were a means by which relationships were entered
into by unrelated persons or peoples on a basis of community of interests and purpose
in order to maintain these interests and fulfill the purpose" (Berkhof and Potter, *Key
Words of the Gospel*, 25).

33. NRSV. Italics added for emphasis.

34. NRSV. Italics added for emphasis.

kindness to strangers were of highest regarded,[35] Abimelech highlighted Abraham's past faults in this area while providing an avenue for immediate rectification. Abraham, accepting Abimelech's request, simply responded "I swear it" (Gen 21:24). This sealed the alliance. After addressing a private grievance regarding a mutual water source (Gen 21:25–26), "Abraham brought sheep and cattle and gave them to Abimelech, and the two men made a treaty" (Gen 21:27). "Set[ting] apart seven ewe lambs from the flock. . . Abimelech asked Abraham, 'What is the meaning of these seven ewe lambs you have set apart by themselves?'" (Gen 21:28–29). In this question, Abimelech highlights the unique cultural differences between the Aramean and Philistine treaty rituals. Explaining his own ritual customs, Abraham responded that by accepting the seven lambs Abimelech bears witness to the fact that Abraham originally dug the well (Gen 21:30). Agreeing to this proof, "the two men swore an oath" and named their location 'Beersheba' (Gen 21:31), which meant "well of seven" or "well of oath."[36] The permanency of the treaty is finally emphasized in the conclusion of the episode with the author(s) notation that Abraham remained in the land of the Philistines peacefully for many years (Gen 21:34).

It is with this understanding of treaty between Abraham and Abimelech that the transference of the blessing of God can be witnessed. As with later Pentateuchal covenants, the cutting of a covenant with God's chosen people placed one under the protection and blessing of their God. Richard De Ridder notes:

> The bond that held Israel together as a people was more than racial: Israel was bound to Yahweh by a covenant bond. For this reason it was always possible for individuals of other nations to be admitted as members of the particularistic covenant with Israel and join with Israel in the service required by her election.[37]

Although De Ridder is referring to the establishment of later covenants between non–Israelites and the nation of Israel, this inherent characteristic of the covenant relationship was still apparent in the earlier period of the patriarchs. For when Abimelech established his covenant treaties, he came under the covering of Abraham's covenant with God. Abimelech was thus protected from the wrath of God and additionally gained the blessing of Abraham as one who was in covenant with Abraham and his descendants. It is through stories such as that of Abimelech that the blessing of God is

---

35. Selman, "Hospitality," 484.

36. Hamilton, "Genesis," 31.

37. De Ridder, *Discipling the Nations*, 47.

transferred from Abraham's family to the nations through the covenant ritual.

MISSIONAL IMPLICATIONS

The fulfillment of the blessing through Abraham in Genesis 12:1–3 reveals several distinctive motifs about the universal purposes of God. First, Abraham's central role as an ambassador of God's grace and mercy to the nations conveys God's overarching plan of redemption. Christopher J. H. Wright explains:

> [Genesis 12:1–3] is the climax of God's promise to Abraham. It is also a pivotal text not only in the book of Genesis but indeed in the whole Bible. So important is it in Genesis that it occurs five times altogether, with minor variations of phraseology. . . . Clearly, therefore, it is not just an afterthought tacked on to the end of God's promise to Abraham but a key element of it. Blessing for the nations is the bottom line, textually and theologically, of God's promise to Abraham.[38]

As a representative of the nations, Abraham becomes a means through which God touches the whole world.

Second, the physical migration of Abraham and his household points to the importance of the literal fulfillment of Genesis 12:3. Initially called from Aram, Abraham moved constantly during his one hundred years following God.[39] The patriarch was already a traveling merchant when God first called him, and he continued his migratory lifestyle up until his death. By living with and among different groups of people, Abraham literally took God's blessing to the nations. It was through Abraham's nomadic wanderings that the blessings and curses of God fell upon the communities around him. God's selection of Abraham both emphasizes and facilitates the outpouring of God's blessing among all people.

Finally, the visible and transformative power of God emphasizes his total authority over heaven and earth. As the nations witnessed God's hand on Abraham, the testimony of God's greatness was spread across the land. In contrast to the local gods, the God of Abraham was not restricted to a single geographical location. Instead, God's authority and power were boundless, present with Abraham as he traveled through the lands of the Arameans,

38. Wright, *The Mission of God*, 194.
39. The book of Genesis records that Abraham was first called by God at the age of 75 years (12:4) and died at the age of 175 years (25:7).

Canaanites, Egyptians, Hittites, Amorites, Amalekites, and the Philistines. God's power even extended beyond the person of Abraham as is evidenced in his interactions with Melchizedek, the king of Salem (Gen 14:18–20), Abimelech the king of Gerar (Gen 20:3–7), and Hagar of Egypt (Gen 16:7–14; 21:17–21). As David Bosch writes, "The entire history of Israel unveils the continuation of God's involvement with the nations. The God of Israel is the Creator and Lord of the whole world."[40]

CONCLUSION

In Genesis the life of Abraham of Ur was permanently transformed by the missional purposes of God. In this chapter, I explored how God's three-fold declaration in Genesis 12:3 was worked out during the geographical journeys of Abraham. Abraham's identity as a migrant was intrinsically bound to the outpouring of God's blessing to the nations. It was through Abraham's nomadic wanderings that the tangible and life-changing blessings and curses of God fell upon the communities around him.

40. Bosch, *Transforming Mission*, 18.

2

Israel's Ancestors as Gerim
A Lesson of Biblical Hospitality

—Timothy A. Lenchak, SVD

Today one can hardly open up a newspaper without reading an article on displacement, migration, and refugees. In 2011 more than 11.5 million people worldwide were officially classified as refugees, but countless others have been internally displaced by war, civil disturbance, and ethnic unrest or have migrated for economic reasons. Throughout history war, famine, drought, and ethnic conflict have led to displacement and homelessness. Migration seems to be a particular characteristic of our modern age. In fact Pope Benedict XVI declared, "One of the recognizable signs of the times today is undoubtedly migration . . ."[1]

Unfortunately the growing numbers of both "legal" and "illegal" migrants have resulted in increasing hostility toward the strangers who seek refuge in another country. More and more governments have placed restrictions on the acceptance of immigrants and asylum seekers. The displaced and the homeless are often seen as a threat. After all, refugees and migrants are outsiders. They do not belong and they are not wanted. There is a strong temptation to blame crime and social problems on them. The United States

---

1. Message of His Holiness Benedict XVI for the 92nd World Day for Refugees and Migrants, 2006. See http://www.vatican.va/holy_father/benedict_xvi/messages/migration/documents/hf_ben-xvi_mes_20051018_world-migrants-day_en.html (accessed August 25, 2013).

has witnessed the establishment of various citizen organizations, which oppose new immigrants and refugees, such as Numbers USA and the Federation for American Immigration Reform (FAIR).

What does the Bible say about migration? How does it view the stranger? This chapter examines the lives of Israel's ancestors Abraham and Sarah in order to discover the attitudes that the Bible or at least the Book of Genesis has towards strangers, migrants, and refugees. We will see that Abraham and Sarah were themselves migrants who sometimes experienced the hostility of the people of the lands into which they immigrated. We will also learn that hospitality is an essential biblical virtue, a virtue well practiced by Abraham, Sarah, Lot, and the people of ancient Israel.

ISRAEL'S ANCESTORS AS *GERIM*

When it comes to strangers and migration, whether authorized or unauthorized, the Bible is both consistent and clear. It proclaims that God loves strangers and expects us to welcome them: "When an alien resides with you in your land, do not molest him. You shall treat the alien who resides with you no differently than the natives born among you; have the same love for him as for yourself; for you too were once aliens in the land of Egypt" (Lev 19:33–34; see also Exod 22:20; Num 15:15–16; Deut 10:19; Ps 146:9; Isa 21:14; Ezek 47:22; Matt 25:35). Without doubt "issues like flight, migration, homelessness, exile and the search for a continuing city (Heb 13:14) belong to the most central traditions of the Bible."[2] To begin with, Holy Scripture acknowledges that God's people were descendants of *outsiders*. Ancient Israel recognized that it developed from "a crowd of mixed ancestry" (Exod 12:38), which included "foreign elements" (Num 11:4). At harvest time Israelites were required to bring their first fruits to the Temple and to declare solemnly: "My father was a wandering Aramean who went down to Egypt with a small household and lived there as an alien" (Deut 26:5). Israel's ancestors—including Abraham and Sarah, Isaac and Rebecca, Jacob and Leah and Rachel—were also displaced persons, that is, they were migrants or even refugees. In narrating their stories the Bible deals with issues such as migration, aliens, economic survival, hospitality, security, and the hostility of host populations.

Abraham and Sarah and their descendants were outsiders who never quite fit into the local Canaanite population. They had no desire to return to their homeland, since they were convinced that God had led them to a new home. They may not have been destitute, but they had to deal with

---

2. Hoffmann, "Solidarity with Strangers," 56.

jealousies, tensions, and conflicts with people who considered them to be foreigners and perhaps even "illegal aliens." In the ancient Near East during the second millennium BCE (roughly the time of Israel's ancestors) there was a special category of people called 'Apiru (in Egyptian) or Habiru (in Akkadian, the language of ancient Mesopotamia). The 'Apiru/Habiru were not an ethnic group but rather a social class, composed of refugees or fugitives, who left their own countries for various reasons. In their new homes they had neither citizenship nor legal protection, and many of them survived by becoming mercenaries or brigands.[3] The words 'Apiru/Habiru may originally have meant "fugitives" or "refugees."[4] It is important to note that many scholars have considered the word *Hebrew* to be related linguistically to 'Apiru/Habiru. It may be significant that in Genesis 14:13 Abraham is called a Hebrew, just as it may be significant that Abraham describes himself as a *ger* (the Hebrew word for "alien resident" or "immigrant") in Genesis 23:4. Various biblical texts call Israel's ancestors *gerim* (the plural form of *ger*) or describe their activities in the land as those of immigrants (Gen 12:10; 19:9; 20:1; 21:34; 32:5; 47:4; 1 Chr 29:15; Pss 39:13; 105:12–13). Other biblical passages indicate that the people of Israel, the descendants of Abraham and Sarah, were also aliens or migrants, especially when they were slaves in Egypt and when they wandered in the wilderness (Gen 15:13; Deut 10:19; 16:11–12; 23:8; 24:17–18, 19–22).

One gets the impression that Israel's ancestors lived lives of insecurity and rootlessness. Abraham and Sarah traveled through the land on a kind of inspection tour (Gen 13:17), but the impression is that they roamed from place to place because they had no real home there. Insecurity motivated many of their movements and activities. For example, Abraham and Sarah had barely arrived in their promised land when they had to abandon it. Famine forced them to enter Egypt as economic refugees (Gen 12:10). However, Abraham did not feel very secure there. He put his marriage and the promise given to him by God at risk by claiming that Sarah was his sister (Gen 12:11–19). Most likely Abraham's deception was motivated by fear, for the Egyptians were sometimes hostile toward strangers. They were not above exploiting and even enslaving the refugees who crossed their borders (Exod 1:8–14). Pharaoh's servants took notice of Sarah's beauty, which must have been exceptional (or the narrative is ironic), considering that at the time she was already 65 years old! Upon his servants' recommendation Pharaoh took Sarah into his palace, certainly to become his wife or concubine. In compensation Abraham "received flocks and herds, male and

3. Gottwald, *The Tribes of Yahweh*, 213, 401, 404–406.
4. Lemche, "Habiru, Hapiru," 7; Finegan, *Light from the Ancient Past* I, 69.

female slaves, male and female asses, and camels" (Gen 12:16). Fortunately God's intervention helped Pharaoh to realize that Sarah was Abraham's wife, and so he angrily expelled them from Egypt. Although enriched by Pharaoh, Abraham and Sarah were forced to seek asylum or resettlement in the land they had previously abandoned because of economic insecurity (Gen 12:20). Throughout their lives Abraham and Sarah continued to seek security and their own "space," that is, their own place in the land promised to them.

This is illustrated by Abraham's purchase of a small plot of land for Sarah's grave (Gen 23:1–20). Abraham was obviously not a full citizen of the place where he was living, since he was landless.[5] As an immigrant or *ger* he seems to have had the right or privilege to dwell in the land but not to own property: "Although I am a resident alien (*ger*) among you, sell me from your holdings a piece of property for a burial ground. . ." (Gen 23:4). Genesis points out that Abraham had to abandon the corpse of his wife (Gen 23:3) in order to negotiate a deal with the local inhabitants. Abraham is at a disadvantage in these negotiations, for bargaining depended on the delicate balance of give and take built upon existing and long-lasting relationships. As a foreigner and a newcomer Abraham had no previous relations with these Hittites and could not expect a positive outcome to his request.[6] After first addressing himself to all the elders at the gate, Abraham politely asks Ephron if he can buy the cave of Machpelah that is on the edge of the Hittite's field. Ephron offers to *give* the field and the cave to Abraham (perhaps a cultural act of politeness that was part of the bargaining process), but Abraham insists on paying for it. He does not want to be under obligation to anyone for Sarah's grave, and perhaps he is even willing to pay an exorbitant amount[7] for a small measure of financial independence.

Despite the purchase of the cave of Machpelah Abraham never really "settles down" in the land promised to him. He remains a migrant, as do his descendants. Abraham's son Isaac seems much more settled in the land than his father (perhaps because he was born there), yet he too is vulnerable when famine once again strikes the land. Like Abraham, Isaac immigrates to the land of Gerar, where he too tries to pass off his wife as his sister (Gen 26:6–11). Some things never change! But the story seems to indicate that Isaac and Rebecca are still strangers, still outsiders, still immigrants. Insecurity and vulnerability are their lot.

5. Vawter, *On Genesis*, 261.

6. Arnold, *Genesis*, 212.

7. We cannot be absolutely sure that 400 shekels was a rather high price for the field, but it would be neither the first time nor the last that outsiders have been overcharged for property or services. See Vawter, *On Genesis*, 264–65.

Isaac's son Jacob is easily *the* migrant of the Bible, for he is constantly on the move. He is the "wandering Aramean" mentioned in Deuteronomy 26:5. Jacob migrates first to Haran, the city of his mother's relatives, when he flees from the wrath of his brother Esau (Gen 28:10). Then, after a long sojourn in Haran, where he acquires two wives, eleven children, and numerous flocks, he again sets off for the land from which he had departed (Gen 31:19–21). Later he makes a third trek, this time to Egypt to settle with his family during a time of terrible famine (Gen 46:1–7). He dies in a foreign land, but his body is returned to Canaan to be buried in the cave of Machpelah (Gen 50:12–13).

BIBLICAL HOSPITALITY

Despite a strong suspicion of strangers, hospitality has always been highly valued in the Near East. Perhaps the deserts of the area encouraged this virtue, since the climate sometimes forced people to rely on each other (even when they did not know one another). Without hospitality survival was more difficult. Even today Arab and Bedouin hospitality is well known, and some hosts will go without eating in order to feed a guest. This kind of hospitality would have been familiar to Abraham, Moses, and David.

Abraham and Sarah, the ancestors of the people of Israel, were in need of hospitality, for they were strangers in the land of Canaan. God called them to leave their own land and culture for an unknown future in a land of strangers: "Go forth from the land of your kinsfolk and from your father's house to a land that I will show you" (Gen 12:1). Eventually Abraham and Sarah become somewhat wealthy (Gen 23:15–16; 24:10, 22, 53), but the Bible does not tell us about their economic situation when they left Haran for the Promised Land. Their wealth increased during brief stays in Egypt (Gen 12:16) and Gerar (Gen 20:14–16), but it is possible that they were poor when they first migrated to Canaan. However, even wealth could not guarantee their security if the population of the land was hostile to them.

Abraham and Sarah were not only *recipients* of hospitality. They could also be gracious hosts and knew how to offer hospitality. Perhaps the most famous example of Old Testament hospitality occurs in Genesis 18:1–15. Abraham saw three men approaching his tent "in the heat of the day" (v. 1). They were strangers, for Abraham did not know them. But he and Sarah were also strangers in the land, so perhaps he was more sensitive and open to other strangers. Despite his age (ninety-nine; see 17:24) and the heat, Abraham *ran* to meet them, so eager was he to show hospitality. He did not wait until they came to him. He recognized their need, for anyone walking in the heat of the day had to be hot, sweaty, dirty, thirsty, and tired. He offered them "a little water" (v. 4) and "a little bread" (v. 5). But actually he not only washed their feet but also served cakes made of three measures of flour (the equivalent of a bushel).[8] Then he offered his guests curds and meat from a calf that had not yet been killed (vv. 6–8). This was no snack but a banquet, and obviously it took more than five minutes to prepare. Abraham himself did not eat with them but rather served them (v. 8: "he stood by them under the tree while they ate"). He was generous, gracious, humble, full of energy, and selfless in his service of others. He is the model of the perfect host.

Whatever conversation took place before and during the meal is not recorded in the story. Perhaps the guests ate in silence, and Abraham patiently waited until the visitors began to speak. Surprisingly, after the meal the first point of conversation concerned Abraham's wife. We have to bear in mind that in that ancient culture men and women normally did not eat together, and Sarah was not present for this meal. Abraham was the host and servant, while Sarah remained within the tent and behind the scenes. Nevertheless, Sarah was involved in the preparation of the meal. A servant killed the calf and prepared the meat, but it was Sarah who baked the cakes, which were served (v. 6). Sarah certainly had servants who could have performed this chore. We know that she had at least one Egyptian slave woman, Hagar (Gen 16:1–16). But it seems that it was important for both Abraham and Sarah to be involved in this special meal. Both were offering hospitality to the three strangers who appeared at their tent one hot afternoon.

It is hard to know what a husband in the ancient Near East would have thought when his guests made inquiries about his wife. Was it merely a matter of courtesy in the culture? Or would it have been an uncomfortable subject for Abraham? How did the visitor know that Sarah was barren? Sarah heard their words from inside the tent. One can easily imagine her sitting on the other side of the tent flap listening to the conversation. She too would want to hear the latest news and find out who these guests were. After such gracious hospitality it seems that the guests wanted to offer a gift to this elderly couple: Sarah will give birth to a son within a year (18:10). When Sarah heard this, she laughed "to herself" (v. 12). After all, "it had ceased to be with Sarah after the manner of women" (v. 11). If that laughter was "to herself," how did the guest know about it? Caught in the act, she was embarrassed and even afraid (v. 15). So she quickly denied that she had laughed, but her denial was simply dismissed.[9] Abraham remained silent, but he had

---

8. Vawter, *On Genesis*, 226.

9. Abraham also laughs in Gen 17:17 when God announces to him that Sarah will

heard this promise from God before (Gen 17:16–21). Since Abraham said nothing, we have no idea what he was thinking. Perhaps he already believed in this promise. Perhaps he was skeptical, since he had heard it all before. Or perhaps he was simply being a polite host by remaining silent.[10]

The strangers in this story are no ordinary visitors, although Abraham and Sarah do not realize this—at least not at first. They are rather mysterious figures, since they say little upon their arrival and do not explain why they are traveling during the hottest part of the day. The reader knows that these are divine visitors because the narrator informs us of this: "The *Lord* appeared to Abraham by the oaks of Mamre . . ." (Gen 18:1). The visitor who announces the birth of a son to Sarah is also identified as "the Lord" in v. 13. By the time the visitors depart Abraham knows that he is speaking with God (v. 22). Normally we do not expect to be offering hospitality to God. However, Hebrews 13:2 warns us that some strangers may prove to be angelic or divine visitors: "Do not neglect to show hospitality to strangers, for by doing that some have entertained angels without knowing it." This is probably a reference to the story of Abraham's hospitality in Genesis 18.[11]

The perfect host, Abraham briefly accompanies his guests when they set out again. Here occurs an interesting dialogue between God and Abraham (Gen 18:16–33). By this time Abraham seems to be fully aware that his visitor is divine. God first reflects on whether or not the divine plan to destroy Sodom and Gomorrah should be revealed to Abraham. God decides that Abraham should be informed, since "all the nations of the earth shall be blessed in him" (v. 18). The following conversation might seem a bit tedious to us, since it describes in detail a kind of bargaining session in which Abraham intercedes for Sodom. With humility, courtesy, and also shrewdness Abraham tries to save the city by appealing to the injustice of destroying the righteous (such as his nephew Lot) along with sinners. Abraham manages to reduce the number of righteous to ten persons before the Lord ends the

---

bear him a son. So both Abraham and Sarah think that parenthood at such an advanced age is more laughable than realistic. Their reaction, of course, will be heard in the name of their son, Isaac (*yiṣḥāq*), which means "he laughs" or "he will laugh." At the birth of Isaac Sarah said, "God has brought laughter for me; everyone who hears will laugh (*yiṣḥāq*) with me" (Gen 21:6).

10. Cotter, *Genesis*, 118.

11. Ancient folklore and mythology frequently relate stories of gods traveling in disguise who receive human hospitality. For example, Ovid and Hyginus tell the story of three Roman gods (Jupiter, Neptune, and Mercury) who grant a son to Hyrieus after receiving hospitality from him (see Vawter, *On Genesis*, 226–27). Early Christian tradition also tells the story of St. Martin of Tours, who divided his cloak in order to give half to a freezing beggar who happened to be Jesus in disguise.

conversation and goes away. Unfortunately, not even ten could be found, although God saves Lot's family from destruction.

The two "men" accompanying God (Gen 18:22: see 19:5, 10, 12, 16) head off to Sodom, where they are now described as "angels" (19:1, 15). Here the narrator recounts another story of biblical hospitality (Gen 19:1–11). This time it is Abraham's nephew Lot who goes out of his way to be hospitable, although his hospitality pales in comparison with that of his uncle Abraham. The two angels arrive in Sodom in the evening, and they decide to spend the night in the public square. Lot has been sitting at the gate of Sodom, and with great courtesy he rises and bows deeply to these strangers, insisting that they spend the night in his home. Lot then "made them a feast" (19:3), but that feast consisted only of "baked unleavened bread"—a far cry from the cakes, curds, and meat offered by Abraham. Does the author deliberately contrast Lot with Abraham, who offered his guests "a little water" and "a little bread" and yet washes their feet and provides them with a splendid banquet? In any case freshly baked bread would still be appreciated by hungry and weary travelers.

At this point the story takes on an ominous tone. "The men of the city, the men of Sodom, both young and old, all the people to the last man" (v. 5) surround the house and demand that Lot hand his guests over to them so that they can sexually abuse the two strangers. Lot is aghast. In the ancient Near East guests come under the host's protection, and Lot's own honor is at stake. So he makes a shocking offer: he is willing to hand over his two daughters to the mob in order to avoid experiencing the shame of his guests being harmed (v. 8). The safety of his guests, an important aspect of Near Eastern hospitality, seems more important than the safety of his own family: "Do nothing to these men, for they have come under the shelter of my roof" (v. 8). For us moderns such an offer is not only shocking but also incomprehensible. The narrator of the story seems to be just as shocked as we are. In no way is this type of hospitality to be emulated.[12]

Lot's desperate act may be the consequence of his own insecure position in the city of Sodom. After all, he and his family were also outsiders, for they were immigrants. It's quite likely that Lot's own sense of hospitality is the result of his experience as an immigrant. The mob quickly reminds Lot that he is an outsider: "This fellow came here as an alien, and he would play the judge! Now we will deal worse with you than with them" (v. 9). The expression "as an alien" translates the Hebrew word *lāgûr*, "to live as an

---

12. Similarly the judge Jephthah's rash vow to sacrifice the first person coming from his house if he is victorious—which leads to the sacrifice of his only daughter—is no good example to follow. Rather it is seen as a foolish and senseless act. See Judg 12:29–40.

alien" or "to be an immigrant." This is the infinitive form of the verb which is related to the noun *ger*. Lot and his family were neither the first nor the last migrants to be threatened because of their outsider status. Migrants are often made to feel that they are unwelcome strangers even after decades of living in a particular place. Sometimes it takes very little for hostility and threats to rise up against outsiders. Even those born in a particular place (were Lot's two daughters born in Sodom?) might be considered outsiders simply because they are the children or grandchildren of migrants.

The people of Sodom were not very hospitable.[13] Perhaps they accepted Lot's family into their city only reluctantly, for they quickly became hostile to these immigrants. Unfortunately Sodom seems to provide a more common model of hospitality than either Abraham or Lot. All too often migrants are treated more as persons who are threats or enemies rather than as persons who are welcomed and valued.

A COMMON HUMAN VIRTUE

Hospitality is an important virtue in the Bible. Certainly the Old Testament distinguishes between various types of strangers, for not all could be integrated into Israelite society, and not all were equally welcome. Those who worshiped idols were normally perceived as enemies, for they were a threat to Israel's religious traditions. But solidarity was possible with those who were willing to worship Israel's God and to accept its ethical and religious standards.[14]

For the ancient Israelites hospitality was an important part of their culture and their lives. They knew what it meant to be strangers, outsiders, and immigrants. Thus they instinctively reached out to the outsider. Hospitality toward others was even built into their legal code. The God of Israel identified with the poor and the outsider and expected the Israelites to favor and even welcome the stranger: "There is but one rule for you and for the resident alien, a perpetual rule for all your descendants. Before the Lord you and the alien are alike, with the same law and the same application of it for the alien residing among you as for yourselves" (Num 15:15–16). Immigrants, along with widows and orphans, were provided special protection and benefits in Israelite law (Exod 20:10; 22:20; Lev 19:10; 23:22; Deut

---

13. Cotter, *Genesis*, 119–20n52, points out that other parts of the Old Testament as well as the Jewish Midrash tend to see the sin of the Sodomites not in terms of homosexuality or of a perverted sexuality but rather in terms of injustice or a lack of hospitality. See Isa 1:10; 3:9; Jer 23:14; Ezek 16:49; and *Pirkei de Rabbi Eliezer* 25.

14. Cardellini, "Stranieri ed 'emigrati-residenti,'" 141, 145–46.

14:29; 16:11, 14; 24:17–21; 26:12–13). In fact, Israelite law did not permit the return of escaped slaves to their foreign masters (Deut 23:16–17). Rather they were permitted to live freely in any part of the country. Such tolerance was not normally found in the other countries of the ancient Near East.

In the United States today hospitality is normally extended to friends and relatives whom we invite into our homes to share a meal or a conversation. Ancient Near Eastern and Mediterranean hospitality was much more likely to involve total strangers. These societies normally viewed strangers as potential enemies, and so hospitality was a necessary process of transforming an outsider into a guest. The guest, however, always remained in a marginal position, since he or she normally was only temporarily on the inside.[15] However, in ancient Israel there was a guest who became a permanent resident: the immigrant or *ger*.

Hospitality is a common human virtue, which is highly valued in many cultures. We ourselves practice hospitality every time we invite someone into our homes, our communities, and our churches. Despite the difficulty of welcoming strangers into our personal world, we do it all the time—at work, in school, on the street, in the shopping center. When we welcome strangers into our world, we also allow them to welcome us into their world. Of course, at the beginning our welcomes are always formal and polite and perhaps not very comfortable, since we don't know our guests very well. But eventually that changes as we become more familiar with them. Mexicans have a lovely expression that they sometimes use when they want a guest to feel at ease: "*Mi casa es tu casa*," that is, "My home is your home." It is unlikely that the Mexican host is literally offering his or her guest a chance to move in. Rather the suggestion is that the guest should no longer feel like an outsider or a stranger.

The proverbs of many cultures suggest that one be cautious about strangers and guests. For example, one South American proverb announces: "*Better a devil you know than a hundred strangers*." The proverb "*Fish and guests smell when they are three days old*" is cited in numerous countries, including Denmark, India, and Rumania. So it may be surprising to learn that the proverbs of some cultures reveal an appreciation of hospitality. A Chinese proverb declares: "*The delicacy of the feast is the learned guest*." A Kurdish proverb proclaims that "*Guests bring good luck with them*." One Iranian proverb seems to indicate that one should not be reluctant to welcome a stranger: "*There are three things that have to be done quickly: burying the dead, opening the door for a stranger, and fixing your daughter's wedding*." A Jewish proverb even makes the startling claim that "*Hospitality is one*

---

15. Malina, *The Social World of Jesus and the Gospels*, 228–29, 235.

form of worship." An Akan proverb (from Ghana, West Africa) states: "*The stranger never makes a mistake.*" Since the stranger has no way of knowing another's customs and traditions, he or she cannot be condemned for saying or doing the wrong thing. Hospitality requires patience. Instead of judging every word or gesture immediately, we need to practice patience until we learn what certain words and gestures might mean in a new culture. In the same way it takes time before others can understand our words and gestures without misinterpreting them.

The same attitude should characterize Americans. After all, all of us come from immigrant roots; even Native Americans are descendants of ancient migrants. All of us have ancestors who were strangers and outsiders. Our nation has accepted and incorporated numerous refugees, outcasts, and poor although they were not always welcomed with open arms. Hospitality has been and should remain an important part of our culture. And if our culture refuses to be hospitable, at least Christians in the U.S. should develop an attitude of acceptance, welcome, and hospitality toward recent immigrants, including those who are labeled as unauthorized or illegal.

CONCLUSION

The Bible leaves us no doubt: God loves the stranger, the immigrant, and those in need. God also expects us to treat the stranger and the migrant with love and respect. Israel's ancestors were migrants who experienced insecurity and hostility. Abraham and Sarah were not full citizens and never really had a place of their own. They were in need of others' kindness and generosity, yet they also knew how to display hospitality perhaps because of their own migrant experiences. Their treatment of the three strangers walking in the heat of the day shows them to be models of hospitality. Lot was also a willing host to two angels, even if his hospitality paled in comparison to that of Abraham and Sarah. The Israelites' experience of slavery in Egypt served forever as a reminder to them to accept, protect, and favor immigrants and even runaway slaves. Although Israelite law recognized that some strangers could never be acceptable, resident aliens or immigrants (*gerim*) were privileged, for they enjoyed the protection of the law and the favor of God.

Hospitality is the opposite of hostility. Although hostility is a natural response to strangers who seem to threaten our security and well-being, hospitality has also been valued in many cultures. Sacred Scripture certainly presents hospitality as an important virtue, a virtue which not only ancient Israelites but also modern Christians should develop. If migration is a particular characteristic of our modern age, hospitality should be a particular characteristic of all those who worship the God of Israel.

3

Coming to Gath

Migration as Mission among the Philistines

—Robert L. Gallagher

The most frustrating experiences of my life were at the hands of the Federal Immigration department. Having come from Australia to study at Fuller Theological Seminary in Pasadena during the early 1990s, I had to annually appear before the immigration authorities in Los Angles to renew my family's documents. I have searing memories of standing in long lines before sunrise waiting for the immigration office to open to be among the accepted daily quota of clients; followed by the human rush to the naked office upstairs where I namelessly filed my documents in a wooden slot to silently wait, never leaving the room for any reason in case my name was called and I missed my opportunity; and finally standing before the wooden authorities to answer questions of my meticulously collected documentation, only to be turned away for neglecting to provide a piece of information that was not listed in the official requirements. I then repeated the proceedings whenever I was able to obtain time off work again.

My own story of migration to the United States is one of thousands in what has become an increasing trend of transglobal migration. These stories of migration, however, are not new. In the Hebrew Scriptures, the themes of migration and intercultural encounter were significant in God's mission. After a brief reflection of the current global trends of migration,

29

the first section of the paper surveys the biblical view of the stranger, and the covenantal responsibility of Israel to love the foreigner. The second part examines the case of David's migration to the city of Gath. David's association with Gath, first as a political refugee and then as a mercenary leader, creates an affiliation with king Achish that discloses the Philistine's confessional language. The final section demonstrates how the union between migration and mission expresses itself in today's world: first, Christians loving the stranger in their neighborhood, and second, Christians in migration becoming global missionaries.

GLOBAL UPHEAVAL AND MIGRATION

We are currently living in an era of global upheaval due to widespread migration.[1] According to the 2013 annual report on global issues by the United Nations High Commission for Refugees, the refugee crisis reached the highest level in two decades with an average of 23,000 people becoming refugees each day and many more seeking asylum. By the end of 2012, approximately 45.2 million people were forcefully displaced because of human rights violations, whether through persecution or conflict. Furthermore, an estimated 7.6 million people were newly displaced across an international border or within their own nation during 2012, the highest level since 1999. Globally there were 15.4 million refugees in 2012 (an increase of 200,000 from the previous year) and 936,740 asylum seekers (up from 895,000). No wonder that there is a surging interest in the study of Christian mission and migration, from academic societies, such as the International Association for Mission Studies who at their 2012 Toronto Assembly focused on the subject, "Migration, Human Dislocation, and the Good News,"[2] to Pope Francis' exhortation, "Migrants present a particular challenge to me, since I am the pastor of a Church without frontiers, a Church which considers itself mother to all."[3]

---

1. See Koser (*International Migration*) for an overview of the migration issue and Johnson, and Bellofatto, "Key Findings of Christianity in Its Global Context," 157–64. Johnson and Bellofatto ("Migration, Religious Diasporas, and Religious Diversity," 3–22) show how the global movement of peoples shapes religious diversity through a number of key issues such as globalization and secularization.

2. Anderson, *Witness to World Christianity*, 125–26, 197.

3. Francis I, *Apostolic Exhortation Evangelii Gaudium* (24 November, 2013), 4: AAS 210 (2013), 164. In particular, Pope Francis stated, "We Christians should embrace with affection and respect Muslim immigrants to our countries in the same way that we hope and ask to be received and respected in countries of Islamic tradition" (*Apostolic Exhortation Evangelii Gaudium* [24 November, 2013], 4: AAS 253 [2013], 188).

BIBLICAL VIEW OF THE STRANGER

These statistics of our contemporary world prime us to ask the question: What is the Christian's role in the midst of such global change and suffering? When turning to Scripture, we discover that the plight of migrants was peppered throughout biblical history from the expulsion of Adam and Eve from the Garden of Eden to the apostle John who was forced to reside on the isle of Patmos.[4] In the Hebrew Scriptures the word *gêr* was used to describe a variety of people—the alien, foreigner, sojourner, and stranger—and was recorded ninety-two times, with the majority of occasions found in the Pentateuch. The Hebrew word *gêr* could be best translated as "guest," which by implication spoke of a "foreigner" or "resident alien," and had its linguistic roots in the concept of a sojourner turning aside from traveling on the road to seek lodging as a guest.[5]

God was continuously seeking to bring the nations to himself.[6] With Israel's exodus from Egypt and the subsequent giving of the Law, God presented an occasion for the "mixed multitude who also went up with them [Israel]" (Exod 12:38) to follow the living God.[7] In the pentateuchal law, God provided an opportunity for the *gêr* of Egypt to participate in the community, together with other peoples that Israel would encounter on their journey.[8] The "stranger" was assumed to be a non-Israelite residing with God's people, and as such, was subject to Israelite law, including the religious decrees. This shows the holistic integration of the *gêr* into the LORD's community. Arie Noordtzij notes:

> In the land of the Lord there could be only one law, viz., that which he had given. This juridical equivalence between alien and native-born was an exception in the ancient world, and in this respect divine revelation was far ahead of the norms of civilization. It took centuries before aliens were humanly treated, and there are often failures in this regard today.[9]

---

4. See Carroll R. ("Biblical Perspectives on Migration and Mission," 9–26) for a consideration of the pertinent biblical material of diaspora mission, particularly the patriarchal narratives of Genesis and Israel's Law.

5. Okoye, *Israel and the Nations*, 155–56.

6. Compare Wright, *The Mission of God*, 159, 422.

7. All scriptural texts are taken from the New American Standard Bible unless otherwise noted.

8. See Carroll R., *Christians at the Border*, 99.

9. Noordtzij, *Leviticus*, 249.

In addition, God desired to use the *gêr* to draw other nations to himself.[10] David I. Smith and Barbara Carvill affirm, "Israel's calling has both an outward and an inward focus. Beyond her borders she is to be a light to the other nations; within her borders she is to be a blessing to strangers, to those from other nations who have taken up residence in her midst."[11]

Love of the Stranger

In Deuteronomy, God clearly outlines Israel's responsibility to the *gêr* framed by the exhortation to walk in all the ways of the LORD and love the foreigner. In communicating the revelation of Mount Sinai, Moses said of God, "He defends the cause of the fatherless and the widow, and loves the foreigner residing among you, giving them food and clothing. And you are to love those who are foreigners, for you yourselves were foreigners in Egypt" (Deut 10:18–19, NIV). God commanded his people to love the foreigner (*gêr*) as they love one another (Lev 19:33–34);[12] and reminded them of their former situation as emigrants in a strange country to conjure empathic memory, as well as a covenantal reminder of God's provision. John E. Hartley says of this passage:

> A powerful motivation was joined to this command. Israel was to remember that she had been a slave in a foreign land when God reached down and delivered her. Memory was a key means for understanding God's demands on his people. Meditation on what God had done for them reminded the community of God's great outreaching love, which had been expressed in his deliverance of Israel from Egyptian bondage and his supplying their needs in trying circumstances. Since God had done so much for his people, he was in a position to ask them to do as much for others. When Israel heeds this call, they were acting like God to others. That is, to those whom they showed kindness they were both communicating God's love and making themselves holy as God.[13]

10. See De Ridder, "Old Testament Roots of Mission," 47; Glasser, *Announcing the Kingdom*, 78; and Kaiser, *Mission in the Old Testament*, 7–9, 20.

11. Smith and Carvill, *The Gift of the Stranger*, 11.

12. The Hebrew word, *'āhab*, meaning "to have affection for," was translated from the First Testament to English language Bibles as the word "love," and was the same word that was used to exhort Israel to love God, neighbor, and stranger (Deut 10:12, 15, 19; Lev 19:18, 34).

13. Hartley, *Leviticus*, 323–24. Also see Biddle, *Deuteronomy*, 179, 183; and Craigie, *The Book of Deuteronomy*, 207.

Israel's love of the foreigner was motivated by their past and the nature of God. Love was synonymous with respect of the LORD and involved actions of service. As God loved the alien, so Israel was to extend its love to the stranger living in their society, and thus share God's concerns and further the program of redemption to the needy.

Compassion to the Stranger

This refrain of Israel's slavery in Egypt was repeated throughout the Pentateuch in their connection with the foreigner as God directed the people not to: mistreat or oppress (Exod 22:21; 23:9), forbid justice (Deut 24:17–18), take advantage by not paying wages on time (Deut 24:14), and give unfair treatment in trials (Deut 1:16–17). Embedded in Israel's covenantal stipulations was God's example of how to love the foreigner as he commanded provision for their physical needs. They were allowed to glean after a harvest (Lev 19:9–10; 23:22; Deut 24:17–22), and every three years the community were to give one tenth of their produce to the foreigner, as well as to the Levites and widows (Deut 14:28–29; 26:12–13). Additionally, Israel was to love the stranger by including them in the feasts of God (Deut 5:14; 16:11, 14; 29:9–14), involving them in the Passover (Exod 12:48; Num 9:14), giving them the right to a Sabbath's rest (Exod 20:10; 23:12), and allowing them to take the harvest produced from the rested land every seven years (Lev 25:6). Hartley elaborates:

> Farmers were not to harvest the corners of their fields in order that the poor, the unfortunate, and foreigners might have the opportunity to come to the fields and gather grain. The formulation of these decrees was amazing in the concern for the dignity of the poor. The poor were given access to a food supply, but not as a hand-out; they had to go out to a harvested field and pick up the gleanings. On their way home they could hold their heads high, for they had labored for that which they were bringing home.[14]

Dignity was maintained in the course of provision. Peter C. Craigie adds, "The farmers who had allowed some produce to remain, were not simply being charitable to those less fortunate than themselves; they were expressing their gratitude to God, who had brought them out of slavery in Egypt and given them a land of their own."[15]

---

14. Hartley, *Leviticus*, 323.

15. Craigie, *The Book of Deuteronomy*, 311.

Religious Observances of the Stranger

The protection and endowment offered the foreigners among God's nation was proportional to their obedience of Israel's religious laws. They needed to know the Law, and live by the Law, to receive the benefit of the Law (Lev 24:22). They would receive the same punishment as Israel for breaking the LORD's covenant agreement, which was excommunication for blasphemy (Num 15:30–31) and death for violating the holiness of God (Lev 24:10–16; 20:2). They were required to be ceremonially clean (Num 10:19), and follow the dietary restrictions (Exod 12:19; Lev 17:10–15) and sexual laws of Israel (Lev 18:6–23, 26). And in doing so, they were afforded the opportunity to participate in the spiritual journey of the nation, as they changed allegiance from their foreign gods to the one, true, living God.

Moreover, the foreigner could offer sacrifices for the atonement of their sin, as well as sacrifices for unintentional sin (Num 15:26, 29). In accordance with the Law of Israel, the stranger was invited to offer sacrifices that enabled them to enter fully into the spiritual life of the community of faith and receive God's mercy (Lev 17:8–9; 22:18–20; Num 15:13–16). Lastly, the foreigner was to gather with the whole assembly of Israel every seven years as the Law was reread during the Feast of Tabernacles (Deut 31:9–13). Iain Provan confirms that one of the most prevalent themes in the Book of Kings was the concept that there was only one true God and that "the LORD demands exclusive worship . . . by Israelite and foreigner alike."[16]

So far we have demonstrated that the LORD's covenant directed Israel to love those who were outsiders as God's people remembered that they also were strangers in Egypt. God continually prompted the holy nation regarding their former situation as emigrants to invoke empathic memory and announce their responsibilities to the covenantal law. As Israel dispensed God's love to the stranger they fulfilled their obligations to the Mosaic covenant. Both challenges were operating simultaneously: love the immigrant by obeying God's instructions; and the corollary, obey the commandments and love God.

Having established a biblical framework of the stranger in the Old Testament, this chapter now turns to the relationship between the resident alien and the mission of God. In particular, we will study David's involvement with the citizens of Gath through the vehicle of migration. David, as an asylee in Gath, became an ensuing influence in that city, resulting in some of the Gittites becoming an important part of God's salvation history.[17] Walter

---

16. Provan, *1 and 2 Kings*, 11–12.

17. A Gittite was an inhabitant of Gath. See 2 Samuel 21:19 and 1 Chronicles 20:5.

C. Kaiser is persuaded that it was God's intent to bless the world by way of David and his dynasty, which was a foreshadowing of the rule of God on earth due to the coming Messiah.[18] The next segment will offer an explanation of the personal history of David with the Philistines of Gath before progressing to observations of David's interface with king Achish. This contact first occurred when David was a political refugee, and then as the leader of a band of mercenaries operating from Ziklag, the town gifted to him by the Gittite monarch. Because of David's migration to Gath he became an agent of transformation in the developing faith of Achish the ruler of the city, which was witnessed in the Philistine king's confessional language.

PERSONAL HISTORY WITH GATH

In the valley of Elah, David, the shepherd boy, defeated Goliath, the veteran warrior. This time the mode of God's rule was not the Ark of the Covenant or milch cows pulling a cart, but a Bethlehemite lad with his slingshot.[19] It started with physical warfare that was implanted in spiritual conflict. God's intention for the battle was that all the earth might know that he existed, and held all things in his control. This included the Philistines.[20] God proclaimed his sovereign purposes through these events in the valley of Elah.[21] Over the years the Philistines remembered this military defeat in association with David and Israel's God. Consistent with historical relations between Israel and Philistia, the instrument of remembrance was a narrative, yet unlike previous incidences, the genre was a poetic song (cf. 1 Samuel 4:8; 6:6).

As Israel's army returned from the battle in triumphant procession, they made their way towards the national capital of Gibeah. Some of the women came out of the villages, dancing, playing musical instruments, and singing a song that would become the number one hit of the Israelite charts. "And the women sang as they played, and said, 'Saul has slain his thousands, and David his ten thousands'" (1 Sam 18:7). In Saul's mind the

18. Kaiser, *Mission in the Old Testament*, 26.

19. See Brueggemann (*David's Truth*, 21–27) for an exposition of "David and Goliath (1 Samuel 17)."

20. Compare Anderson, *1 & 2 Samuel*, 137, 203; and McCarter, *II Samuel*, 256, 435.

21. David took the head of Goliath and displayed it at the Jebusite stronghold of Jerusalem declaring that after 500 years of resistance to the Israelites, the days of Jebusite occupancy were numbered (1 Sam 17:54). Psalm 132 was David's explanation of the vision God gave him for the Ark to be installed on Mount Zion in Jerusalem. The first royal action of David was to attack the Jebusite stronghold and possess it (2 Sam 5:6–10 and 1 Chr 11:4–9). David's second decree was to search for the lost Ark that had been missing for over 20 years and bring it to Jerusalem (2 Sam 6:1–12 and 1 Chr 13:1–14).

song triggered an emotional spiraling of anger, suspicion, rage, fear, and dread towards David, since he deduced, "Now what more can he [David] have but the kingdom?" (1 Sam 18:8).[22] What then began as an attempted murder of Saul's beloved armor bearer, ended in paranoia and depression, as the counterfeit king sought the guidance of the medium of En-dor and committed suicide on Mount Gilboa.

POLITICAL REFUGEE IN GATH

In desperate fear of his life, David made a series of unwise decisions that God accommodated. One of those choices eventually led to a continuance of intercultural encounters between David's family and the people of Gath that resulted in generations of Philistines submitting to the Reign of God. For the next ten years, however, David was a political refugee protecting himself from the tyrannical Saul in isolated pockets of Israel and the region of Gath. Under life-threatening conditions, David and his family and friends migrated from place to place hiding from Saul's dictatorship.

When David realized that Saul, his former patron, was determined to murder him in Gibeah, he sought the wisdom and protection of Samuel, his spiritual mentor. From Ramah David scrambled back to the national capital to design political intrigues with Jonathan, Saul's son, and then fled to Nob to seek the security of Israel's priesthood. David failed to recognize the divine protection of God, running as a little bird seeking refuge from his attacker. Through his scheming he nearly got Jonathan killed, and indirectly caused the massacre of the priestly community of Nob by Doeg the Edomite. David, the fugitive escaping from Saul, then went into hiding in Gath, the home town of Goliath, the renowned soldier he had killed only months before. Why was David scuttling to the enemies of Israel for protection? And why hide in Gath of all places? Why not seek refuge in one of the other four confederate cities of Philistia? How could he possibly think that he could conceal himself among a beardless Aegean people who were unusually tall and had olive complexion while David himself wore a beard, was probably much shorter, and had a ruddy complexion?

In Gath, David quickly discovered that it was difficult to hide among these Philistine giants. The servants of Achish, the king of Gath, saw the Israelite and proclaimed to their ruler, "Is this not David the king of the land? Did they not sing of this one as they danced, saying, 'Saul has slain

22. See Saul's range of emotions in 1 Samuel 18:8, 9, 10, 12, 15, 29 concerning his full realization that David was his replacement as the king of Israel, even though the LORD had forewarned Saul (1 Sam 13:13–14; 15:23, 26, 28, 35; 16:1; 28:15–19).

his thousands, and David his ten thousands?'" (1 Sam 21:11). The national song of Israel had crossed the adversary's border carrying the message of the saving power of the Hebrew God.[23] On recognizing David, the leaders of Gath incorrectly thought that he was their enemy's king, yet accurately remembered the song. Bill T. Arnold points out that the Philistines' identification of David as "a king of any kind was ironic," and shows the fact that all of these events were a part of God's divine plan.[24]

Again, David in great fear of his life, decided to lie his way out of his dangerous predicament; this time not through words, but by drama. David pretended to be insane by dribbling on his beard and scribbling on the doors of the city's gates, knowing that the Philistines believed that the gods spoke through the mentally unstable; and thus would not imprison or slay him.[25] Reinforcing this false portrayal was the Israelite belief that the beard was the symbol of masculine dignity and worth. It was shared cross-cultural knowledge that no Israelite male in his right mind would ever spit on his beard.[26] Hence, Achish released David (with sarcastic humor), and an intriguing relationship began between the two leaders. Ralph W. Klein summarizes this episode: "Thanks to David's wild behavior, the Philistine king did not execute David or imprison him, but sent him on his way unharmed. Would not the narrator see in this protection by a foreigner the hand of YHWH, just as the priest Ahimelech had delivered David by giving him food and a weapon?"[27]

MERCENARY LEADER OF GATH

David returned to Israel and the irrational king Saul relentlessly continued to pursue the one who threatened to remove him from power. It was because of this baseless hunt of David's life that in his last dialogue with Saul, the refugee acknowledged that if the chase continued he would be forced to live beyond the reach of Saul; in a place where the LORD was not worshiped.

---

23. The irony was that the song was carried to Israel's enemies across national borders, which expressed the unlimited geographic authority of the Hebrew God. This was a continuation of the manifestations of God's power when the Ark was brought as a trophy of war to the temple of Dagon (1 Sam 5:1–12).

24. Arnold, *1 & 2 Samuel*, 311.

25. See Malony, "Mad," 1960–61; and Harrison, "Madness," 220–21. Also see Ackroyd, *The First Book of Samuel*, 173; Brueggemann, *First and Second Samuel*, 156; Klein, *1 Samuel*, 216–18; and McCarter, *1 Samuel*, 355–58.

26. See Reed, "Beard," 368. Compare 2 Samuel 10:4–5, and contrast Nelson, *First and Second Kings*, 17.

27. Klein, *1 Samuel*, 218. See Halpern, *David's Secret Demons*, 20.

David was being driven from God's presence and forced to live where pagan gods were served. As David once fled from Gibeah and the royal court of Saul, he was now compelled to escape from the desert hideouts of southern Judah. This was David's last and only hope of survival.[28]

David now revisited Gath with six hundred mercenaries, and offered his mobile army for Achish's service. For sixteen months David pretended that he was attacking the enemies of Gath, yet in reality he was helping to protect his own people. In the midst of such deception, Achish only saw David's loyalty, and consequently offered him the city of Ziklag and an opportunity to be his "bodyguard for life" (1 Sam 27:6, 12; 28:2).[29] Baruch Halpern asserts, "He [David] becomes the chief of the bodyguard of Achish, king of Gath. He is the ruler of Ziklag, a town subordinate to Gath. David has made the transition to abandoning his true ethnic loyalty. At least on the face of things, he is a traitor."[30]

Further, when the Philistines came to fight against Israel with the intent of thrusting their army into the Jezreel Valley, Achish took David and his mercenaries to the battle.[31] The other four confederate kings reacted in disbelief and anger at the thought of David alongside them in combat. In explanation, Achish emphasized the length of David's betrayal of king Saul while simultaneously acknowledging the loyalty of his protector. David's defeat of the Philistine armies at Elah, however, was still graphic in the kings' memories—sustained by the song of David that was rehearsed in Israel and Philistia. Hence they asked the king of Gath, "Is this not David of whom they sing in the dances saying, 'Saul has slain his thousands, and David his ten thousands'?" (1 Sam 29:5). The rhetorical question was evidence that the song, indelibly etched in the national mind of Philistia, continued to carry an understanding of David's military prowess and by implication God's sovereignty.

---

28. 1 Samuel 26:19–20. See Arnold, *1 & 2 Samuel*, 359–60.

29. P. Kyle McCarter (*1 Samuel*, 415) states that the translation of "my servant for life" (1 Sam 27:12) literally means "a slave of eternity." That is, Achish believed that David was voluntarily surrendering himself to serve him for life. Further, Peter Ackroyd (*The First Book of Samuel*, 208) notes that when Achish used the phrase "bodyguard for life" in 1 Samuel 28:2, it literally means "keeper of my head." This would indicate that the Philistine king was completely entrusting his personal safety to David.

30. Halpern, *David's Secret Demons*, 23.

31. See ibid., 78–80, 295.

ACHISH'S CONFESSIONAL LANGUAGE

We have seen that the political turmoil created by Saul of Israel forced David to immigrate to the city of Gath. This provided David an opportunity to intermingle with the Philistines that he never previously experienced. The case of David's migrations to Gath, first as a political refugee and then as a leader of a mercenary band of warriors, reveals an Old Testament example of the connection between migration and mission. The following section will demonstrate how the migrant David became a missionary of transformation as king Achish of Gath developed an awareness of the Hebrew God. Whether purposeful or unintentional, David shows that migration played a role in the mission of God.

A dialogue unfolded between David and king Achish following the Philistine kings' suspicion of David's troops participating in the battle array. In this discourse, Achish revealed his possible trust in YHWH and sincere appreciation of David, and the question remains as to what deception the Israelite was undertaking.[32] David the protagonist becomes a double agent. In interpreting this passage Walter Brueggemann reflects, "It is ironic that only Achish, most loyal to David, was the one deceived. Neither the Philistine lords nor we are taken by David's ruse."[33] The record of 1 Samuel 29:6–7 follows:

> Then Achish called David and said to him, "As the LORD lives, you *have been* upright, and your going out and your coming in with me in the army are pleasing in my sight; for I have not found evil in you from the day of your coming to me to this day. Nevertheless, you are not pleasing in the sight of the lords. Now therefore return, and go in peace, that you may not displease the lords of the Philistines."

When David objected to this dismissal from the battle, Achish addressed him, "I know that you are pleasing in my sight, like an angel of God; nevertheless the commanders of the Philistines have said, 'He must not go up with us to the battle'" (1 Sam 29:9). Achish thought that he was disappointing David by driving him away. In fact, he had become God's instrument of delivering David from an impossible losing position.[34] Halpern correctly

---

32. See David's defensive response to Achish in 1 Samuel 29:8. Mary Evans (*1 & 2 Samuel*, 122) suggests that for Achish, a recovered madman may even be seen as a token of good luck (in regards to the Ancient Near Eastern connection of madness and spiritual revelation), which would perhaps explain his readiness to accept David at face value as an enemy of Saul.

33. Brueggemann, *First and Second Samuel*, 197–98.

34. Arnold, *1 & 2 Samuel*, 387.

acknowledges, "Achish's confidence in him [David] is unbounded: Achish has made David responsible for guarding his person. And David protects his loyalty, pleading to join Achish in battle. The suspicions of the other Philistine monarchs thus rescue David from betraying either his countrymen, the Israelites, or his adopted protector."[35] The poetic song, "Saul has slain his thousands, and David his ten thousands," thus saves David from himself.

Before the battle the king of Gath used Israel's confessional language in his response.[36] Because of David's positive character traits of living an upright life, Achish acknowledged, "As the LORD [*YHWH*] lives." Could it be that because of the presence of God's person in Gath that the polytheistic king changed his religious allegiance to YHWH? The confession, "As the LORD lives," was an echo of the words of David in 1 Samuel 17:26 and 17:36 when he spoke of "the living God." Did Achish learn this declaration from his vassal lord, and was it an admission of a spiritual conviction? In other words, was Achish a convert to David's God? Quite possibly, since theological terms were used in the conversation. Reminiscent of Achish's confession was Ittai the Gittite's response to David in 2 Samuel 15:21, "As the LORD lives, and as my lord the king lives, surely wherever my lord the king may be, whether for death or for life, there also your servant will be." In this case, Joyce G. Baldwin maintains, "From his response, Ittai reveals himself to be a believer, for whom love and faithfulness were paramount."[37] Baldwin's persuasion that the commander of the Gittite forces was a "believer" stems from his oath, "As the LORD lives." Could this also be true of Achish who utters the same oath? Brueggemann admits, "David [was] moved and convinced by the foreigner's [Ittai's] words."[38]

It was not expressly stated that Achish's encounter with David led to his religious conversion. Absent from the narrative was the type of confession of Jethro the Midianite who declares in Exodus 18:11, "Now I know that the LORD is greater than all the gods." Neither was it explicitly announced that the Philistine king surrendered his cultish practices or understood the ways of God such as Naaman the Syrian in 2 Kings 5:15–17 who confesses, "I know that there is no God in all the earth, but in Israel . . . as the LORD lives . . . your servant will no more offer burnt offering nor will he sacrifice to other gods, but to the LORD." None of this was in evidence

35. Halpern, *David's Secret Demons*, 23–24.

36. Compare Peterson, *First and Second Samuel*, 209 where he discusses the same confessional language from the lips of Ittai the Gittite in 2 Samuel 15:21.

37. Baldwin, *1 & 2 Samuel*, 260.

38. Brueggemann, *First and Second Samuel*, 303.

with Achish. Nonetheless, there are further linguistic considerations that need exploration.

In the first instance, Achish used the term, *YHWH*, the covenantal name of God, instead of David's earlier phrase, *Elohim*, referring to the God of Israel as the God of the nations. Later, the Philistine king used *Elohim* to describe what David meant to him as one sent as God's messenger: "like an angel of God [*Elohim*]" (1 Sam 29:9). Does Achish's use of the personal name of the LORD indicate that he had found faith in the covenantal Yahweh, the God of the nations? Klein recommends, "Achish had to pass the negative word on to David. First, he affirmed his own respect for David, underscoring it with an oath in the name of YHWH. It is not clear whether the reference to YHWH was just a slip, or whether it was intended to show special courtesy."[39] Mary Evans augments, "His [Achish] comparing of David to an angel of God and his use of the name of Israel's God in verse six as part of an oath shows how much he wanted to back up his sincerity" in his confident belief that David was innocent.[40]

The text does not unequivocally indicate either way, yet there were clues that would suggest the likelihood that a change had occurred in Achish towards his understanding of David's God. Baldwin acknowledges the possibility when she states, "*As the Lord lives* was unexpected in a Philistine oath; can it be that Achish had committed himself to David's Lord, or was he being courteous to David in not swearing by Philistine gods?"[41] We shall probably never know, yet we should certainly entertain the question.

In summarizing this pericope, Klein believes, "No explicit theological statement marks this chapter, except for an incongruous Yahwistic oath from a pagan's mouth. But the biblical narrator surely sees here the providential hand of God and not just another lucky break."[42] David's successes were the LORD's own deed. Besides, Achish, son of Maacah, was the king of Gath before David's flight from Nob until the beginning of Solomon's reign.[43] During David's rule in Jerusalem he captured Gath (1 Chr 18:1; 2 Sam 8:1), yet Achish remained as the city king throughout this period (1 Kgs 2:39–41). This means that Achish was a vassal lord under David's suzerain authority. In fact, the city of Gath continued subject to Judah to the time of Rehoboam, who fortified it (2 Chr 11:8). Halpern underscores this

39. Klein, *1 Samuel*, 277.

40. Evans, *1 and 2 Samuel*, 127. Evans later reinforces the view that Achish used the name of Yahweh, the LORD, probably out of respect for David rather than because he had given allegiance to God (129). Also see McCarter, *1 Samuel*, 427.

41. Baldwin, *1 & 2 Samuel*, 165. See 1 Sam 17:43.

42. Klein, *1 Samuel*, 278.

43. See 1 Kings 2:39–40. Compare 1 Samuel 21:10; 27:2–3.

issue: "All the signs thus point to a long and sincere Davidic commitment to the Philistines of Gath."[44] The longevity of this relationship would lend more credence to the possibility of Achish's maturing spiritual journey towards the LORD.

In summary of the case, in David's migrations to the city of Gath and subsequent intercultural encounters, Achish, the Philistine king, fostered an awareness of the LORD. This instance of David therefore provides an example of migration and mission in the Old Testament. As a consequence of migration, there developed a cross-cultural relationship between the Israelite and Philistine leaders that provides contemporary missiological implications. David in immigrating to the region of Gath showed that migration played a role in the mission of God and should be considered as a strategy of the church.

LOVING THE STANGER TODAY

In this chapter we have seen that in the Hebrew Scriptures, migration served an important function in the mission of God in two major aspects. First, as detailed in the Mosaic covenant, God's people were to love the stranger and in so doing offer an invitation to participate in the community. Second, God's people in migration were to be agents of transformation, stimulating faith in those with whom they came into contact, and to draw them towards a relationship with the living God. Each of these two perceptions will be developed in the remainder of this paper in regards to the function of the church today.

We are living in a time of unparalleled global movements of people, and the church is being called to be a light to those who are displaced. God commanded the people of Israel to care for the strangers in their community. Arthur F. Glasser recognizes that the oppression faced by the Israelites in Egypt "was to serve as a constant reminder that they were not to be exploiters and dehumanizers of persons in the way Pharaoh's people had treated them. Freedom and justice for all were to be the hallmarks of God's land."[45] Inasmuch as the Israelites were once slaves of Egypt, we too were once slaves to sin. As the author of Ephesians said, "You are no longer strangers and aliens, but you are fellow citizens with the saints, and are of God's household" (2:19). The Israelites were to love the gêr as a neighbor in remembrance of the Exodus, and so the church is to love the foreign

---

44. Halpern, *David's Secret Demons*, 294; see also 150, 281, 287, 296, 302, 306, and 330–331, which support the notion of David's continued allegiance with Gath.

45. Glasser, *Announcing the Kingdom*, 86.

neighbor out of gratitude to God's liberation. Patrick D. Miller claims, "The experience of being slaves and strangers marks forever the way those who have been released and given a home treat those whom they encounter as slaves and strangers. Love the Lord and love the stranger—that is indeed the greatest of the commandments."[46]

As the new Israel, the Christian community is similarly obligated to fulfill God's directive to bestow his love to the foreigner in their midst, with the Old Testament Law serving as a model of contemporary diaspora mission (1 Pet 2:9–12). As the local church inevitably comes in contact with refugees, immigrants, and exiles in its own backyard, it should draw these people into a protective community of involvement. These guests need the welcoming kindness of the church where they may have their immediate societal needs met, and an opportunity to explore the gospel: to choose to accept the good news and become a part of a loving connection, or move on.

COMING TO AMERICA AS MISSION

The second Old Testament perception of migration and the mission of God was that Israel, as the stranger, was to represent the LORD of the nations among the nations. Sarita D. Gallagher alleges that only in analyzing Abraham's cross-cultural encounters as a migrant, does the full significance of Genesis 12:3 emerge. "And in you all the families of the earth shall be blessed." Gallagher says, "Abraham's identity as an immigrant also highlights the universal intentions of God. It was through Abraham's presence as a stranger in the land that God's mission to the nations was fulfilled."[47] The immigrant Abraham "becomes a means through which God touches the whole world."[48] Underscoring this reflection in the New Testament case of Priscilla and Aquila, vanThanh Nguyen argues that "from the very beginning, Christian expansion and migratory movement were forcibly and intimately intertwined."[49] He maintains that as an immigrant, every follower of Christ has the opportunity of being a prospective missionary. Nguyen concludes, "If every Christian migrant is a potential missionary, then migration could provide enormous prospects and opportunities for evangelization.

---

46. Miller, *Deuteronomy*, 127.

47. Gallagher, "Blessing on the Move," 151.

48. Ibid., 160. See Okoye, "The Blessing of Abraham: Genesis 12:1–3," *Israel and the Nations*, 43–55.

49. Nguyen, "Migrants as Missionaries," 205.

When Christian immigrants travel, they bring their religion with them, or more personally, their God literally migrates with them."[50]

Somewhat parallel to David immigrating to Gath, recent statistics indicate that the majority of emigrants to the United States were followers of Christ. In May 2013, the Pew Forum on Religion and Public Life released a report that found that in the twenty years from 1992 to 2012 approximately one million immigrants came to the United States each year. At the start of this period sixty-eight percent were Christian, which then tapered to sixty-one percent in 2012. Moreover, the United States has a total of about forty-three million foreign-born inhabitants, of whom seventy-five percent were legal and twenty-five percent illegal immigrants. The religious composition of the two groups was significantly different, whereby, of the approximately eleven million unauthorized immigrants residing in the U.S. in 2011, about eighty-three percent were Christians, mainly from Latin America, and less than one in ten belonged to a non-Christian religion.[51]

There has been an influx of Christians from around the world to New York City, for instance, who have given vitality to other Christians to live their faith and bless their neighborhoods. In 2009, immigrants and their families composed fifty-five percent of New York City's population. No longer coming from Europe, the latest wave of immigrants arrived from Africa, Asia, Latin America, and the West Indies, regions of the world where Christianity is flourishing. Mark R. Gornik and Maria Liu Wong contend that as people move to New York City, "many are bringing their churches and distinct ministry practices. Of course, migration as a primary means of church expansion is not a new trend, but . . . because of technology and greater access to air travel, this movement runs in both directions. . . . The centers of Christian life and growth are increasingly found where immigration has had the greatest impact."[52]

This phenomenon may also be witnessed in the Nigerian diaspora, "as the vision of African Christianity not only finds a foothold in Europe and North America, but also challenges the very expression of Christianity in those continents."[53] Allan L. Effa contends that post-Christian westerners

---

50. Ibid., 206. Also see Hanciles, *Beyond Christendom*, 378.

51. "Majority of Immigrants to the United States are Christians," 218. Also see Johnstone, *The Future of the Global Church*, 4–5.

52. Gornik and Wong, "Christ in the Capital of the World," 40.

53. Effa, "Releasing the Trigger: The Nigerian Factor in Global Christianity," 217. Also see Hanciles, "Migrants as Missionaries, Missionaries as Outsiders," 71–74 where the author reflects on the problems challenging African immigrant churches in the West; and Hanciles, *Beyond Christendom*, 364–73; see also Asamoah-Gyadu, "To the Ends of the Earth," 23–44.

are being led "back to a living, transforming faith in Jesus Christ" by West African-initiated churches through their Bible centeredness, evangelistic passion, dependency on prayer, and sacrificial giving.[54]

CONCLUSION

Israel's personal experience as a dislocated people evoked an awareness of the need to demonstrate covenantal love to the stranger. When David conquered Goliath of Gath, he had no idea that in a short time he would be estranged among the archenemies of Israel. Because of the political unrest within Israel, David first immigrated to the city of Gath as a political refugee, and then again as a military leader, allowing him to intermix with the Philistines of the region. As a consequence, it would appear that king Achish was brought to an understanding of the Hebrew God, which influenced the evolving destiny of the inhabitants of the city. Equally, many in the church, having immigrated to different parts of the world as strangers, should also be mindful of dispensing God's transforming love as they have been loved.[55] Whether a follower of God is on the move to Gath or America, migratory movements continue as an important aspect in the global spread of the Christian faith to bring about the missional purposes of God; impacting both the people of God and society towards a renewing faith. Parker J. Palmer concludes, "The stranger is not simply one who needs us. We need the stranger. We need the stranger if we are to know Christ and serve God, in truth and in love. For it is by knowing the truth and by serving in love that we ourselves will be set free."[56]

---

54. Effa, "Releasing the Trigger," 214–17.

55. See Escobar, "Mission Fields on the Move," 28–31.

56. Palmer, *The Company of Strangers*, 65.

4

Jesus' Migrations and Liminal Withdrawals in Matthew

—Paul Hertig

> "The human story is a migration story. We all are, or have been migrants, immigrants, refugees, or asylum seekers."
>
> —JOAN M. MARUSKIN

With the world rapidly surpassing a population of eight billion people, natural disasters and displacement are on the rise. Mass migration in an era of globalization will increase as never known before. Politicians politicize. Pundits analyze. Sociologists scrutinize. Theologians theologize. But the problems, the pain, and the politics, become more pressing with each passing day. Where do we turn for interpretation and understanding? "The great movements of refugees and migrants are not just random occurrences in our modern world. We must interpret these massive and often tragic human dramas from God's perspective in Scripture," declares Ray Bakke.[1] And, when we do turn to Scripture, there may be no better foundation than to explore Jesus' own migrant journeys.

Jesus' earliest migratory experience occurs when Herod the Great orders the murder of male infants in the Bethlehem vicinity (Matt 2:16). Jesus and family flee from the holy land and find safety and refuge in Egypt of all places. Contrasting sentimental Christmas pageants, the scriptural reality depicts Jesus slipping "quietly into a world of brutal rulers and hard-pressed refugees" in which "the central characters in the Christmas story are a rural peasant couple displaced by powerful political, economic, and military forces in Roman Palestine."[2] In this dark, dangerous context surrounding Jesus' birth, Joseph relies on dreams to navigate through a world of woe; one wrong move could be the very last.

We now explore the six withdrawals in Matthew, beginning with the first three withdrawals that occur during Jesus' childhood in the context of political turmoil in the Roman-occupied Holy Land. We then explore the subsequent three withdrawals in the context of religious turmoil surrounding Jesus' ministry and through the anthropological lens of liminality. Each of Jesus' withdrawals in his ministry signals a key phase of migration that opens up liminal space for an unrestricted stage of ministry.

THE FIRST THREE WITHDRAWALS: JESUS' CHILDHOOD MIGRATIONS

Twice Jesus' family withdraws from danger during his early childhood (2:14, 22). Warned in a dream, Joseph "having risen, took the child and his mother by night, and *withdrew (anechōrēsen)* to Egypt, and he was there till the death of Herod, that it might be fulfilled what was spoken by the Lord through the prophet, saying, 'Out of Egypt I did call My Son.'"[3] (Matt 2:14–15). This was the first family withdrawal. The term for withdrawal means "to depart from a location," or "to go away."[4]

Once Herod died, an angel of the Lord appeared in a dream to Joseph in Egypt and said, "Get up, take the child and his mother and go to the land of Israel, for those who were trying to take the child's life are dead" (2:20). So he got up, took the child and his mother and went to the land of Israel. However,

1. Bakke, *The Urban Christian*, 82.
2. Myers and Colwell, *Our God is Undocumented*, 159–60.
3. Young's Literal Translation.
4. Bauer and Danker, *A Greek Lexicon*, 75.

danger lingered. When Joseph heard that Archelaus reigned over Judea in place of his father Herod, he was afraid to go there and being warned in a dream, he again *withdrew (anechōrēsen)*, this time to the district of Galilee, settling in Nazareth (2:22). This was the second family withdrawal.

This passage elicits a contrast between the Moses' story and Jesus' family migration. In Exodus, the king of Egypt is the enemy of Israel; here, a king of Jerusalem is the enemy of Jesus. In Exodus, Moses flees for safety *out of* Egypt and then returns; here, Jesus is taken *into* Egypt for safety and then returns. For Moses, Egypt and Pharaoh represent unbelief, oppression, and violence; for Jesus and his family, Jerusalem and Herod fulfill this role of unbelief, oppression, and violence.

Furthermore, even prior to public ministry, Jesus was unwelcome in Jerusalem or Judea, but welcome only in Egypt and eventually "finds his abode in Galilee of the Gentiles, continuing the theme that the Messiah of God's presence has no home in God's holy city."[5] Whether among rushes or under starlight—displacement, withdrawal, exile, and return are dynamic themes in the infant lives and eventual missions of Moses and Jesus.

This interplay of Jesus' family migration with the Moses story contains an important continuity: "It seems that the thrust of the movement of Matthew 2 is to have Jesus as the Son of God go into Egypt in order to come out of Egypt, which clearly alludes to Israel's exodus and liberation."[6] This allusion, in both cases, is in the context of danger and oppression. In the case of Jesus' family, Herod the Great conjures a sinister plot to kill Jesus, while masquerading as a man who wants to worship him (2:8, 13). A ruthless ruler who came to power through bloodshed, he eventually killed his own wife and her two sons; he created an atmosphere of apprehension and trepidation throughout his vast kingdom that oppressed the Jews. This cruel dictator, when outwitted by the Magi, ordered the killing of all the boys, two years old and under, in Bethlehem and its vicinity (Matt 2:16). In this context, Jesus' family, and many others, suddenly become refugees.

This context of displacement was relevant at the time that Matthew's Gospel was written, around 80 CE, about a decade after the Temple at Jerusalem was destroyed. At that time, due to the violence that surrounded this event, many followers of Christ had become refugees. The story of Jesus' flight in and out of Egypt was of deep relevance and comfort. Many followers had crossed borders to settle in Antioch and Syria, possible locations from where the Gospel was written. These Christians formed new communities

5. Kupp, *Matthew's Emmanuel*, 66.

6. Nguyen, "In Solidarity with the Strangers," 222.

in new contexts. As in the context of Jesus' family, crossing borders became a passageway to safety and stability.

In the context of Jesus' family, migration and return migration represent temporary responses to danger; there is no indication that Jesus' flight across borders for safe haven, although this is an argument from silence, is unusual or in violation. In the two withdrawals of the infant Jesus (2:14, 22) into regions of safety, there is no indication that actual boundary or border crossing is a dangerous enterprise. The night flight has to do with the danger posed by Herod in Jerusalem. In fact, the border does not represent a barrier, but a gateway to safety and stability for the family of Jesus.

By the double usage of the term *withdrew* (*anechōrēsen*), Matthew wants to highlight that Jesus is a migrant from early childhood, who must cross borders not only to survive, but, eventually, to initiate and fulfill his mission (4:12–25). Jesus, the migrant Messiah, will eventually call into being a community of migrant disciples, who are sent out to the world by faith, without possessions and dependent on the hospitality of strangers.

We can infer from the text of the withdrawal into Egypt that "Jesus, Mary, and Joseph become asylum seekers in Egypt. Without travel documents, they cross the border, looking for safety and sanctuary. Someone takes them in. Someone welcomes them and protects them."[7] Meditation on the dangers of the journey in the Franciscan tradition of the medieval period helps us to consider the challenges faced by Jesus' family:

"Jesus was carried to Egypt by the very young and tender mother, and by the aged saintly Saint Joseph, along wild roads, obscure rocky and difficult, through woods and uninhabited places—a very long journey. They are said to have gone by the way of the desert which the children traversed and in which they stayed for 40 years. Where did they rest and spend the night? Have pity on them. Accompany them and help to carry the child Jesus and serve them in every way you can. Here there comes a compassionate meditation. Make careful note of the following things do they live or did they beg? You must contemplate all these things."[8]

THE THIRD WITHDRAWAL: NAZARETH

When Jesus' family return migrated from Egypt to settle in the land of Israel and learned that Herod's son reigned over Judea, the family "withdrew to

7. Maruskin, *The Bible as the Ultimate Immigration Handbook*, 8.

8. O'Kane, "The Flight into Egypt," 40. This quote is originally found in Franciscan writings in the Pseudo-Bonaventure tradition, entitled, "The Meditations of the Life of Christ."

the district of Galilee, and lived in a town called Nazareth" (2:21–23). This third withdrawal (*anechōrēsen*) into a safer region previews Jesus' discord with the political and religious authorities, highlighted in Matthew through an eventual series of withdrawals and heightened tensions. Jesus' withdrawal into Galilee from dangers in Judea reverses the traditional association of Galilee with darkness and death, and the Judean homeland with safety and security. Galilee is now safe;[9] Judea has become dubious.

Following the death of Herod the Great in 4 BCE, great political and economic upheaval occurred in Jerusalem and the surrounding area, including Galilee. Jewish inhabitants of Sepphoris revolted against Roman rule. Herod's son, Herod Antipas, became Tetrarch in 1 CE, and established Sepphoris, just five kilometers from Nazareth, as his center of government, declaring Sepphoris as "the ornament of all Galilee."[10] It is postulated that Joseph, a *tektōn*, a woodworker or builder,[11] returned to Galilee and settled with his family in Nazareth to become employed in woodworking, an opportune time for this trade in Sepphoris and the surrounding area, including Nazareth.

As in his introduction to Jesus' *childhood*, Matthew's introduction to Jesus' *ministry* is laced with migrant language: "Now having heard that John was arrested, he *withdrew* into Galilee. And *having left behind* Nazareth, *having come, he settled* in Capernaum a way leading to the sea in the *borders* of Zebulun and Naphtali" (Matt 4:12–13, italics and translation, mine).

In this passage, the migrant verbs are: *withdraw, leave behind, come,* and *settle* among borders. The first verb is critical to this text, and to the overall migration motif of Jesus in Matthew. This key verb, withdrew (*anechōrēsen*) into Galilee means to "go away, to depart, often to escape danger."[12]

Matthew utilizes the verb "withdraw" six times, signaling Jesus' rite of passage from one region to another. The previous three usages indicated withdrawals from danger into regions of safety. Now that Jesus begins his ministry, we shall see that each subsequent withdrawal signals a key phase of migration that opens up liminal space for a new and unrestricted stage of Jesus' ministry.

---

9. Galilee is not always a place of safety; John was beheaded there, and Jesus pronounced woes on specific Galilean cities due to their lack of repentance (11:21–24). According to Josephus, John the Baptist was beheaded at the fortress of Machaeus, located south (today's Jordan) and on the other side of the Dead Sea. John was probably captured in Galilee and probably brought to Machaeus.

10. Horsley, *Galilee*, 163.

11. Rogers and Rogers, *The New Linguistic and Exegetical Key*, 31.

12. Ibid., 7.

WITHDRAWALS AND LIMINALITY

Arnold van Gennep originally described liminality as a detached state from normative culture in pre-industrial societies. Liminality depicted the middle of three phases of rites of passage: separation, liminality, and incorporation.[13] This dynamic in-between state allowed for inner and outer transformation toward a new status, a passage from one destiny to another. While in the liminal state, the individual loses status and authority according to culture's classifications. This loss of identity, a crucial phase in a rite of passage, leads to new potential or loss.

In this case of Matthew 4, the withdrawal inaugurates Jesus' ministry and thus leads to new potential. But it is an unusual way to begin a ministry: to "withdraw," rather than "go forth!" This strange beginning signals a Matthean agenda that continually unfolds in the subsequent withdrawals of Jesus. The quote from Isaiah 9:1–2 that justifies Jesus' geographical locations indicates a defensive response to John's imprisonment—Herod's interruption of John's ministry—but also a nuance of new beginnings, the first phase of Jesus' ministry: "Land of Zebulun and land of Naphtali, the way to the sea, along the Jordan, Galilee of the Gentiles—the people living in darkness have seen a great light" (4:15–16). This marks a magnificent reversal for Galilee, from darkness to light. The good news of the kingdom quickly becomes a light to the nations (4:23–25).

In one brief literary sequence following the wilderness temptation, Jesus returned to Galilee, specifically stopping by his hometown of Nazareth, and then settled in Capernaum, where he begins calling his disciples to follow him on his itinerant journey in Galilee and beyond its borders.

Galilee is rooted in a history of migration, intrusion, exile, and return. Jesus, through personal experience, enters that multicultural and migratory context. The backdrop of Matthew's unique New Testament phrase "Galilee of the Gentiles" (4:15) is the Assyrian deportation of the Jews of Galilee from the region of Zebulun and Naphtali, which opened the door for an influx of migrants, in particular, Canaanites and Sidonians. Matthew's reference to "Galilee of the Gentiles" (4:15) derives from the Hebrew *galil ha-goyim* (Isa 9:1) meaning "circle of the nations," referring to the surrounding peoples and city-states, which vied for political and economic power in the region.[14]

13. Van Gennep, "Rites of Passage," 11.

14. Horsley, *Galilee*, 20.

THE FOURTH WITHDRAWAL: FROM PHARISEES TO MASSES

Migrating through grain fields on a journey of mission, on the road to healing a man with a withered hand in a synagogue, Jesus and his disciples pluck
and eat heads of grain (12:1–10). The religious leaders charge the disciples
with violating the Sabbath. His loving action, demonstrated through healing, supersedes temple duties; the priestly privileges have been widened to
include all people.[15] Jesus chooses mercy over sacrifice (12:7).

This creates a symbolic turn of events. The Pharisees depart from the
synagogue to deliberate on how they might destroy Jesus (12:14). They are
now on the outside and Jesus is on the inside, an insider-outsider reversal.
Jesus, aware that they are plotting to kill him, "withdraws" from the scene
altogether and "many crowds followed him" (12:15). This is Jesus' fourth
withdrawal.

Jesus' withdrawal (*anechōrēsen*) into a new liminal space places him
among the masses. Mathew emphasizes the perfection of the situation,
stating that he "cured all of them," demonstrating the power of liminality
occasioned by Jesus' separation from the old restrictions and his entrance
into a new and vital mission experience. Jesus' alternative vision emerges
in non-retaliatory, liminal space. In fact, "Jesus' withdrawal in the face of
threat is not a matter of cowardice or strategy, but represents the divine
response to human violence that will ultimately lead to the cross, in which
human violence is met with divine self-giving."[16]

In summary, after the Pharisees seek to restrict his Sabbath healing
in "their synagogue," Jesus withdraws to the multitudes, whose existence
reflects pharisaic leadership. The shepherds have not tended to the sheep;
however, Jesus, the good shepherd, heals all indiscriminately. The scripture
makes reference to Jesus' healing, *not some*, but *all* in the crowds (12:15).
This unrestrictive healing takes place after the religious authorities seek to
restrict his healing and plot to kill him. Even that healing was unrestricted. Jesus "completely healed the man's hand, just as sound as the other"
(12:13–15).

Furthermore, in addition to healing everyone to wholeness (12:18),
the scope of Jesus' mission broadens as he proclaims justice to the nations,
which will put their hope in him (12:21). His healing, justice and salvation
are indiscriminate, available to all, contrasting particular Pharisees' injustice
and lack of compassion that constrict God's mercy and grace. Jesus' healings

---

15. Levine, *The Social and Ethnic Dimensions*, 248.

16. Boring, "The Gospel of Matthew," 280.

represented a protest against temple discriminations, which deemed certain persons impure and untouchable. Restoring people's physical honor enabled persons who are healed to reestablish themselves as members of communities.[17]

Furthermore, the wholeness of human communion "cannot be programmed or manufactured through structure, but spontaneously emerges precisely when programs and structure are left behind and when individuals are freed to relate to one another completely on an egalitarian ground."[18] Liminality is a space of creativity and freedom that alters the status quo and creates an alternative community. Liminality provides an open space of detachment. It is "essentially ambiguous, unsettled, and unsettling,"[19] and consequently, "subversive."[20]

THE FIFTH WITHDRAWAL: A LONELY PLACE

In the violent context of John's beheading, the disciples took John's body and buried it; then they went and told Jesus. "Now when Jesus heard this, he *withdrew* (*anechōrēsen*) to a lonely place. But when the crowds heard it, they followed him" (Matt 14:12–14). This fifth liminal withdrawal serves as a transition from hostility to healing.

While grieving, Jesus has withdrawn to be alone, but the crowds find him again, entering their own liminal space. They are harassed and helpless, sheep without a shepherd, due to the political and religious leaders, who have just played their role in the murder of John and are plotting against Jesus. Jesus expresses compassion in the midst of grief. In the role of a new Moses in the wilderness, Jesus provides bread for all, leaving none hungry: "and all ate and were filled"[21] (14:20). Just as Manna was God's provision for all, the unrestricted, unhindered Jesus provides for all.

This liminal moment is unplanned and spontaneous. Jesus has retreated in order to grieve, but crowds follow him in order to be healed. Liminality goes hand in hand with *communitas* in Victor Turner's observation of anti-structure. Turner described *communitas* as a spontaneous and unstructured community that provides "a greater wisdom, for human beings are responsible to one another in the supplying of humble needs, such as food,

17. Herzog, *Jesus, Justice, and the Reign of God*, 184.

18. Lee, *From A Liminal Space*, 9.

19. Turner, *The Ritual Process*, 274.

20. Lee, *From A Liminal Space*, 10 and 44.

21. France, *The Gospel of Matthew*, 559.

drink, clothing, and the careful teaching of material and social technique."[22] In this lonely location, Jesus creates mutual responsibility, not allowing the disciples to send the crowds away, but, in a moment of shared crisis, makes their limited resources unlimited (20:15–20). To summarize:

> Communitas breaks in through the interstices of structure, in liminality; at the edges of structure, in marginality; and from beneath structure, in inferiority. It is almost everywhere held to be sacred or "holy," possibly because it transgresses or dissolves the norms that govern structured and institutionalized relationships and is accompanied by experiences of unprecedented potency.[23]

From the beginning, the disciples had resisted this liminal state of *communitas*, stating, "This is a remote place, and it's already getting late. Send the crowds away, so they can go to the villages and buy themselves some food" (14:15). To this resistance of both *communitas* and Gentile mission, Jesus replied, "They do not need to go away. You give them something to eat" (14:16). Jesus not only included the outsiders and incorporated them into the community, but he involved the disciples in their lives, imploring them to feed the crowds. This liminal experience was life changing for the disciples, who can only state the obvious, "We have here only five loaves of bread and two fish" (14:17). And then, the miracle occurs: "Bring them here to me," Jesus says (4:18). Suddenly, food scarcity becomes abundance. Lack of community becomes *communitas*. Thousands are fed from meager beginnings, and there are plenty of leftovers. The Rabbi, his ragged disciples, and throngs of strangers come together, break bread, eat, and enter into an enchanted new community of faith and transformation: *communitas*.

THE SIXTH WITHDRAWAL: THE CANAANITE WOMAN

As a prelude to Jesus' encounter with the Canaanite woman, the text states, "Jesus withdrew to the region of Tyre and Sidon" (15:21). He specifically withdrew from certain Pharisees and Scribes who came from Jerusalem to interrogate him about matters of the law. Jesus calls these religious leaders "hypocrites," whose traditions "make void the word of God." He also states that what comes out of the heart defiles a person; "but to eat with unwashed hands does not defile" (15:1–20). His withdrawal from the Jerusalem leaders serves as an entrance into the Gentile territory of Tyre and Sidon. As in

---

22. Turner, *The Ritual Process*, 139.

23. Ibid., 112.

his other withdrawals, Jesus' migration appears effortless. He simply "withdraws" across the Galilean border into a Gentile region.

Matthew's use of "withdraw" signals a liminal transition *from* the context of Jewish obsession with personal cleanliness, *to* a context of social uncleanliness. Jesus has, for the first time, departed from Galilee, and migrated into Gentile territory. Ironically, Tyre and Sidon is in Syrian-Phoenicia, which Jesus had previously avowed as more bearable on judgment day than the Galilean cities of Korazin and Bethsaida (11:21). This Phoenician homeland represented Israel's ancient enemies.

The border is crossed. A Canaanite woman approaches, shouting and begging him to heal her demon-possessed daughter. Jesus and the disciples appear reluctant to deal with this woman, yet she does not concede, knowing the compelling connection between her dilemma and Jesus' power.[24] Jesus' initial statement, "I was sent only to the lost sheep of Israel," refers to a boundary that he just broke moments earlier when he crossed the border! He seems to use this statement as a point of departure, rather than an ultimatum.

Kneeling before him, she halts his movement and holds her ground. This leaves Jesus with the choice of responding or walking around her.[25] But Jesus again speaks of a boundary that he is about to break: "It is not right to take the children's bread and toss it to their dogs" (15:26). Jesus initiates a harsh saying that connotes a traditional Jewish nuance of primacy, echoing the Pharisees and Scribes whom he just called hypocrites and whom he left behind on the other side of the border. An interesting reversal: Jesus is typically the recipient of a hostile remark and then responds with a correction or reproving question. But in this case, Jesus initiates a hostile saying, and the woman responds with a witty comment of her own. Levine notes that "his insult is in part a commentary on her physical position: kneeling, or heeling—begging like a dog—is not the proper position for someone about to receive the master's food."[26]

In fact, the tone of the dialogue, in the midst of this critical moment becomes surprisingly playful. Giving highest honor to Jesus with, "Yes, Lord" the desperate woman somehow affirms Jesus' words and wittingly continues her plea, "for even the dogs eat the crumbs that fall from the master's table" (15:27). Here, the woman acknowledges and does not challenge Jesus' stated priority to the lost sheep of Israel. But she also seeks access "by

---

24. Sanders, *Ministry at the Margins,* 89.

25. Levine, "Matthew's Advice," 36–37.

26. Ibid.

laying claim to the 'crumbs.'"[27] Jesus' phrase, "the children's food," is likely a reference to the covenantal term "children of Israel" (Deut 14:1; Matt 5:9).[28] Since bread and food form themes of the two previous stories about conflicting traditions (12:7, 8; 15:1–20), of which Jesus is not bound, food represents God's unrestricted provision. Thus the woman kneels before Jesus, claiming the crumbs, connecting herself to the promises of Israel through faith. Ched Myers interprets that, in this public context, Jesus' Jewish male dignity is "seriously affronted by a gentile woman who 'bests' him" and this is "precisely the problem with honor culture" that "requires winners and losers."[29] However, instead of this narrative ending with winners and losers, the honor of the Jewish people yields to a solidarity with all people, rising above the game of winners and losers, depicted in this embrace of a woman furthest from Jesus' own social location.[30]

The Canaanite woman responded to Jesus' recognition of her social reality of inferiority and turned it to her own advantage. "This is the role of the trickster, the person without power, the colonized subject. This is the role of the Cynic, the social critic who calls householders to accountability." After all, "Cynics take their name from the Greek for 'dog'; that the woman's retort also plays on the aural connection between 'Canaanite' (*Kananaia*) and 'dogs' (*kynaria*) may be more than happy accident."[31]

Jesus creates a scenario in which this woman has an opportunity to express herself. She challenges the prevailing theology of Judaism, and Jesus offers a compassionate response. A fundamental frustration of the migrant, or, one on the "other side" of the border, is a dehumanization that elicits voicelessness and powerlessness. The violation of their rights "just happens."[32] Jesus ultimately forbids injustice to follow its blind course and initiates a process that reverses the dehumanization of the Canaanite woman, a reality that he earlier expressed without mincing words.

In summary, after choosing to respond to her cries and ignore the disciples' pleas, Jesus enters into a conversation with the Gentile woman across the border. His last words to her are literally, "let it be to you as you desire," and he heals her daughter (15:28). Not only the Canaanite, but also the Centurion, are the only two Gentiles found within the healing narratives who "are positively portrayed, engage in dialogue with Jesus, and have their

27. Sanders, *Ministry at the Margins,* 89.

28. Carter, *Matthew and the Margins,* 324.

29. Myers and Colwell, *Our God is Undocumented,* 135.

30. Ibid., 135.

31. Levine, "Matthew's Advice," 39.

32. Boff, *Faith on the Edge,* 43, 54.

requests granted."[33] In this liminal space, the disciples' wish is not granted, and hers is; surprisingly, Jesus engages in conversation with a Gentile woman in public space. She expresses herself freely and is theologically engaging. She acknowledges Jesus as Lord, and her wish of the healing of her demon-possessed daughter is granted.

Levine observes that the term "to withdraw," referring to Jesus' trek across the border, has both ethnic and political associations: Ethnically, the term foreshadows the mission to the gentiles, and it indicates to future missionaries that gentile territory can be a place of refuge. Politically Jesus' withdrawing implies a deliberate separation of his mission from the agendas of the Pharisees and the Herodians.[34]

Having separated himself from the Pharisees and Herodians in order to redirect his mission and include Gentiles, Jesus crossed over a threshold (*limin*) and engaged in healing in Gentile territory.

The border crossing migration of Jesus has broadened the seeds of mission, once prioritized on the lost sheep of Israel, now planted in new ground among people of other nations. The border crossing fits the immediate Matthean context of Jesus' withdrawal from restrictions imposed by the religious leaders into unrestricted mission that extends to all nations, as indicated by his interaction with a Gentile woman, whose faith is celebrated and contrasted by the faith of the religious leaders, whose theology cannot restrict the movement of God into "unclean" territory. The story has relevance for ancient and modern audiences:

The story serves to challenge the sexism and racism of hearers and readers, ancient and modern, who tend not only to consider those of different gender and ethnicity as "the other," somehow more distant from God and the divine order and plan than our own group. . . . The story invites readers to place themselves in the role of the other to struggle not only with God but also with our own perceptions of the other, and pronounces such enduring struggle to be great faith.[35]

Sociologists recognize that fixed boundary lines of cultural and religious identity do not exist in real life and are social constructions. We continually move in and out of various cultural groups, though our own cultural groups often deny this reality. However, Jesus' disciples, sought to draw clear boundaries, and, as in other cases, resisted the mission to Gentiles. From the moment the woman began shouting, the disciples urge Jesus to send her away. In fact, the imperfect tenses of the verbs indicate that they make

33. Levine, *The Social and Ethnic Dimensions*, 131.

34. Ibid., 134.

35. Boring, "The Gospel of Matthew," 338.

continual demands to "send her away" in response to her continual "crying out" for her daughter to be healed. The woman immediately understands Jesus' saying about the children's bread and further develops the saying by augmenting it to include the crumbs that fall from the master's table.[36] She has now made the theological argument for the inclusion of Gentiles in Jesus' mission.[37] As a result, the woman's daughter is healed. In contrast, the disciples did not want to engage with her at all. Yet, it becomes a critical liminal experience for them. They have now crossed a border into Gentile territory and observed Jesus conversing with a Gentile and performing a miracle among Gentiles, whom they have resisted. It prepares them for the very next liminal experience, when they join Jesus for three days of further miracles among the multitudes and participation in a second mass feeding (15:29–38, cf. 14:13–21). The two mass feedings, one before and one after the story of the Canaanite woman, shed further light on the unfolding of the Gentile mission of Jesus in Matthew. The prologue to the second feeding describes Jesus "along the Sea of Galilee," ministering to "great crowds" who "praised the God of Israel" (15:29–31), implying that Gentiles were in the crowds. Jesus heals and feeds indiscriminately. The woman's "crumbs" thus "point to an extravagant note of abundance as some four thousand people miraculously eat and are filled, with seven baskets full of leftovers gathered."[38] Food and feeding become the physical and metaphorical manifestations of the messianic banquet to come, which is signaled by Jesus in his very first encounter with a Gentile, the Centurion, when he states, "I have not found anyone in Israel with such great faith. I say to you that many will come from the east and the west, and will take their places at the feast with Abraham, Isaac and Jacob in the kingdom of heaven" (8:10–11).

SUMMARY OF JESUS' WITHDRAWALS

The withdrawal into Galilee of the Gentiles, a liminal separation from the old and preparation for the new, that initiates Jesus' mission, hints at the multicultural nature of that mission. Of the six uses of "withdraw" in Matthew (2:14, 2:22, 4:12–15, 12:15–18, 14:13, 15:21), five have direct associations

---

36. Gene Smillie points out, "Readers throughout the centuries have been disturbed, even appalled, by these words. But the Canaanite woman apparently is not. She tacitly agrees with the conventional nationalistic principles the Jewish Messiah has been articulating ('Yes, Lord'), and yet parries with the riposte, 'but even the dogs feed on the crumbs which fall from their master's table' (v. 27)." Smillie, "Even the Dogs," 93.

37. Robinson, *Jesus and the Religions*, 100, 106–8.

38. Ibid., 154.

with the Gentiles, and one has indirect associations. The disciples, often resistant to contact with Gentiles, discover a new paradigm when following Jesus into liminal space.

Since the rules of the game change, liminality "becomes a place of undefined potential," for transformation.[39] Matthew's use of the expression "to withdraw" implies the necessity of separation from fixed, religious paradigms and the entrance into a liminal state that leads to a new paradigm of mission. Levine concludes that Matthew's use of withdraw provides a veiled hint that, for the church to survive, future disciples must remove themselves from the influence of those whose positions are characterized by stasis. In other words, while the members of the establishment reside in cities, palaces, and synagogues, Jesus and his followers withdraw into places apart from the center, where refuge is found.[40]

Withdrawals thus indicate places of undefined potential where a new paradigm is formulated, always separate from the center, always inclined to the peripheries. Jesus' withdrawals are not mere retreats from danger, but intentional departures from old patterns and arrivals at new possibilities.

Jesus' migrant movement across borders, boundaries, and barriers, discharges restrictions imposed by the religious order that would prevent him from healing every day of the week, ministering to people of all nations, and feeding all who are hungry. In so doing, he declares justice to all nations, heals all, and feeds all. His migrant mission shatters every barrier, boundary, border—allowing his ministry to be unrestrained, unbridled, without limitations. He crosses borders, enters new regions, overcomes all restrictions, engages in his ministry of justice to all nations, healing all, and feeding all.

CONTEMPORARY RELEVANCE

Reflecting upon Jesus, the migrant God who empowered liminal people on the move, we now move to the contemporary scenario. One way of empowering migrant people in a liminal state is through the annual ritual of *posada* at the California border of San Diego and Tijuana.

A *posada*, meaning, inn, is a Catholic-Mexican procession that reenacts the story of Joseph and Mary seeking shelter in Bethlehem. Participants carry a doll that symbolizes the baby Christ, journey through neighborhoods, and seek lodging. The participants are turned down many times until they finally receive hospitality, at which time a great celebration breaks

---

39. Roxburgh, *The Missionary Congregation,* 32–33.
40. Levine, *The Social and Ethnic Dimensions,* 134.

forth. The *Posada Sin Fronteras* is an interfaith adaptation of the *posada* that commemorates the stories of migrant families who have attempted to cross the U.S.-Mexico border. During the advent season, diverse groups of people meet on both sides of the border fence and encounter the sacred in the lives of the other—in a spirit that transcends the border.[41]

They feel that "their Christian identities and beliefs dictate inclusion, equality, and hospitality."[42] They reflect upon what Jesus would do and say if standing at the border. "Surely there is room for everyone on God's earth," said one woman. "It does not belong to us; it belongs to all of his children." A man stated his belief in the biblical injunction to help "aliens" and to "Remember you were an alien yourself in Egypt."[43] Here, we have contemporary people participating in a liminal experience that recollects the first liminal experiences of Jesus and family, connecting with them through time and space at a border fence, acknowledging that we are all migrants on this earth.

This diverse group of people from various ethnicities and all walks of life, shared *communitas* on both sides of the border. They shared a sense of hope, unity, healing, transformation, and transcendence. The walls metaphorically broke down. One Latina stated that the border became "invisible" during the *posada*. It was more sacred, real, empowering, and experiential than a routine church service.[44]

The ritual of the *posada* reconnects us with a long Judeo-Christian heritage of a migrant God who calls a wandering people who are on the move. Rituals create people connections across time, space, borders, and boundaries. In this case, they create space to connect with the immigrant poor and "know them not as statistics, but as human beings who endure extraordinary hardship and trauma in their struggle just to survive."[45] We do well to familiarize ourselves with the Scriptural stories, our own stories, and the stories of others in contemporary life—stories of people on the move. Only then might we begin to journey through the maze way of complexities that surround our modern day borders and often separate people by race, ethnicity, and social class.

When he entered the world, Jesus shattered the boundary between God and humanity. From childhood and on into adulthood, he lived as a perpetual migrant, and he called disciples to follow in his footsteps. After

41. Hondagneu-Sotelo, et al., "There's a Spirit that Transcends the Border," 134–43.
42. Ibid., 146.
43. Ibid., 147–48.
44. Ibid., 154.
45. Myers and Colwell, *Our God is Undocumented*, 15.

departing from this earth, he sent the disciples to all nations. It is from this story that we must begin our reflections in a contemporary world of mass migration that results in the dislocation of human beings. The annual ritual of *posada* locates the dislocated with Jesus, his family, and their own border crossings. At the intersection of their own dislocation and Jesus, migrants find meaning beyond their own predicament.

CONCLUSION

In meditating on Jesus and his family who crossed the desert, one cannot help but reflect on contemporary people who, squeezed by economic and political powers, desperately cross dangerous borders, deserts and mountains, for their survival. Do stricter laws or unswervingly following the letter of the law provide the answer to protect borders? Do we find empathy for the plight of our neighbors who are crossing borders? Or, do we find a balance between two polarized perspectives? In answering these questions, it might be helpful to ponder the paradox "that in Jesus' day, there were more open borders than at the end of the 20th century. The holy family was able to return from Egypt to Palestine. The repatriation of refugees is a right and not a courtesy."[46]

Through the concept of "withdrawals" early on in Jesus' life, and at key turning points in his ministry, we have discovered in the Gospel of Matthew that human boundaries and borders are not obstacles, but gateways for unrestricted opportunities of transformation. His withdrawals open up space for creativity and freedom that alter the status quo and create an alternative community. His vital themes of justice, salvation, empowerment, and healing to wholeness, surround the context of his liminal withdrawals. Jesus' retreats were not defeats; they propelled him forward.

46. O'Kane, *Borders, Boundaries, and the Bible*, 59.

5

Migrants as Missionaries

The Case of Priscilla and Aquila

—*vanThanh Nguyen*

This chapter argues that early Christian migration, whether stimulated by mission or caused by persecution, was historically a prime factor in the spread of the Good News of Jesus Christ and the church. The case of Priscilla and Aquila will demonstrate that migration and mission were closely intertwined. This Judean Christ-believing-couple was constantly on the move for the cause of the gospel. They first settled in Rome, were then forced to migrate to Corinth because of the Edict of Claudius in 49 CE, relocated in Ephesus for the purpose of evangelization, and finally returned to Rome after Claudius' death in 54 CE. They relocated both their home and their trade at least three times in three different locations. Their home was as movable as the tents they erected. Yet, they never faltered in their commitment to preach the Gospel of Jesus Christ, risking everything because of their faith. Like any immigrant who experiences the trauma of displacement and uprootedness, they knew the importance of being welcomed and finding shelter. Their homes became house churches. It is no surprise that Pope Benedict XVI called this best-known married couple in the New Testament "models of conjugal life" (Pope Benedict XVI).[1]

---

1. For a copy of the translation of Pope Benedict XVI's address at the general audience on February 7, 2007, see http://www.ewtn.com/library/papaldoc/b16ChrstChrch29.

In order to understand and appreciate the impact made by this immigrant missionary couple, which was honored by three different New Testament authors, ministered in three important cities in the Roman Empire (Corinth, Ephesus, and Rome) and was appreciated by "all the churches of the Gentiles" (Rom 16:3), it is necessary to first examine the situation of the Jews in Rome and their civic status in the Roman Empire. In this first section, we will also discuss the evidence for the expulsions of the Jews from the imperial capital and the reasons underlying these expulsions that impacted Priscilla's and Aquila's migrations. The second section examines the references to Priscilla and Aquila, who appear six times in the New Testament: three times by Luke (Acts 18:1–3, 18–19, 26–27); twice by Paul (1 Cor 16:19; Rom 16:3); and once by a Deutero-Pauline (2 Tim 4:19). The last section will show that the history of Christian missionary expansion and migration movement were intimately connected. Since migration is at an all time high and since every Christian migrant is a potential missionary, migration could have enormous prospects and opportunities for evangelism today.

JEWS IN ROME DURING THE FIRST CENTURY CE

We know from isolated inscriptions, archaeological finds and literary references that diaspora Jews lived in many parts of the Mediterranean world during the Second Temple period: Egypt, Syria, Cyprus, Greece, Asia Minor, and Italy, just to name a few.[2] But the question of interest is: What do we know about Jews in Rome? According to Valerius Maximus, a historian of the early first century CE, Jews were already expelled from Rome in 139 BCE, which indicates that there could have been Jews living in Rome at least since the middle of the second century BCE. Historians however question this early date because of insufficient evidence.[3] A much more reliable date seems to be 63 BCE, when Pompey conquered Palestine, forcing many Jews to emigrate or to be sold into slavery. Consequently, the first Jews in Rome could have been slaves or prisoners of war.[4] Other historians suggest that the

---

htm [accessed on June 4, 2012].

2. See Barclay, *Jews in the Mediterranean Diaspora.*

3. Valerius Maximus referred to an expulsion of Jews in 139 BCE by praetor Cornelius Hispalus. The report has been widely questioned; see Barclay, *Jews in the Mediterranean Diaspora,* 285. Leonard Victor Rutgers ("Roman Policy toward the Jews," 97) however seems to trust Velarius Maximus' account and therefore suggests that Jews may have reached Rome as early as the middle of the second century BCE.

4. This date seems to be the most accurate. According to Barclay (*Jews in the Mediterranean Diaspora,* 286), the earliest secure information on the Jews' presence in Rome

earliest Jews to have arrived in Rome were merchants and not necessarily slaves.[5] The arrival of the Jews in the imperial capital is an ongoing debate. What is certain is that by the early first century CE there were Jews living in Trastevere, between Porta Collina and Porta Esquilina. Philo indicates that by Augustus' time a large Jewish population settled mainly on the right bank of the Tiber in a poor residential area of the city.[6]

Literary as well as archaeological evidence suggest that the Jewish community in Rome prospered during the Augustan period, both in terms of number and social significance.[7] No one knows for sure what the exact population of the Jewish community was in Rome at the time of the expulsion by Claudius in 49 CE. We can only give an estimate deduced from various sources and incidents. Josephus, a first century Roman-Jewish historian, says that in 4 BCE eight thousand Roman Jews accompanied a Jewish delegation from Palestine to appear before Caesar Augustus.[8] According to another report, four thousand Jews, who were Roman citizens or had Junian status capable of taking up arms, were sent to fight in Sardinia during the reign of Tiberius.[9] These figures help historians to estimate that there might have been approximately twenty to thirty thousand Jews in Rome at the time when Claudius expelled Priscilla and Aquila from Rome.[10]

---

is to be found in Cicero's speech in defense of Flaccus (59 BCE).

5. Rutgers ("Roman Policy toward the Jews," 97) says that when the Jewish slaves arrived from Palestine, the Jewish community in Rome was already well established.

6. Brändle and Stegemann, "Formation of the First 'Christian Congregations' in Rome," 120; Barclay, *Jews in the Mediterranean Diaspora*, 290.

7. For the sources about the history of the Jews in Rome, see Brändle and Stegemann, "Formation of the First 'Christian Congregations' in Rome," 120; Barclay, *Jews in the Mediterranean Diaspora*, 282–95.

8. See *Antiquities of the Jews* (17.299–303) and *The Jewish Wars* (2.80). These two important ancient works were written by Josephus, who was also known as Titus Flavius Josephus (37–*circa* 100 CE). *Antiquities of the Jews* (*circa* 94) recounts the history of the world from a Jewish perspective for an ostensibly Roman audience. *The Jewish Wars* recounts the Jewish revolt against Roman occupation (66–70 CE). These works provide valuable insight into first century Judaism and the background of Early Christianity. For an online resource of the works of Flavius Josephus, see http://www.biblestudytools.com/history/flavius–josephus/ [accessed on August 31, 2012].

9. This incident is mentioned in various ancient sources: Josephus, *Antiquities* 18.8.1–84; Suetonius, *Tiberius* 36; Tacitus, *Annals* 2.85. See also Brändle and Stegemann, "Formation of the First 'Christian Congregations' in Rome," 120; Barclay, *Jews in the Mediterranean Diaspora*, 294.

10. Brändle and Stegemann, "Formation of the First 'Christian Congregations' in Rome," 120; Barclay, *Jews in the Mediterranean Diaspora*, 295. Keller (*Priscilla and Aquila*, 9) suggests that there were as many as 40–50,000 Judeans living in Rome by the time of Augustus. I think this number is a bit too large.

Jews in Rome during the first century CE belonged to one of three categories: slaves, free *peregrini* or *Latini Iuniani*,[11] or Roman citizens. First, some were definitely slaves. According to Cicero, prisoners of war should be freed after six years of slavery, but this was probably a rare exception since most slaves were not able to acquire their freedom so quickly. Slaves were subject to criminal law, and in case of criminal offenses, they could be severely punished by their master or by the Roman senate. Second, some Jews were free *peregrini* or *Latini Iuniani*, who had acquired an informal manumission, so their status was inferior to that of the Roman citizen. Third, some Jews were Roman citizens, who could only be expelled after they had been found guilty of a criminal offense in a Roman court. As a privileged Roman citizen, he or she had the right to appeal to a higher authority, namely to the emperor, after having been convicted.[12]

Jews enjoyed special privileges under the Roman legal system. Around the second half of the first century BCE, under the peaceful reign of Augustus Caesar, Roman magistrates passed "the *Acta Pro-Judaeis*," which consisted of a number of decrees granting the Jews in the Empire the freedom to practice their religion. The decrees allowed the Jews to gather freely (for example in a synagogue or *thiasoi*), observe the Sabbath and other Jewish festivals, send money to the temple in Jerusalem, and enjoy autonomy in their communal affairs. The Jews were also exempt from being enlisted in the Roman military.[13] Obviously, being a Jew in the early first century CE had its advantages and privileges. It also demonstrates that the Jews must have had social significance and remarkable influence at that time.

The situation of the Jews in Rome changed significantly after the peaceful reign of Augustus. As a matter of fact, the Jews in Rome experienced something of a backlash during the rule of the next three emperors: Tiberius (14–37 CE), Gaius (also known as Caligula)[14] (37–41 CE), and Claudius (41–54 CE). Noticeably, from the reigns of Tiberius to Claudius, the Jews were twice expelled from Rome. The first expulsion happened in 19 CE when Tiberius (or, more exactly, the Senate) enlisted 4,000 Jews into

11. *Peregini* is the plural form of *perigrinus*, which in Latin means "foreigner" or "one from abroad." It is a term used during the early Roman Empire to denote free individuals who were not Roman citizens. As for *Latini Iuniani*, these were slaves who had acquired freedom by manumission but did not become Roman citizens.

12. Rutgers, "Roman Policy toward the Jews," 98.

13. Ibid., 94.

14. Gaius (also known as Caligula) seemed to have little respect for Jewish practices and religion. During his reign, he intended to erect his own statue in the temple of Jerusalem, which caused no small uproar and resistance. The Jews in Palestine were willing to die rather than have their sacred temple contaminated. Fortunately, the emperor died before the project was ever completed.

the army to fight in Sardinia and banished many others from its capital.[15] Josephus recounts that the incident was incited by a Roman noblewoman, named Fulvia, who was the wife of a prominent senator. She adopted Jewish practices under the influence of four Jews in Rome, who then stole the money and purple cloth that they persuaded her to donate to the Jerusalem temple.[16] However, Dio Cassius records that the expulsion took place because the Jews were converting many Romans to their customs.[17] The sources disagree as to why the expulsion really took place.[18] Some argue that Jews and devotees of Isis were expelled for religious reasons, while others assert that Rome acted purely to maintain law and order.[19]

The second Jewish expulsion from Rome, which is more related to our present topic, happened in 49 CE under the reign of Claudius. We have a few sources referring to this event: Suetonius, Dio Cassius,[20] Orosius,[21] and Luke in Acts 18:2.[22] Several important questions loom before us concerning the Edict of Claudius, namely, what was the cause of the expulsion, who was expelled, and how many? Suetonius says that the Jews were expelled because "they constantly made disturbances *impulsore Chresto*" ("at the instigation of *Chrestus*"). Suetonius's famous phrase, *impulsore Chresto*, is not easy to interpret. Opinions differ greatly among the sources as well as historians as to what he meant by the phrase and what actually caused the disturbanc-

---

15. Barclay, *Jews in the Mediterranean Diaspora*, 298; Rutgers, "Roman Policy toward the Jews," 98–99.

16. See Josephus, *Antiquities of the Jews* 18.81–84.

17. See Dio Cassius, *Roman History* 57.18.5a. Dio Cassius was a Roman historian, c. 150–235 CE, who wrote the *Roman History* (*Historia Romana*) covering a period about 1,400 years, beginning with the arrival of the legendary Aeneas in Italy (c.1200 BCE) and ending with the historical events of the year 229 CE.

18. For a summary of the various sources, see Barclay, *Jews in the Mediterranean Diaspora*, 298–301.

19. Rutgers ("Roman Policy toward the Jews," 102 and 104) suggests that the expulsion of the Jews in 19 CE was primarily because of political rather than religious reasons.

20. While Dio dated the event to 41 CE, which is the year of Claudius' inauguration, scholars think that he must have meant 49 CE as Orosius has it. This date also fits with the time and sequence of Priscilla and Aquila's arrival in Corinth in 50 CE when they met up with Paul. See Brändle and Stegemann, "Formation of the First 'Christian Congregations' in Rome," 125–26.

21. Paulus Orosius was a fifth century CE historian and theologian and a student of St. Augustine of Hippo. His most important apologetic work is the *Seven Books of History Against the Pagans* (*Historiarum Adversum Paganos Libri VII*).

22. Suetonius, *Claudius* 25.4; Dio Cassius 60.6.6; Orosius, *Adversum Paganos* 7.6.15–16. It is interesting to note that this important event is not recorded by Josephus or Tacitus.

es.[23] According to Dio Cassius, Claudius did not expel the Jews since they were too numerous, but rather only prohibited them from holding private gatherings in order to prevent potential unrest.[24] The problem with Dio's account is that he dated the event in the year 41 CE. Orosius, on the other hand, asserts that Josephus records Claudius' expulsion of Jews in his 9th year, which is 49 CE. The difficulty with Orosius' statement is that there is no such report found in Josephus. Perhaps Luke might give us a little more information. He states, "After that, Paul left Athens and went to Corinth. There he found a Jew named Aquila, a native of Pontus recently arrived from Italy with his wife Priscilla. An edict of Claudius had ordered *all Jews* to leave Rome" (Acts 18:1–2a; emphasis mine). Acts 18:2 at least confirms the Edict of Claudius and the date was likely 49 CE based on the sequence of events in Acts. Luke however does not specify the reason for the expulsion.

From the sources, we can only surmise that at the end of the year 40, during the reign of Claudius, intense conflicts arose between Jews and Jewish believers who professed that Jesus is the Christ. The confrontation caused such a disturbance in the capital that police action was necessary to maintain law and order and even the emperor himself had to intervene. Perhaps in the beginning (in 41 CE, if Dio is reliable) Claudius only suppressed but did not expel the Jews. Later, when the situation got a bit out of hand and clearly threatened law and order, he decided to expel the Jews. The silence about this expulsion in other important sources, such as Josephus, Tacitus, and Dio Cassius, could indicate that the number was small or insignificant, for to expel "all Jews" as Luke records it would amount to twenty to thirty thousand people.[25] Such an expulsion would have caused disorder and a logistical nightmare. Some historians therefore propose that only (and perhaps only certain) Christian Jews or possibly only "ringleaders" were expelled but definitely not all.[26] There were other Christians who are called, "God-fearers," that remained in Rome after the expulsion.[27] Paul's farewell greetings in Romans 16, which includes many Jews and non-Jews, indicate that the Christian community in Rome endured quite well and was

23. Rutgers, "Roman Policy toward the Jews," 105.

24. Barclay, *Jews in the Mediterranean Diaspora*, 304.

25. Ibid., 105–6.

26. Rutgers, "Roman Policy toward the Jews," 106. Acts 28:15 indicates that there was already a thriving Christian community in Rome when Paul arrived at the capital. Much speculation has been made as to who founded the Christian community in Rome. The fact is that we cannot know due to the limited sources. See Brändle and Stegemann, "Formation of the First 'Christian Congregations' in Rome," 127.

27. Brändle and Stegemann, "Formation of the First 'Christian Congregations' in Rome," 126.

thriving when he wrote to them in the mid-50s. Furthermore, Paul's letter also presupposes that Jewish Christians, among them Priscilla and Aquila, eventually did return to Rome after only a few years when the situation had improved.

PRISCILLA AND AQUILA

Priscilla and Aquila are mentioned six times in the New Testament by three different authors: three times by Luke (Acts 18:1–3, 18–19, 26–27); twice by Paul (1 Cor 16:19; Rom 16:3); and once by a Deutero–Pauline (2 Tim 4:19). Priscilla, as Luke consistently calls her, is the affectionate diminutive of Prisca.[28] Paul however prefers to address her by her formal name, Prisca. Throughout this chapter, I will use Priscilla as Luke affectionately calls her. Four out of six times and by all three authors, Priscilla (Acts 18:18, 26; Rom 16:3; 2 Tim 4:19) is named before her husband. Showing such precedence over her husband was certainly unusual in the ancient world. Scholars have postulated various reasons for such an unconventional occurrence. Some suggest that it was her wealth and social status (for example from noble birth) that gave her precedence.[29] However, since Priscilla worked manually alongside her husband (Acts 18:3), Murphy-O'Connor indicates that she neither outranked her husband in social status nor by independent wealth. A woman of noble origins would not be accustomed to the heavy needle and palm work of tentmakers. Furthermore, a woman with wealth would not have to work. Consequently, most scholars, including Murphy-O'Connor,[30] think that the preference of Priscilla's name is probably judged by her greater prominence in the life of the church.[31] In other words, Priscilla possibly played a greater role in ministry and leadership. However, the alternating order of their names (twice Aquila's name appears first) could simply reinforce the "mutuality of this couple's relationship."[32] Whatever the case might be, this married couple is inseparable and a model of collaboration, for apart from each other they do not appear at all.

---

28. Walker, "Portrayal of Aquila and Priscilla in Acts," 489. According to Walker, Luke intentionally changed "Prisca" to "Priscilla" as a way to downplay her role as a leader in the church. Walker also argues that Acts reflects a distinctly anti-feminist bias (490).

29. Keller, *Priscilla and Aquila*, xiii.

30. Murphy-O'Connor, "Prisca and Aquila," 40–51.

31. See Keller, *Priscilla and Aquila*, xiii–xv.

32. Ibid., xv.

We know a lot about this extraordinary migrant and missionary couple. What follows is a brief examination from all three available sources, namely, Luke, Paul and Deutero-Pauline (or First Timothy). Since Luke provides us with the most information, we shall start with the book of Acts. The references are as follows:

- "After this [Paul] left Athens and went to Corinth. There he met a Jew named Aquila, a native of Pontus, who had recently come from Italy with his wife Priscilla because Claudius had ordered all the Jews to leave Rome. He went to visit them and, because he practiced the same trade, stayed with them and worked, for they were tentmakers by trade" (18:1–13);

- "Paul remained for quite some time, and after saying farewell to the brothers he sailed for Syria, together with Priscilla and Aquila. At Cenchreae he had his hair cut because he had taken a vow. When they reached Ephesus, he left them there, while he entered the synagogue and held discussions with the Jews" (18:18–19);

- "He began to speak boldly in the synagogue; but when Priscilla and Aquila heard him, they took him aside and explained to him the Way (of God) more accurately. And when he wanted to cross to Achaia, the brothers encouraged him and wrote to the disciples there to welcome him. After his arrival he gave great assistance to those who had come to believe through grace" (18:26–27). (*NAB Rev*)

Luke gives us three separate descriptions of this married couple. The first description (Acts 18:1–3) describes four important details about them. First, Aquila and Priscilla are a married couple and probably free *peregrini*. They seemed to be legally married, and marriage based on Roman law existed only between two free citizens.[33] However, the fact that they were expelled from Rome without due process may imply that they did not have the full status of free citizens but only as free *peregrini* or *Latini Iuniani*. Luke also tells us that Aquila is a diaspora Jew, "a native of Pontus."[34] Second, this married couple was expelled from Rome due to the Edict of Claudius in 49

33. How they were married and ended up in Rome is all a matter of pure speculation (see Keller, *Priscilla and Aquila*, 3–4). One interesting theory proposes that Aquila was an independent businessman–adventurer (who could be a free man, slave, or freed slave of the Roman Acilian family), whose work led him to the house of Priscilla, who was a free woman living in Rome.

34. Luke mentions in Acts 2:9 that there were people from Pontus present at Pentecost. It is possible that those who were present at that occasion could have brought the faith to Pontus. It could also be possible that Aquila himself was present at that event and was converted.

CE. Third, they immigrated to Corinth and settled there by the spring of 50 CE as tentmakers (and/or leatherworkers).[35] Fourth, Paul met up with them in Corinth and resided in their home, and the three worked together as tentmakers. We believe that Paul arrived at Corinth sometime in mid to late 50 CE. This scenario fits well with Paul's appearance before Gallio, the proconsul of Achaia, in 51/52 CE, recorded in Acts 18:12. The couple seemed to have been Christ believers before they left Rome. As mentioned previously, only Judean Christ believers and perhaps only "ringleaders" were expelled. It is also unlikely for a Judean who had been expelled because of Christ to associate with anyone who is a Christ believer, for example Paul, unless that person is already a Christian.[36] If our scenario is correct, Priscilla and Aquila therefore established the Christian community in Corinth, since they arrived in Corinth before Paul.[37]

In Luke's second description (Acts 18:18–19), we learn that Priscilla and Aquila were missionary companions of Paul and founders of the church in Ephesus. After having spent eighteen months (18:11) working side by side with Paul in Corinth, the couple uprooted themselves again. Priscilla and Aquila sacrificed everything they had built up in Corinth to accompany Paul on a 250 mile journey across the Aegean Sea to Ephesus. Luke says that Paul left them at Ephesus as soon as he arrived, which indicates that the migrant couple must have founded the church in Ephesus.[38]

Luke's third description (Acts 18:26–27) credits Priscilla and Aquila as the catechizers who taught the great preacher Apollos, a Judean native of Alexandria. Apollos was not just any convert to the faith; he was as an eloquent speaker, who was well versed in the scriptures (18:24). Their teaching was so effective that after only a brief time Apollos wished to move on to Achaia, perhaps to bring the Good News there also.

---

35. Murphy-O'Connor ("Prisca and Aquila," 50) suggests that Priscilla and Aquila were expelled from Rome in 41 CE and that they had lived in Corinth for some ten years.

36. Murphy-O'Connor, "Prisca and Aquila," 47; Keller, *Priscilla and Aquila*, 12. Keller suggests that perhaps Aquila, a native of Pontus, might have been in Jerusalem during Pentecost and then brought the Good News to Rome. The silence about their baptism also indicates that they were already baptized before they arrived at Corinth. Some suggest that the couple was baptized in the early 40s.

37. Murphy-O'Connor even proposes that the couple could have migrated to Corinth since 41 CE during the first wave of expulsions by Claudius. Evidence supporting this hypothesis is weak. Keller (*Priscilla and Aquila*, 27) is convinced that this couple was responsible for establishing the community in Corinth.

38. Maloney, "Priscilla and Aquila Set Out Again," 8. Luke however positions Paul as the real initiator of the new mission as recorded in Acts 18:19. See Keller, *Priscilla and Aquila*, 23.

Paul has two references about the couple:

- "The churches of Asia send you greetings. Aquila and Prisca together with the church at their house send you many greetings in the Lord" (1 Cor 16:19);

- "Greet Prisca and Aquila, my co-workers in Christ Jesus, who risked their necks for my life, to whom not only I am grateful but also all the churches of the Gentiles; greet also the church at their house" (Rom 16:3–5a).

The first occurrence is found in the farewell greetings of the letter to the Corinthian church (1 Cor 16:19). Paul probably wrote First Corinthians in the mid-fifties from Ephesus, where Priscilla and Aquila were residing at the time. After arriving from Corinth, Paul left this couple in Ephesus to establish and build up the church there as he went on to Antioch, Galatia, and Phrygia (Acts 18:21). Paul rejoined them sometime later, supposedly on his third missionary journey (Acts 19:1). Priscilla and Aquila were left to build up the community, teach about Jesus the Christ (as they did for Apollos and presumably many others), and continue to provide fellowship or meals in their home. The detail mentioned by Paul in his address, "together with the church in their house," (1 Cor 16:19) could very well indicate that Paul resided in their home when he wrote 1 Corinthians.[39] The greetings from Priscilla and Aquila would have been very well received by the Corinthian community since they had shared so much during their time in Corinth.

Paul's second reference about the couple occurs in the farewell greetings of the letter to the Romans (16:3–5a). The letter was probably written in 56 or 57 CE, when Priscilla and Aquila had already returned to Rome.[40] In this brief description, Paul highlights four outstanding features about this missionary couple. First, Paul regards them as his "co-workers" in Christ Jesus. Second, they risked "their necks" for his life, perhaps because they had defended Paul and remained faithful to him. Third, Paul and "all the churches of the Gentiles" are grateful to them. And fourth, believers are meeting in their home in Rome,[41] just as they had while they were in Ephesus (1 Cor 16:19) and in Corinth (Acts 18:1–3).

---

39. For the significance of house church in early Christianity, see Keller, *Priscilla and Aquila*, 30–50.

40. The couple, along with other Judean Christ believers, could have returned soon after the death of Claudius in the fall of 54 CE.

41. The church of Prisc(ill)a and Aquila in Rome is built on top of an ancient house church believed to have been the home of this missionary couple. Inside the church, there is a fresco depicting Peter baptizing Priscilla.

The final reference concerning this extraordinary lay couple appears in Second Timothy: "Greet Prisca and Aquila and the family of Onesiphorus" (4:19). This highly contested letter is considered to be a Deutero-Pauline text by many biblical scholars, meaning that it is not written by Paul himself but by a disciple of Paul who claims to be Paul. Pseudonymity, or writing under an "alias" name, is not uncommon in ancient literature. Whatever the case might be, the author of this letter sends greeting to Priscilla and Aquila who are depicted as "faithfully ministering with Timothy in Ephesus."[42] The letter to First Timothy (1:3) indicates that Timothy resides in Ephesus. From this seemingly insignificant reference, we are informed that by late first century or early second century, when these pastoral letters were written, the missionary couple had once again immigrated to Ephesus. Furthermore, being listed first in the greetings testifies to the enormous respect and regard the author and early believers had for them.

The six references to Priscilla and Aquila by three New Testament authors tell us a lot about this extraordinary immigrant missionary couple. As a way to summarize, here is a list of what we know about them:

- A married couple who convert from Judaism
- Expelled from Rome for being Christ believers and perhaps "ringleaders"
- Tentmakers (and/or leatherworkers)
- Refugees living in exile in Corinth and Ephesus
- Missionary companions and "co-workers" of Paul
- Founders (and/or co-founders) of the churches at Corinth and Ephesus
- Mentors and catechizers[43] of the great preacher Apollos
- Teachers, leaders, and hosts of the local church in their own home or house-church (Corinth, Ephesus, and Rome)
- Collaborators of Timothy in Ephesus
- Respected by Paul, Timothy, and all the churches of the Gentiles

One noticeable conclusion from the list above is that Priscilla and Aquila were exemplary immigrant missionaries who did not hesitate to bring the faith with them wherever they went. Aquila was originally from Pontus and immigrated to Rome where he might have met and married Priscilla. While in Rome, the couple was forced to migrate to Corinth because of the

---

42. Keller, *Priscilla and Aquila*, 55.

43. A catechist is one who gives religious instruction. The word comes from Greek *katechesis* or "oral instruction."

persecution by Claudius (49 CE). They then moved to Ephesus (53 CE) to accompany Paul in his travels and to establish a new Christian community and center in the capital of Asia Minor. After Claudius' death, they returned to Rome (58 CE). According to First Timothy, they eventually moved back to Ephesus (circa 64 CE). This couple was frequently on the move. With basic portable tools (awl, needles, and thread), they were able to relocate with ease, making mobility more possible. During their journeys, whether voluntary or involuntary, this migrant couple planted churches in at least three different cities, collaborated with the apostle Paul and Timothy, and catechized Apollos and presumably many others. Their homes became house churches and hospitality centers. The case of Priscilla and Aquila therefore provides a paradigm of migration and mission in early Christianity and also for today. Whether it was by force or by missionary strategy, Priscilla and Aquila showed that migration could be part of God's great plan and a means for the expansion of the church.

MIGRANTS AS MISSIONARIES

Migration was a key factor in the expansion of the church in the New Testament times.[44] In the book of Acts, Luke records numerous stories of Christian missions advanced in the context of migration. Early Hellenistic Christians who were scattered because of religious persecution founded churches in Samaria (8:1), Damascus (9:2), Phoenicia, Cyprus, and Antioch (11:19). In other cases, voluntary immigrants moved with a missionary purpose in mind. The efforts of Peter, John, and other itinerant missionaries succeeded in planting new communities in various towns throughout the regions of Judea, Galilee, and Samaria (9:31; 10:1–48). Paul, Barnabas, and their traveling companions were sent out on various missionary journeys to establish and build up the Christian communities in Celicia, Illyricum, Asia Minor, Macedonia, and Achaia (Rom 15:19, 23–24). Paul's list of farewell greetings in Romans 16 likewise gives us a glimpse of his successful mission endeavor, reaching all the way to the imperial capital. We are told that he even planned to travel to Spain (Rom 15:24) to evangelize to the edge of the known world.

44. The link between migration and mission is already found in the life of Jesus. Hanciles states that "Jesus' life and ministry embodied the interconnection of mission, boundary–crossing movement, and the alienation of exile and migration" (*Beyond Christendom*, 150). For a brief survey of the theme of migration in the Bible, see Nguyen "Asian in Motion: A Biblical Reflection on Migration," and how Jesus is depicted as an infant refugee and an itinerant preacher, see Nguyen, "In Solidarity with the Strangers: The Flight into Egypt."

Jehu Hanciles correctly notes that "Christianity is a migratory religion, and migration movements have been a functional element in its expansion."[45] Hanciles observes that the six ages or phases of Christian history that were identified by Andrew Walls were shaped in one way or another by migratory movements.[46] From the very beginning, Christian expansion and migratory movement were forcibly and intimately intertwined. In a more comprehensive study, Hanciles' book explores the massive consequential connection between migration and mission in the history of Christian missionary expansion, starting with the age of European migrations in the sixteenth century.[47] The book successfully demonstrates that migratory movement was and remains a prime factor in the global spread of Christianity, Islam, and other world religions. What he says in the concluding section of the book bears truth and wisdom, "Every Christian migrant is a potential missionary."[48]

Statistics show that we are undeniably living in "the age of migration."[49] The global (im)migrant population is estimated to be around 214 million people.[50] According to the estimation of the International Organization for Migration (IOM), that is one out of every thirty-three people on the move worldwide today. However, based on the religious composition of international migrants in 2010, approximately 105 million international migrants were Christians.[51] This equals 49 percent of all international migrants on the planet. Statistics clearly indicate that Christian immigrants are the largest population on the move. The top two favorite destinations of Christian immigrants are North America (72 percent of 43 million immigrants) and Europe (57 percent of 40 million immigrants).[52] Noticeably, 85 percent of

45. Hanciles, "Migration and Mission," 149.

46. Ibid., 148–49. For a complete study, see Walls, *The Missionary Movement in Christian History*, 16–25. See also Walls, "Mission and Migration," 3–11.

47. Hanciles, "Migration and Mission," 157ff.

48. Ibid., 378.

49. Castles and Miller, *Age of Migration*.

50. For more facts and figures, see the IOM's website: http://www.iom.int/jahia/Jahia/about–migration/facts–and–figures/lang/en [accessed on June 11, 2012].

51. For the religious composition of internal migrants in 2010, see http://www.statista.com/statistics/221157/religious–composition–of–international–migrants/ [accessed on August 30, 2012]. According to this figure, the top seven religious affiliations of international immigrants are as followed: Christian (105,670,000); Muslim (58,580,000); Unaffiliated (19,330,000); Hindu (10,700,000); other religions (9,110,000); Buddhist (7,310,000); and Jewish (3,650,000).

52. For charts and other pertinent statistics, see http://www.statista.com/statistics/221384/immigration–to–north–america–by–religion/ [accessed on August 30, 2012].

immigrants to Latin America and the Caribbean are Christians.[53] If every Christian migrant is a potential missionary, migration then could have enormous prospects and opportunities for evangelism. When Christian immigrants travel, they take their religion with them, or more personally, their God literally migrates with them. As people in transition, who experience the pain of homelessness and uprootedness, "they are usually open to new commitments and ready to assume faith in a personal way."[54] The case of Priscilla and Aquila is a good example for lay Christian immigrants scattered all over the globe to emulate, for their displacement, whether voluntary or involuntary, can serve as an opportunity for church planting, hospitality, mission and evangelism. Furthermore, the story of Priscilla and Aquila also serves as a reminder for the church to realize that Christian immigrants, voluntary and involuntary, can fall within the plan of God and become a key factor in the expansion of the church.

53. See, http://www.statista.com/statistics/221400/immigration-to-latin-america-and-the-caribbean-by-religion/ [accessed on August 30, 2012].

54. Escobar, "Mission Fields on the Move," 31.

6

Paul and Barnabas in Lystra
Lessons for Crossing Cultural Boundaries in Ministry

—Amy C. West

Fleeing from stoning in Iconium, Paul and Barnabas crossed cultural boundaries and entered the region of Lycaonia (Acts 14:6). It is not unusual for people to cross boundaries; they have crossed them from the time boundaries were formed. God's people frequently cross cultural boundaries—some willingly, such as Abram who was commissioned by God to leave his ancestral home in Ur for a country "that I shall show you" (Gen 12:1 NRSV). God commissioned Paul, formerly known as Saul of Tarsus, to be his chosen instrument to go to the Gentiles (Acts 9:15). Paul and Barnabas were later sent by the church to take the gospel to new places, which often required crossing cultural boundaries (Acts 13:1–3). Jesus himself instructed his followers to cross borders, even to the remotest parts of the earth (Acts 1:8). Others crossed boundaries unwillingly, such as Daniel who was taken by force to Babylon (Dan 1:3–7). Persecution scattered yet others, for example the Christians scattered from Jerusalem (Acts 8:1). In each of these new cultural contexts, God's people encountered beliefs and rituals, often very different from those at home.

This chapter examines the story of Paul and Barnabas in Lystra (Acts 14:6–23).[1] The aim is to uncover lessons for God's people today, specifically those engaging in ministry across cultural boundaries. First, I discuss what in Lystra ignited the peoples' reaction to Paul and Barnabas (Acts 14:8–13) and then look at the apostles' response (14:14–18). Next, I will apply two lessons from this event for today. The first is the necessity of understanding peoples' underlying beliefs and ritual relationships; rituals are themselves a window on beliefs and relationships. The second lesson is the necessity of addressing from Scripture a peoples' underlying beliefs and ritual relationships, seeking to direct their hearts to God.

SUPERNATURAL HEALING IN LYSTRA (ACTS 14:6–18)

Having fled to Lystra, Paul and Barnabas continued to preach the gospel. One day, Paul observed a cripple listening to him. Perceiving that this man had faith to be healed, Paul addressed him directly and in a loud voice ordered him to stand up. The cripple leaped up and walked around, astounding those watching as they knew he had been unable to walk since birth. The people responded to this obviously supernatural event in accordance with their culture's experience and perspective. They knew a ritual was needed, a sacrifice to their gods. Paul and Barnabas, on the other hand, sought to turn the Lycaonians' focus from their traditional response to expressing gratitude to the living God.

Lycaonians' Cultural Response

When the crowd saw the man, who was crippled from birth, suddenly stand up and walk around, the people intuitively understood the healing to be a supernatural phenomenon. They assumed their city's deities, Zeus and Hermes, had arrived.[2] Concluding that Barnabas was their guardian deity Zeus, while Paul, the main speaker, was Hermes, the messenger of the gods, they sent for the priest of Zeus. He went into action, bringing oxen

1. Lystra had been made a Roman colony by Caesar Augustus in 6 BCE. Army veterans and their families were moved there to live among the population of "mostly uneducated Lycaonians, who came from a small Anatolian tribe and spoke their own language. The ruling class was made up of Roman army veterans while education and commerce were controlled by a few Greeks. Jews also lived there (16:3) but their influence seems to have been minimal" (Longenecker, "Acts," 434).

2. The literary evidence in Ovid, along with two inscriptions and a stone altar discovered near Lystra, indicate that Zeus and Hermes were worshipped together as local patron deities. See Stott, *The Message of Acts*, 231.

and wreaths to the city gates, intending to make an appropriate sacrifice. The peoples' actions in response to this healing open a window into their underlying beliefs and their ritual relationships to which they turn when an obviously supernatural event occurs.

Underlying Beliefs

A peoples' belief system forms the basis for how they as a society develop and perform rituals. Belief systems are formed through a people's social interaction, combined with reflection on this experience. Belief systems help a people determine what is real and what is false, what is important and what is not. Beliefs regarding the reality of an unseen, supernatural realm and of supernatural beings determine if and how that realm is included in a culture's ritual practices. Beliefs such as these are what "frame the context— definitions, meanings and motivations—of our daily lives."[3] The people of Lystra, like others in the first century Greco-Roman world, had culturally defined beliefs about their gods being the source of fortune and misfortune.[4] They believed the gods "could help them in practical ways for their earthly needs and, in many instances, bring them a blissful afterlife."[5] These beliefs created the foundation upon which the people of Lystra structured their cultural response. They had "a body of rules telling what had to be done or avoided in order to influence the gods for good."[6]

The quick action of the inhabitants of Lystra was most likely influenced by their fear of angering the gods. Socio-biologists point out the preeminence of heart over head in times of crisis, noting that "our emotions . . . guide us in facing predicaments and tasks too important to leave to the intellect alone—danger, painful loss, persisting toward a goal despite frustrations, bonding with a mate, building a family."[7] Finn notes of Greco-Roman culture:

> To be sure, the gods were felt to be ever present with people, but so was their anger, anger that could flash out at any act of omission that disturbed the right relation between them and human beings—especially a ritual act of omission. The welfare

---

3. Lingenfelter, *Agents of Transformation*, 219.

4. Arnold, *Powers of Darkness*, 58–60, 64, 65; Ferguson, *Backgrounds of Early Christianity*, 213–18; Malherbe, *The World of the New Testament*, 24.

5. Arnold, *Powers of Darkness*, 35.

6. Jeffers, *The Greco-Roman World of the New Testament Era*, 90.

7. Goleman, *Emotional Intelligence*, 4.

of individual and empire depended on maintaining the right relationship with the gods.[8]

Accordingly, the fear of offending the gods kept those in Lystra, as with other Greco-Romans, sensitive to any possible omissions.

The Lystran crowd's swift actions may also have been in response to their belief that they needed to show proper respect to the gods. Respect was needed to avoid the dire consequences of those who had failed to do so in ages past. Many commentaries point to Ovid's account of a previous visit to the area by Zeus and Hermes.[9] That account, passed down from the ancestors, told how these same gods, Zeus and Hermes, had come into the area disguised as humans. During that visit, however, people had not recognized them and so failed to treat them with due respect. Only two people, Philemon and Baucis, had welcomed the disguised deities into their home. Consequently, the gods retaliated, destroying the area with a flood; Philemon and Baucis were the only ones saved.[10] Stories like this, passed down from generation to generation, contribute to what people believe and influence their responses in certain situations. This local legend may well explain the Lycaonians' fear and hence their quick response. They may have believed that the gods would retaliate should they not respond appropriately this time.

Lystran beliefs in the reality of spiritual beings and in the supernatural power of those beings open a window of understanding as to why they responded the way they did to the healing of the cripple. They understood what needed to be done to maintain a right relationship with their gods.

Ritual Relationships

The Lycaonians related to both social and spiritual beings. These relationships had to be maintained to preserve equilibrium in their lives. Lingenfelter points out how the relationships we value and to which we give priority are what assist us to accomplish our interests.[11] One's interests focus on meeting biological, economic, social, and spiritual needs. Cultures have structured systems for its people to achieve those interests. Relationships ultimately affect how we think about the world and how our ideas

8. Finn, *From Death to Rebirth,* 48.

9. See Ovid, *Metamorphoses* 8.620–724 . Also detailed in Boice, *Acts,* 255; Bruce, *The Book of the Acts,* 276; Stott, *The Message of Acts,* 230–31.

10. Many animistic cultures have myths about a flood that wiped out humanity. The Balangao in the northern Philippines tell how the flood happened right there.

11. Ibid., 226.

are shaped. The people of Lystra turned to both their social and spiritual relationships to achieve their interests. Assuming the gods were the source of the miraculous healing, they turned to the priest of Zeus for help in performing the essential ritual. It was critical that they make a proper ritual response to gods who had power over human affairs—their well-being was at stake. The priest of Zeus brought what was necessary for the traditional sacrifice—oxen decorated with traditional garlands. He led them to the city gates where most likely the temple of Zeus stood.[12] The Lycaonians' ritual response to this supernatural event flowed from their traditional beliefs regarding what needed to be done to maintain their relationship with the gods. We turn now to the response of Paul and Barnabas to those actions, a response permeated by Scripture.

Response of Paul and Barnabas

When they saw the oxen being brought for a sacrifice and realized that the Lycaonians thought they were gods, Paul and Barnabas moved quickly to stop the peoples' traditional response to their deities. They tore their clothes—a Jewish sign of horror at blasphemy (Matt 26:65; Mark 14:63–64). Rushing into the crowd they cried out, "Friends, why are you doing this? We are mortals just like you" (Acts 14:15). Paul spoke immediately to their core value—the gods. He began to introduce new information about one greater than their gods, namely the living God, who created the heavens and the earth, seeking to redirect their focus onto him rather than on their lesser gods.[13] Thus, Paul confronted the Lycaonians' underlying beliefs and associated ritual relationships by using insights from the Scriptures.

Addressing the Underlying Beliefs

The Lycaonians believed that some of the gods held sway over the heavens, some over the earth, and still others over the underworld. Paul, realizing that they were proceeding to pay ritual respect to their gods for this miraculous healing, continued with further information about God's supernatural powers, information they did not yet have. Trained under Gamaliel (Acts 22:3), Paul was very familiar with the Scriptures. Even in the midst of the Lycaonians' excited response, he focused his thoughts and used Scripture to

12. Barnes, *Acts of the Apostles*, 218.

13. Many commentators attribute what is said in 14:15–17 to Paul even though the text does not specify him alone. Arnold, *Acts*, 134; Boice, *Acts*, 255; Stott, *The Message of Acts*, 231.

address their beliefs and actions. He contrasted their gods with the Creator God. He told them he brought good news and exhorted them to turn from their useless gods (Deut 32:17, 21; 1 Sam 12:21; Jer 14:22) and turn to the true source of their well-being, the living God, the creator of the heavens, the earth, the sea, and all things that are in them (Exod 20:11; Ps 146:6; Acts 14:15). Paul continued by expounding on the true God, that although in past generations God had "all the nations to follow their own ways" (Acts 14:16), God was still personally involved in human history and had not left them without evidence of himself (Acts 14:17). Here Paul develops the verification of God's witness, that this good God sends rain from heaven, makes crops grow, gives food and makes hearts glad (Lev 26:4; Deut 11:14; Ps 65:9–10; 104:14–15, 27; 147:8, 18; Acts 14:17). Paul thus exhorted the Lycaonians to redirect their ritual response of gratitude to this living God rather than to their vain gods.

Addressing Ritual Relationships

The Lycaonians had turned to the priest of Zeus to perform the required sacrifice to the gods. He was the one they traditionally trusted for help in avoiding any possible reprisal of the deities. Paul, using insights from Scripture, tried to persuade them that their gods were worthless. Their gods were not the ones who healed the cripple—nor had they provided anything else. It was to the living God that a respectful relationship was due. Switching allegiance from their gods to the living God would bring them into direct conflict with their society and with their social networks that were important to them for achieving their interests. Those social relationships were culturally strong and wielded a powerful influence. Any Christians in the area would be marginalized, considered "outsiders to the normal flow of daily living, no longer paying respect to the gods and goddesses who protected household and city."[14] Paul knew it was vital for those who switched allegiance to the living God to have a network of trusted relationships of support for each other. There was, in fact, a body of believers that had been developing in Lystra, and Paul understood the need to strengthen them. Later he and Barnabas returned to encourage those believers to continue in their faith, and he appointed elders for the church (Acts 14:21–23). He acknowledged they would face many tribulations, and so sought to focus them on the kingdom of God (14:22).

Cultural beliefs and traditional ritual responses are often deeply ingrained in society. Despite their best efforts, Paul and Barnabas found it

14. Doran, *Birth of a Worldview*, 65.

exceedingly difficult to dissuade the Lycaonians from offering sacrifice to them (Acts 14:18). This incident and the response of Paul and Barnabas provide lessons that can be applied to those engaged in contemporary ministry across cultural boundaries. We see the need to understand peoples' rituals with their associated beliefs and relationships and the need to verbalize and address those beliefs and relationships with Scripture.

CONTEMPORARY APPLICATION

Appropriate ways to relate on social levels, on spiritual levels, and to ritual beliefs are deeply ingrained from childhood. Thus, an important part of redirecting a people's focus and influencing their choices is to recognize the complexity of the internal negotiation process in which they engage for decision-making. The transformation of ingrained ritual responses is almost always accompanied by intense struggles. A powerful fear of reprisal drives people to continue in their established patterns.

Peoples' rituals are formulated for specific reasons and can have serious social and spiritual consequences if neglected. Rituals are essential elements in both the formation of social communities and the maintenance of their belief systems.[15] As Hiebert says,

> Rituals . . . give expression to and reinforce social structures, communicate information about the culture's cherished beliefs, feelings and values, and provide a sense of personal and corporate identity to those involved either as participants or as audiences.[16]

As teaching activities, rituals are a means whereby generations "learn of their heritage, reinforce their relationships to one another and to God (or gods) or their ancestors. Ritual takes many diverse forms, yet all rituals have symbolic importance to the participants."[17] Even after their symbolism is lost and participants no longer know the meaning behind a ritual, Lingenfelter asserts that "the mere performance of ritual often sustains the social purpose for which it was originally created."[18] Rituals are thus windows on a society's beliefs and relational networks.

As in Lystra, people are not easily swayed from what they know needs to be done. For transformation to happen, God's people must first

---

15. Hiebert et al., *Understanding Folk Religion*, 283.

16. Ibid., 290.

17. Lingenfelter, *Agents of Transformation*, 166.

18. Ibid., 166.

understand the underlying beliefs and relationships behind traditional practices and then address those from Scripture.

Seek to Understand

People generally are not consciously aware of all that underlies their rituals. While they generally know what needs to be done on given occasions, rarely do they think about the beliefs underlying those rituals or the reasons why those rituals must be done. Those in cross-cultural ministry need to study rituals in their context and so gain understanding of the peoples' beliefs and the relationships to which they turn for their well-being. To address rituals adequately, the cross-cultural worker must get a clear picture of what the ritual accomplishes for the people and what kind of pressures enforce it. Then those need to be addressed with Scripture.

Paul, throughout his ministry, addressed the core issues of people's beliefs that were reflected in their ritual practices (Acts 17:16–31 ; 1 Cor 8:1–13 ; Gal 3:1–29 ; Eph 3:1–13 ; Col 2:16–23). Those in contemporary ministry can apply lessons from the apostle Paul's approach. He spoke to the peoples' specific beliefs as the entry point for preaching the gospel. And in addressing those issues, he made Scripture foundational in his approach, both to the Jews and to the Gentiles.

Address with Scripture

Having been socialized within a culture, people typically accept their traditions implicitly, leaving them unanalyzed. It is only when those traditional beliefs and relationships are brought to the surface that they can be intentionally challenged by Scripture. When verbalized they are brought to conscious attention, and any possible contrast with Scripture becomes apparent. Thus, Paul, steeped in the Scriptures and relying on the Holy Spirit, addressed peoples' beliefs and relationships with Scripture that challenged their gods. In contemporary ministry, God's people also encounter thorny situations. Fernando points out that those in cross-cultural ministry will be faced with what feels like desperately complex situations that are replete with issues that need Scriptural answers.[19] He exhorts God's people to seek biblical answers prayerfully, encouraging them to be saturated in the Scriptures so they are ready with a response to challenging issues.[20] When people

19. Fernando, *Jesus Driven Ministry*, 98.
20. Ibid., 90.

discover that the Scriptures speak to their beliefs, their relationships, and their ritual needs, a new window of understanding is opened to them. It creates a legitimate reason for them to grapple with their traditional responses and consider who God is and what God has done.

When this information about God is new, those wanting to align their lives with God will encounter a paradigm shift that will most assuredly stir up intense inner tensions. Gushee challenges Christians to think beyond just transforming beliefs to transforming the very way people live and relate. He contends, "Christianity is more than an event, an experience or a set of beliefs. It is a way of life characterized by moral seriousness and the quest for holiness."[21] The paradigm shift that is required can shake persons to the core, regardless of the culture within which they have been socialized. It is particularly difficult for those from group-oriented cultures, where community pressures effectively compel them to conform to traditional expectations. Their social networks wield powerful influences on their decisions. When anyone strays from traditional practices, it has the potential of affecting the whole society. Consequently, society, too, has a vested interest in forcing adherence to traditional rites. Christians, therefore, are vulnerable. They need strong support if they are to focus their lives on honoring the living God. Relationships that can be trusted are critical for them to stand firm. Paul and Barnabas returned to Lystra to strengthen and encourage the disciples, helping to establish a structure for continuance in the faith (14:21–23). Likewise, those in contemporary ministry must do the same.

Just as the Scriptures inform beliefs, they must also inform relationships. God gives clear instructions regarding how his followers are to relate to each other. They are to love one another (John 15:12), to build one another up (Rom 14:19), to care for one another (1 Cor 12:25), to bear one another's burdens (Gal 6:2), to comfort one another with truth from Scripture (1 Thess 4:18), to comfort each other and edify one another (1 Thess 5:11), to pray for one another (Jas 5:16) and to serve one another (1 Pet 4:10). The relationships we strongly value influence our thinking and ultimately our decision-making.[22] When Christians are in vulnerable situations, they need strong relationships with fellow believers who will stand with them, reminding them of truths from Scripture. Insights from Scripture that address peoples' underlying beliefs and their ritual relationships are vital for helping them evaluate their traditional rituals in light of the living God.

21. Gushee, "Our Missing Moral Compass," 88.

22. Lingenfelter, *Transforming Culture*, 226.

CONCLUSION

In this paper I have discussed insights gained from the encounter of Paul and Barnabas with the Lycaonians' ritual system. Underlying peoples' ritual actions, a complex interplay takes place between traditional beliefs and social relationships. As Paul was ready to address Lycaonian beliefs and relationships with Scripture, so too, God's people moving across cultural borders need to be ready to address traditional beliefs and relationships with Scripture. Those beliefs and relational interests have emotional components that accompany them. Accumulated input from family and community passed down through the generations, also strongly influences the process. Adding to the societal complexity of the new context, God's people bring their own beliefs, relationships and ritual focus.[23] Endeavoring to understand the reasons for actions can present an opportunity for people to evaluate why they respond in a given manner. This creates an opportunity for God's people to generate dialogue and introduce Scripture to the process.

Thus, two lessons can be learned from the Lystra incident that are helpful to those in contemporary cross-cultural ministry. First, God's people need to understand the underlying beliefs embodied in peoples' rituals, and how information passed down through the generations influences those beliefs. Important relationships associated with those beliefs also need to be understood.

Second, God's people need to saturate themselves with Scripture. The Scriptures equip one to speak specifically to the critical beliefs and relationships that one encounters. Only then can one be prepared to point people to the living God who created everything, remains in control of all that happens, and is the One who is truly due people's gratitude and honor in each and every situation.

---

23. It should be noted, though it is beyond the scope of this paper, how important it is for those in cross-cultural ministry to be aware also of the influence on their own thinking of their childhood culture's beliefs, relational networks, and traditional ritual responses.

PART II

Contemporary Issues of Migration
and Mission

7

Undocumented Workers in the U.S.

A Challenge from the Good Samaritan

—Timothy A. Lenchak, SVD

TWO STORIES

Quelino Ojeda Jimenez arrived in the United States in 2007. Born in a small village in the state of Oaxaca, Mexico, he came to the U.S. to seek work. After all, someone had to support his wife, child, six sisters, parents, and grandmother. He worked for a time in South Carolina and Georgia. In August 2010 he moved to Chicago, where he found work as a roofer. One day while working he pulled hard to remove a sheet of metal from the roof. Unfortunately the metal was not fastened, and he fell backward over 20 feet to the ground. Three days later he woke up in the hospital, a near quadriplegic and connected to a ventilator. The hospital managed to save his life and to stabilize his condition. Just over twenty years old, he now speaks only with difficulty and still cannot breathe on his own. He can barely move his fingers and toes on one side.

On December 22, 2010, the hospital staff quickly disconnected him from the equipment in his room and told him he was going home. An airplane ambulance flew him from Chicago to the city of Oaxaca. Then he was transferred to a small hospital in a town four hours from his family. But they have spent little time with him because they cannot afford either transportation or hotels. And the hospital itself is so poor that it cannot afford new filters for his ventilator. Instead the staff there cleans the filters daily and reuses them. Ojeda said that he had no idea that the hospital in Chicago was planning on moving him to Mexico, and the Mexican consulate in Chicago was not informed about his transfer (the hospital was not legally obliged to do so). The hospital claimed that it had spent $650,000 on Ojeda's medical care and another $60,000 to bring him to Mexico. Normally U.S. hospitals would transfer such a patient to a rehabilitation center once he is in a stable condition. But no rehabilitation center or nursing home would accept him. He is an "illegal" or "undocumented" or "unauthorized" laborer in the U.S. He has no medical insurance. He has no way of paying for his care. The firm which hired Ojeda has since ceased to exist, and no one seems to know if it carried workers' compensation insurance.

In Illinois alone more than 272,000 undocumented Latino immigrants were uninsured in 2008. Only emergency medical care is given to those without insurance, and then they are on their own. The Mexican Consulate in Chicago reports that each year ten to fifteen medical repatriations occur. What makes Ojeda's case "completely unorthodox," according to the consulate, is the fact that he was repatriated against his wishes.[1]

A similar case is that of Jose, who slipped across the Rio Grande in 1997, when he was 18. Since he has numerous relatives in the U.S. who are citizens, he was able to stay with them until he found a job in Arkansas. For twelve years he worked in various factories. Eventually he married, and he and his wife now have three children—all born in the United States, all less than seven years of age. Using someone else's social security number, Jose was able to get a driver's license. He never got a ticket or was involved in an accident. But he was unable to renew his driver's license, because it was discovered that someone else had the same social security number. So now he drives to work without one, which causes him great anxiety. Recently he was rushed to the hospital for an emergency appendectomy. The hospital bill came to $49,000. He has no medical insurance (none is provided with his job), and he makes only $300 each week, which he needs to support his family. He fears that eventually he will be arrested and sent back to Mexico.

These are but two stories describing the difficulties of economic migrants who come to the U.S. without documentation and who develop medical problems. With these stories in mind I will examine the situation of undocumented Mexican laborers who have come to the United States because of their own financial situation. Unfortunately there is a common

---

1. Reported in the *Chicago Tribune*, February 7, 2011, 1, 4.

human tendency to demonize strangers, and in the U.S. this tendency has resulted in the habit of calling unauthorized workers "illegal aliens." This term identifies undocumented economic migrants as dangerous and criminal rather than as fellow human beings who are in need. Finally I will examine Jesus' Parable of the Good Samaritan, which challenges present American attitudes toward undocumented migrant workers.

HOW DO WE TREAT THE UNDOCUMENTED?

Ours is an age of migration, and there are numerous reasons why both authorized and unauthorized migration will continue into the near future. Almost all migration has some economic dimension to it. That is especially true today, since the migration of labor has been one of the bases of the capitalist world market. Whether we admit it or not, migrant workers have provided both skilled and unskilled labor for developed nations—including the United States—which have found it useful or necessary to exploit this labor. Economic factors (great differences in wealth between the North and the South, the phenomenon of globalization, and the movement of commodities and capital) are not the *only* reasons for migration, yet they are often crucial.[2]

> Over the last 30 years, economic restructuring in rich countries has been linked to a new international division of labor, in which migrant workers play important but varied roles. . . . It is disadvantaged and vulnerable groups of workers—migrant women, irregular workers, ethnic and racial minorities—who end up in the most precarious positions. Deprivation of human and worker rights for groups that lack legal status and market power seems to be an integral aspect of all advanced economies today.[3]

Economic factors don't just affect national and regional economies. They also influence the individual men and women—especially the young—who emigrate in search of work. Immigrants seek higher income, better opportunities, and professional advancement. Often they are fleeing situations of poverty, economic stagnation, and political oppression in their native lands. Too often they also experience hardship, prejudice, and exploitation in their country of adoption, yet these conditions may be better than those at home.

2. Castles and Miller, *The Age of Migration*, 123–24.
3. Ibid., 243–44.

Many migrate because they have little choice—they need to survive.[4] They are not so different from the millions of immigrants who arrived in the U.S. during the nineteenth and twentieth centuries.

Some Statistics

As of March 2010 there were 11.2 million unauthorized or undocumented immigrants living in the United States or 3.7% of the nation's total population. This figure is actually below the peak level of 12 million in 2007. Nearly half of these undocumented immigrants arrived in 2000 or later. In fact, although the number of unauthorized immigrants is below 2007 levels, it is three times the number of 1990 (when it was 3.5 million), and it has grown by one-third since 2008, when it was 8.4 million. Approximately eight million unauthorized immigrants are part of the U.S. workforce (5.2% of the total). According to some experts the U.S. economy needs immigrants, since most job growth is projected in those areas where native-born Americans have no interest in working.[5] A major problem for these workers is that U.S. labor laws often do not cover them. It is estimated that approximately three million agricultural workers, one million domestic employees, and seven million persons working for independent contractors are not covered by the National Labor Relations Act. To make things worse, the labor union movement, which defended workers' rights to a decent wage, insurance benefits, and the forty-hour work week, is notoriously weak in the twenty-first century.[6] States seeking to attract businesses and jobs are increasingly passing "right-to-work" laws. Modern economies tend to favor business and to pit worker against worker. The labor of immigrant workers (especially the undocumented) is often rewarded with suspicion, poverty, exploitation, and an insecure future.

Mexicans are the largest group of unauthorized immigrants in the United States, 6.5 million or 58% of the total. Mexicans also make up the largest number of legal immigrants, approximately the same number as illegal immigrants. The worst-paid laborers in the U.S. today are migrant farm workers, and the majority of these are Mexicans. Many immigrants work at jobs that do not provide health care benefits. Of the 45 million U.S.

4. Ibid., 5, 221; Groody, "Fruit of the Vine," 305.

5. Passel and Cohn, "Unauthorized Immigrant Population." The Department of Homeland Security and the Center for Immigration Studies gave a total of 10.8 million unauthorized immigrants in early 2009. See Camarota and Jensenius, "A Shifting Tide"; Kerwin, "The Natural Rights," 197–98; Trumbull, "Illegal Immigrants."

6. Kerwin, "The Natural Rights," 198–99.

residents who lack health care, 13% are native-born, 34.5% are foreign-born, and 45.3% are noncitizens. Eighteen per cent of immigrant children lack health care, while 7.5% of children of native parents have the same problem. Too many immigrants also work in dangerous jobs, often without worker compensation for injuries. Mexican migrants are 80% more likely to die on the job than native-born Americans. In some states a Mexican worker is four times more likely to die on the job than a native-born American worker. Some have called the deaths of undocumented workers in the U.S. an epidemic.[7]

Strangers and Illegal Aliens

Do unauthorized workers have rights? Many do not think so, since they are here illegally. But can we deny human rights to someone simply because he or she has crossed our borders without a visa? Do illegal immigrants have a right to medical care? Do they have a right to medical insurance? A market economy, which is basically that recognized by U.S. law, does not seem to recognize such rights. In a market economy all must offer their skills or labor to those who have need of them. No laws guarantee a match of skills and needs, no laws guarantee a decent wage (although some guarantee a "minimum" wage to those who work legally), no laws guarantee a job, and at least until recently no laws have guaranteed health insurance. Even native-born U.S. citizens have few if any *rights* to medical care.[8] Globalization has increased the competition for jobs on a worldwide basis, and certain businesses require *cheap* labor. Despite laws, prejudice, and harassment, illegals still manage to find jobs—at low salaries and without benefits such as health insurance or workers' injury compensation. In order to have inexpensive chickens and tomatoes and orange juice we often close our eyes to the exploitation of these desperate workers for the sake of our market economy.

A problem with unauthorized workers is that they are *strangers*. They do not belong to our families, to our neighborhoods, or to *our* culture. There is a natural tendency to be suspicious of strangers. They often look different from us, they do things differently, they eat different kinds of food, and they may speak a language which we do not understand. Thus we have a tendency to see strangers as "other," as foreign, as suspicious, and even as dangerous. Are strangers always a threat? Are unauthorized workers and

7. Castles and Miller, *The Age of Migration*, 120; Groody, "Fruit of the Vine," 309; Kerwin, "The Natural Rights," 198. See Pritchard, "A Mexican Worker."

8. To the best of my knowledge not even the Affordable Health Care for America Act of 2010 states that health care insurance is a human or legal right.

undocumented immigrants a threat to us? They certainly are if we treat them as dangerous, if we allow their differences to annoy us, disturb us, and to threaten us. One can easily make a monster of the unknown and to make an enemy of the stranger. The only way to avoid this is to integrate the stranger into our world and thus to cancel his or her "strangeness."[9]

Unfortunately there is a natural tendency to demonize strangers, especially those who cross our borders without a visa in order to seek work. We even call them "illegal aliens."[10] This term automatically puts them outside the law, outside our culture, and outside our sympathy. Illegal activity is assumed to be criminal activity, and thus it must be rooted out and punished. But we forget that laws—and even definitions—are made to conform to the needs and understandings of those who make them and that they can be changed when new needs and understandings develop. It is interesting that the term "alien" today is often used for extraterrestrial beings. Applying this term to undocumented immigrants gives the impression that they are somehow inhuman, repulsive, and threatening. For some it may be important to deny them a human face. Otherwise they might attract our sympathy as suffering fellow human beings. This especially seems true for immigrants from the Third World, since we don't normally call English or Irish or German immigrants to our shores "aliens." Neither do we associate such groups with terrorists. Does racism somehow enter into our vocabulary and into our minds when we seek to use such terms for Mexicans, Latin Americans, Asians, and Africans seeking to enter our country? Immigrants from the past are often looked upon as heroes, and Ellis Island is a monument to their courage. Mexicans did not pass through Ellis Island and therefore are somehow "aliens" rather than heroes.[11]

Legal Strategies

Most countries have made efforts to halt the movement of unauthorized people crossing their borders. But an increase in police officers and border

9. Bonora, "Lo 'Straniero' in Deuteronomio," 25.

10. Although the English word "alien" can refer simply to a person from another nation, it is often connected with what is "strange" and "foreign." *Merriam Webster's Collegiate Dictionary*, 10th ed. (1993), 29, even defines "alien" as "differing in nature or character typically to the point of incompatibility." The noun "alien" is related to the verb "alienate," which means "to make unfriendly, hostile, or indifferent where attachment formerly existed," and to the noun "alienation," which can mean "estrangement." Thus hospitality, which is the acceptance of that which seems alien, is the opposite of alienation.

11. Campese, "¿Cuantos Más?" 275–76.

patrols, numerous arrests, and new sophisticated fences built along the Mexican border have all failed to stop the flood of illegals looking for work, a better life, and greater security. Expensive technological gadgets and strategies aimed at criminalizing undocumented migrants have not succeeded in stopping them. Battistella says:

> The unsuccessful attempts to stop the movement of people have resulted in bringing additional violence against the migrants and in strengthening the tie of migrant smuggling with criminal trafficking. Thus unauthorized migration has become a quagmire where aspiration for dignity and freedom is intertwined with violence and criminality and the security response is paradoxically diminishing security precisely for the people who most need it, the migrants.[12]

The new strategies to stop migrants have only increased the death rate of those crossing our borders illegally. It is estimated that since 1993 an average of 1.25 migrants has died each day—a rather high price for the "serious" crime of wanting to improve their lives and provide for their families. American politicians frequently criticized the shooting of East Germans who sought to cross the Berlin Wall and flee communism. Yet there is little criticism by politicians of the fact that our fortified border with Mexico "has been more than 10 times deadlier to migrants from Mexico during the past nine years than the Berlin Wall was to East Germans throughout its 28-year existence."[13]

Criminalization

The current U.S. policy is to criminalize those without proper documentation. Thus unauthorized immigrants who come to the U.S. to join their families, many of whom may already be in the U.S. legally, are automatically considered criminals. If they later apply for a visa or for other documentation or even for citizenship, they can easily be denied because they have technically already broken U.S. law. Thus they are criminals. Any American citizen—including relatives or church workers who hope to relieve some of the suffering of illegal immigrants—can also be accused of breaking the law and aiding criminals. Two generations ago they would have been heroes. Today they are the enemy.

12. Battistella, "The Poor in Motion," 70. See also Kerwin, "The Natural Rights," 197.

13. Cornelius, "Controlling." See also Campese, "¿Cuantos Más?" 277; Hoover, "The Story of Humane Borders," 161.

This tendency to criminalize and demonize unauthorized workers helps us to ignore their suffering and the fact that thousands have died trying to enter the U.S. It's their fault, so what can we do? We usually forget that American laws and policies have forced needy immigrants to seek ever more dangerous ways to enter the country. The death and suffering of these unauthorized immigrants are simply "unintended consequences" of our laws or "collateral damage," a phrase our military likes to employ when our armed forces unintentionally kill innocent civilians in Afghanistan or in other troubled countries. One might ask if these deaths are truly "unintended." Even if they are, they are the consequence of an attitude of refusing to recognize the humanity of illegal migrants. After all, they are only criminals and aliens—even if they need medical attention.[14]

THE CHALLENGE TO CHRISTIANS TODAY

The church has often tried to face the issue of unauthorized migrants. Sometimes the church cannot help but become involved, since it regularly and charitably responds to human suffering. The church cannot simply dismiss undocumented laborers as "illegal aliens," since many illegal workers also join or form Christian communities in the receiving countries. Rather they are brothers and sisters. So what should the churches do? Obviously Christians too must deal with their own prejudices, fears, and hostility toward the stranger. Happily most Christian churches have welcomed these new if illegal members, seeing in them the "migrant" Christ—who was born in a stable far from home because there was no room for his parents at the local inn, who became a refugee in Egypt as a baby because of political violence, and who spent most of his ministry wandering from place to place. Christians have sought to be true to the nature of the church, which accepts everyone. As Pope John Paul II said, "In the Church no one is a stranger, and the Church is not foreign to anyone, anywhere."[15] Catholic tradition recognizes the right to migrate, and it has often worked with both refugees and economic migrants.[16]

The Catholic Church also needs to be involved because many if not most Mexican and Hispanic migrants are Catholic. It is estimated that at least 39% of Catholics today are Hispanic, and that number increases to 45% for those under the age of 30. Since the Hispanic population in the U.S.

14. Campese, "¿Cuantos Más?" 281.

15. Pope John Paul II, "Message for the 1995 Day of Migrants," 5. See Baggio, "The Migrant Ministry," 48.

16. Kerwin, "The Natural Rights," 193.

continues to grow (partly because of undocumented workers), the future of the church will be Hispanic.[17]

We know that hospitality was an important part of the ancient Israelite and Jewish culture. The Israelites knew what it meant to be strangers, outsiders, and immigrants. Their ancestors Abraham and Sarah, Isaac and Rebecca, and Jacob and Leah and Rachel were never quite at home in the land promised them by God. Their descendants were first aliens and slaves in Egypt and then wanderers in the wilderness. Once settled in their own land, the Israelites instinctively reached out to the outsider. Hospitality toward others was even built into their legal code, since immigrants were provided special protection and benefits. For example, the "resident alien" or immigrant had the same right to rest on the Sabbath as did any native Israelite (Exod 20:10). Like the widow, the orphan, and the poor Levite, the immigrant was permitted to reap the gleanings of the harvest (Lev 19:10; Deut 24:19–21) and shared in the tithes required by law to feed the poor (Deut 14:29; 26:12–13). The immigrant was also welcome to join religious festivities (Deut 16:11, 14). Generally speaking, the immigrant was equal to the native before the law (Num 15:15–16). In fact, God tells Israel, "When an alien (immigrant) resides with you in your land, do not molest him. You shall treat the alien who resides with you no differently than the natives born among you; have the same love for him as for yourself; for you too were once aliens in the land of Egypt" (Lev 19:33–34).

The same attitude should be characteristic of Americans, or at least of American Christians. After all, all of us come from immigrant roots; even Native Americans are descendants of ancient migrants. All of us have ancestors who were strangers and outsiders. Our nation has accepted and incorporated numerous refugees, outcasts, and poor although they were not always welcomed with open arms. Hospitality has been and should remain an important part of American culture. And if our culture refuses to be hospitable, at least Christians in the U.S. should develop an attitude of acceptance, welcome, and hospitality toward recent immigrants, including unauthorized workers.

In witnessing to the Reign of God the church is called to highlight universal inclusiveness and openness to diversity. Today's globalization is marked by exclusiveness and a lack of openness to difference. Globalization has emphasized an economics which seems universal in scope but actually excludes and abandons those who do not fit—especially the poor and marginalized. At the same time it promotes uniformity and attempts to eliminate diversity. The Reign of God, however, is open to everyone and

17. Murphy, "The Ninety-Nine Sheep," 145 and 153.

excludes no one. It values the particularity of every person and culture. Thus it should be natural to the church to offer hospitality to the stranger and to comfort those who may be labeled as "illegal aliens."[18]

Of course, hospitality becomes complicated when it involves economic and health issues. Who should pay for the health care of unauthorized workers? It does not help that our health care system is no longer a non-profit one, and hospitals whose purpose is to provide profits for shareholders cannot afford to accept expensive charity cases. But perhaps we can be challenged by a story that Jesus told to the people of his time, a story of a stranger with health issues: the Parable of the Good Samaritan (Luke 10:25–37).

THE GOOD SAMARITAN

Jesus narrates the Parable of the Good Samaritan as a response to a lawyer who knows the Law well but seeks to define "neighbor." The lawyer's question should not be dismissed. Every society, including that of Jesus, feels the necessity of defining its boundaries and regulating the relationships between insiders and outsiders, men and women, the powerful and the marginalized. The lawyer would certainly agree that he has obligations toward and responsibilities for his neighbor. But, like the citizens of most nations, he probably feels that there should be some limitation to these obligations and responsibilities. "Neighbor" would hardly include "stranger"—much less "enemy." In telling the story Jesus redirects the focus of the question. It is not important to ask about the "insiders," about those who belong to God's people and who deserve attention and care. Rather our focus needs to be on what is our responsibility as members of God's people and as disciples of Jesus to *outsiders*.[19]

Jesus tells us that "a certain man" fell victim to robbers. He does not identify this victim as a Jew, but the context presumes it. Jews from the Holy City would certainly have recognized the dangers of traveling on the twelve-mile stretch of road between Jerusalem and Jericho. Sooner or later almost everyone in the city went down to Jericho or to the Jordan Valley. But even Jews from Galilee would be familiar with the road, since many of them traveled that narrow and winding thoroughfare from Jerusalem to the Jordan Valley in order to avoid journeying through Samaria, the land of a hostile, alien, and unclean people. We have no idea what the man was doing on that particular road, but like some economic migrants today he was left destitute and badly injured. Without assistance he probably would have died there.

18 *Documents of the XV General Chapter SVD 2000*, 29–30.

19 Culpepper, *The Gospel of Luke*, 229; Karris, "The Gospel according to Luke," 702.

Quite likely from afar he appeared to be dead—which could explain why both priest and Levite avoided him. To touch a dead body meant to become unclean and to be excluded from the Temple, which neither would have wanted (see Lev 21:1–4; Num 6:9–12; 19:11–16; 31:19; Ezek 44:25–27). For them the unfortunate victim left lying on the road did not qualify as a "neighbor." Perhaps they thought that he even deserved his fate. But the fact that Jesus introduced the victim first and in a very generic fashion ("a certain man") could easily induce his audience to identify with this character. Do we identify with him?

There are five characters in this story (if we don't count the robbers): the victim, the priest, the Levite, the innkeeper, and the Samaritan traveler. Except for the victim and the Samaritan, each appears and disappears quickly from the narrative. It seems that the characters have been carefully chosen.[20] The hero of Jesus' parable is a Samaritan—an outsider in the Jewish society of that day. Since Samaritans were normally hostile to Jews and Jews were hostile to them (see Luke 9:52–54; John 4:9), it would have been highly unusual and even shocking for Jesus to present a Samaritan as the hero of his story. Unlike the priest and the Levite, the Samaritan took pity on the man who had been beaten and robbed (Luke 10:33–35). He gave the man first aid and brought him to an inn. The next day he left a deposit with the innkeeper to care for the injured traveler, and he promised to reimburse the innkeeper should the costs exceed what he had given (v. 36). Caring for this unknown stranger cost the Samaritan a minimum of two days' wages (the denarius was the usual daily wage of a laborer), not to mention his time and some of his provisions. The Samaritan went out of his way to help a stranger who was injured and penniless. He is far more sensitive to others than the rich man, who did not even notice the beggar Lazarus at his own gate (Luke 16:19–31). Perhaps his own outsider status motivated the Samaritan to act in this fashion. In any case he showed that it is possible to care for strangers with health issues.

This story is a challenge to our own wealthy society, which has problems expending funds on its own ill and injured members, much less on strangers and undocumented immigrants. We still have great difficulty in seeing outsiders, especially "illegal aliens" who have no rights in our society and who are in fact considered criminals, as neighbors. Let them go back where they belong. Let's not waste our tax dollars on them. The lawyer who challenged Jesus reluctantly admitted that the Samaritan acted as a neighbor to the victim. The question remains whether or not we can learn the same lesson.

20. Abogunrin, "Luke," 1407.

CONCLUSION

Every society defines its boundaries and its relationships with outsiders, including citizens of other nations. Thus it would seem logical to reject the needs and requests of those who do not belong—all the more so if they have entered the country illegally and are "taking away our jobs." However, such a view fails to recognize our own role in creating economic need in other nations and in attracting the poor to our country in order to do the hard work we ourselves refuse to do, at wages which cannot sustain a family. Few undocumented immigrants in the U.S. can afford health care, and most of their employers offer neither workmen's compensation nor health insurance. Thus injury or sickness can be disastrous to "illegal aliens."

Can Christians accept an attitude which demonizes immigrants? They may be undocumented, but they are also our brothers and sisters. Jesus challenges the view that we must necessarily exclude strangers, foreigners, and outsiders—especially when we are the ones who make the laws and define the relationships. The Parable of the Good Samaritan demonstrates that we too need to learn to be a neighbor to those who are in need—perhaps especially those who have become a part of our national identity, even if they did so without our permission. We pride ourselves on being a nation of immigrants (*E pluribus unum*). The Reign of God is open to everyone and excludes no one. The challenge is to figure out what that means for us Christians today as we face the issue of unauthorized immigration.

8

Mission in an Urban Culture of Displacement

A Missional Theology of Place for the North American Church

—*Craig S. Hendrickson*

Where are you from? I must admit that every time I am asked that question I go through some mental gymnastics before answering the well-meaning person who asked me. Does he or she mean where was I born? What is my hometown? Where do I live now? What seems like an innocent question with a relatively simple answer, for me, becomes a multi-layered question demanding an in-depth response to adequately represent my conception of where I am really from. Living what some would call a migrant lifestyle, I am currently residing in my twelfth city during my relatively short lifespan, with the result that I can no longer easily answer the question, "Where are you from?"

Like many others in my generation, my highly mobile lifestyle has been driven primarily by the pursuit of a better life, initially just for myself, but now for my family as well. And while I have usually acquired jobs with either more financial security, or that have allowed me to live out my calling with more congruence, our mobile lifestyle has come with a cost. My family and I have become "displaced by our own mobility,"[1] with the result that we often feel like wandering nomads without a sense of rootedness in any one place that we can call home. This sense of rootlessness has contributed towards an adult life largely devoid of the meaningful kinds of relationships that characterized my youth. Consequently, while I have a house that I live in with my family, I really have no specific place I can call home. I am a postmodern migrant.

My experiences as a postmodern migrant are characteristic of an increasing number of my contemporaries in the North American urban context. We are in fact a generation of migrants; a generation of displaced persons with "little more than a romantic attachment to place and home" driven by the pursuit of economic security, adventure, or simply searching for something new.[2] This culture of displacement has created a significant challenge for local churches seeking to participate with God in his redemptive mission in America's urban contexts. The challenge is not simply trying to figure out how redemptively to engage postmodern migrants with the gospel in ways that are meaningful, however. The greater challenge is that many in our churches are characterized by the same nomadic existence as those we are trying to reach. Accordingly, many local churches have themselves become placeless. They maintain a physical presence in their communities through a building to be sure, but all the while they are becoming more relationally detached from their local contexts as people relocate in pursuit of better homes and neighborhoods, jobs, or education.[3] The result has been the rise of the commuter church, with people driving in on Sundays to consume religious goods and services, all the while becoming more and more detached from other church members and their former (and often current) neighbors. The consequences of this trend have been inevitable; countless churches are in decline in America's urban centers due to little or no meaningful social connection in their contexts.

The solution to this problem, I believe, is helping churches located in America's complex urban environments to recapture and embody a sense of place within their local contexts. This is no easy task to be sure, as it requires more than a simple change in mission strategy. It requires addressing what Ronald Heifetz and Marty Linsky refer to as an adaptive problem;[4] one, which cannot be addressed by simple shifts in strategy, programs, or skills of the leader. Instead, it requires the entire congregation to learn and adopt

---

1. Bouma-Prediger and Walsh, *Beyond Homelessness*, 257.
2. Ibid., 267.
3. Branson and Martinez, *Churches, Cultures, and Leadership.*
4. Heifetz and Linsky, *Leadership on the Line.*

new values, practices, and ways of being. In other words, those leading and participating in local congregations will need to re-envision the nature, identity, and mission *praxis* of the local church in ways that run counter to the universalizing tendencies and placelessness characteristic of modernity.[5] In this chapter I will attempt to lay the foundations for this adaptive leap by developing a missional theology of place for churches located in North America's complex urban environments. I carry out this task by first briefly exploring how we got here, that is, highlighting how place has been deconstructed and de-valued in the North American urban context through the influence of various forces characteristic of modernity and late capitalism. I then propose a pathway forward for churches located in North American urban environments by examining the themes of placement (land), displacement (exile), and re-placement (homecoming) in the biblical narrative. I suggest in this discussion that God's desire is for local congregations to participate in the *missio Dei* as a placed people in the current urban culture of displacement. Finally, I recommend that this will require both leaders and congregants of local churches to dwell among our neighbors in humanized relationships characterized by reciprocal hospitality, mutuality, and interdependence, which can ultimately lead us towards embodying God's *shalom* in our communities together.

FROM PLACE TO PLACELESSNESS IN NORTH AMERICAN URBAN SOCIETY

Numerous scholars have argued convincingly that one of the defining characteristics of modernity and late capitalism in Western society has been the loss of place.[6] This phenomenon has contributed significantly toward the culture of displacement characterizing the North American urban mission context that I briefly described above. But what exactly do these scholars mean when they suggest this erosion of place? Are they referring to physical locations that people live in or visit? Or does the concept of place connote something more?

The common understanding held by many everyday people, and some scholars as well, is that place is simply a way of describing specific locations, the various settings where life and embodied social activities occur.[7] Place is simply a container, so to speak, where things happen. At one level,

---

5. Casey, *The Fate of Place*; Foucault, *Of Other Spaces*.

6 See Casey, *The Fate of Place*; Foucault, *Of Other Spaces*; Inge, *Christian Theology of Place*; Bouma-Prediger and Walsh, *Beyond Homelessness*.

7 Rodman, *Empowering Place*, 204.

this understanding is reasonable. The concept of place carries with it this connotation of geographical location where life unfolds. The problem, however, is that when place is restricted to this type of functional and generic understanding, it can easily become taken for granted. Place's role in shaping human experience, meanings, and memories is lost, and we are left with the idea that certain phenomena can happen just as easily and certainly in one place as in another.[8]

This universalizing approach characteristic of modernity has been refuted through the ethnographic work conducted on place by a number of anthropologists,[9] as well as by the theoretical work conducted by postmodern geographers,[10] and philosophers.[11] People and places are not the same everywhere. Rather, places are "politicized, culturally relative, historically specific, local and multiple constructions" that are brought into being through a convergence of voices.[12] They are complex social constructions that bring together social history, selective memory, and personal and social experience to link people from a given locale together into a shared history and identity.[13] Various places, then, are unique and carry within them meanings that are shaped as much by the people within the place as the place itself. As such they are much more than geographical containers. They are in fact sites of culture construction, shared memory, and lived experience.

This phenomenological understanding of place suggests, then, that specific locales are not just physical spaces that people inhabit, but that they are in fact inherently relational. John Inge asserts that the human experiences that occur in various places shape stories that are unique to each. These placed stories are distinct and recognizable, somewhat like a personality, and make distinguishing specific places from the communities associated with them an impossible task.[14] This relationship between place and the specific community within that place is what conceptually distinguishes place from space. As sites of lived experience and shared memory, places are particular, specific, and unique, while space is more abstract and undifferentiated. Interestingly, this conceptual divergence is what gave space primacy over place for over two millennia extending from 400 BCE to modern times.

---

8. Inge, *Christian Theology of Place*, 5.

9. See Feld and Basso, *Senses of Place*; Low and Lawrence-Zuniga, *Space and Place*; and Rodman, *Masters of Tradition*.

10. See Soja, *Postmodern Geographies*; and Tuan, *Space and Place*, and *Making Place*.

11 See Casey, *The Fate of Place*; Heidegger, *Building Dwelling*.

12. Rodman, *Empowering*, 205.

13. Kahn, *Your Place and Mine*, 167–68.

14. Inge, *Christian Theology of Place*, 26, 124–25.

Edward Casey traces the battle of space versus place back to the Hellenistic and Neo-Platonic philosophers of ancient Greece. Neo-Platonic philosophers such as the Atomists became fascinated by the conceptual possibilities that the idea of space brought to explore the infinite, the absolute, and the open-endedness of the universe. Unsatisfied with the limits and boundaries provided by Aristotle's "place as a container" philosophy that 'located' all things material, they abandoned questions of location and boundary to pursue questions surrounding the immense and the undelimited. Not surprisingly, space won this initial skirmish in the larger philosophical war and began a period spanning over two millennia, extending from 400 BCE to the mid-20th century, where space increasingly dominated the discussion.[15]

While these philosophical developments meant very little to everyday people who were mostly bound by their places through the centuries, space made further gains over place in philosophical thought during the medieval period. Leaders of the Church in Europe, especially the Bishop of Paris, extended a series of condemnations against Aristotelian philosophies that could limit God's power. If God's power is truly unlimited, they reasoned, then God must in fact be able to move the entire universe through space. Because Aristotle's philosophies suggested a finite amount of matter in the universe, however, this suggested limits to the universe and thus limits to God's power. The decree then was that space must be infinite, which allowed God to exist outside of time and space and maintain authority and unlimited power over the universe.[16]

According to Michel Foucault, this intermingling of theology and philosophy secured the environment necessary for the scientific discoveries of Galileo and Newton to relegate place to secondary status behind space. In this, he suggests that the real scandal of Galileo's work was not the discovery that the earth was not the center of the universe. Rather, it was the establishment of an infinitely open space that relegated the concept of place prevalent in the Middle Ages to nothing more than a point in a thing's movement.[17] In other words, specific places simply became components of the larger entirety of absolute space and retained no importance in and of themselves.[18]

The scientific environment brought about by this unlikely marriage between theological and philosophical thought provided new freedom for

15. Casey, *The Fate of Place*, 77.
16. Inge, *Christian Theology of Place*, 7.
17. Foucault, *Of Other Spaces*, 23.
18. Inge, *Christian Theology of Place*, 7.

the Enlightenment thinkers like Immanuel Kant and John Locke who would soon follow. Their advancements would further solidify space's primacy, but would also introduce a new partner into the mix that would subjugate place even further, namely time. Building on Gottfried Leibniz's understanding that time must necessarily precede space in philosophical thought, Kant argued, "that objective succession of time is the schematic expression of causality in the physical world order."[19] Kant's influential work, coupled with the widespread distribution of the mechanical clock and the invention of the marine chronometer in the 18th centuries, would ultimately subjugate space to time, a trend that would continue for the next two-and-a-half centuries. Thus, according to Inge, a new hierarchy was established in Western academia that also colonized the life-worlds of everyday people in Western societies during the period of modernity, time, over space, over place.[20] Casey agrees, suggesting that place has been actively suppressed in Western society over the past three centuries, as the natural and social sciences focused almost exclusively on space and time; the "two colossal cosmic partners towering over modernity."[21]

Martin Heidegger further suggests that this cosmological hierarchy of time and space over place has been strengthened, and extended, into everyday experience during the modern period through the development of technology relating to travel and digital communication networks. Speaking even before the development of the Internet and mass distribution of high-speed computers, smart phones, electronic media, and faster transportation methods utilized by large percentages of the population in American cities over the past twenty-five years,[22] he observes that advancements in these areas have shrunk the world, allowing people to reach places in hours that formerly took days, and sometimes months, of travel. Further, we now receive information about events in minutes that people in past generations might only learn of months or years later. The irony in all of this for Heidegger, however, is that this demolition of distance does not bring nearness. Instead, the uniformity resulting from everything being both near and far renders everything "together into uniform distancelessness [sic]."[23] Anthony Giddens agrees, suggesting that specific places are now shaped by social in-

19. Kant cited in Inge, *Christian Theology of Place*, 8.
20. Inge, *Christian Theology of Place*, 8–9.
21. Casey, *The Fate of Place*, xiv.
22. The notable exception to this, of course, is the urban poor who remain locked in place due to their lack of economic means. For an analysis of this situation see Gottdiener and Hutchinson, *New Urban Sociology*, 66; Savage, Warde, and Ward, *Urban Sociology*, 198; or Caldeira, *Fortified Enclaves*.
23. Heidegger cited in Inge, *Christian Theology of Place*, 13.

fluences from a distance, completely devoid of any face-to-face interaction. Relationships are fostered between distant others, and space is increasingly torn away from place as technological advances like televisions and computers become information highways, further weakening the relationship between sociality and place.[24]

As if these philosophical, scientific, and technological developments haven't eroded the value for and experience of place in Western society enough, there are also transnational and cultural forces impinging on North American urban environments. The phenomenon of globalization, for example, driven by capitalism's quest for profit and wealth, has also contributed toward the devaluing of local places in everyday experience for many American urban dwellers. According to Mike Savage et al, globalization's effects are most profoundly felt through the homogenization of various urban environments through the import and export of brand names, the proliferation of global businesses, the use of similar architectural styles, and especially through the reproduction of "non-places"[25] like malls, airports, hotels and leisure facilities, and interstates and motorways. As the built environments of various urban locales throughout North America begin to take on a similar character architecturally and structurally, city dwellers are divorced further and further from the distinctiveness of place as they experience the "placeless city" during their travels.[26]

A second key factor is the unprecedented migration between cities and nations that has been occurring in the 20th and early 21st centuries. While a great deal of this people movement is due to geopolitical dynamics such as war, genocide, and persecution that displace people from their homelands, a large percentage is also related to the pursuit of wealth or economic security.[27] This is especially true of inter-city migration within the United States as postmodern migrants move from town to town in pursuit of wealth and adventure. Bouma-Prediger and Walsh note that this American migrant spirit is legendary and deeply rooted in the American value of individual autonomy. It is this desire for autonomy that drives capitalist ventures in pursuit of expansion and profit, and that leads individuals to neglect civic virtues and responsibility toward place for the higher calling of upward mobility and accomplishment. Bouma-Prediger and Walsh note that,

24. Giddens, *Consequences*, 18.

25. Auge refers to "non-places" as functional sites out of which commodities and mobility occur. They are characterized by uniformity, functionality, and common architecture.

26. Savage, Warde, and Ward, *Urban Sociology*, 146–47.

27. See Bouma-Prediger and Walsh (*Beyond Homelessness*, 250–53) for a more in-depth discussion of this global phenomenon.

The idea of staying put, being content with one's place, having a deep sense that one has 'enough' and needs no more, seems somehow unpatriotic and even crazy in a capitalist society like America. . .To stay in one place for life is often interpreted as being unambitious, unadventurous, a negation of American values.[28]

If the picture I have painted here is true, that North America has become a place of highly mobile and rootless strangers with little attachment to place and home, and that this cultural value of placeless has in fact colonized the North American church as Bouma-Prediger and Walsh propose; what hope is there of rediscovering the role of a "placed" faith in contemporary urban society? Walter Brueggemann suggests that this hope lies in the failure of an urban promise; the promise that people can live lives of endless choice free of attachments, characterized by "the virtues of mobility and anonymity."[29] This promise will always come up empty, he asserts, because the human heart longs to be placed . . . an understanding that flows directly from his belief that a sense of place is a primary category of faith in the Scriptures.

GOD'S PLACED, DISPLACED, AND REPLACED PEOPLE

In his landmark work *The Land*, Walter Brueggemann asserts that the Bible is written to address the primary problem of humanity, homelessness (*anomie*).[30] Because of this, he makes the bold, yet not unfounded claim, that land is the central theme of biblical faith.[31] From the beginning, Brueggemann notes, God's people were meant to be a placed people. This is evidenced right away in the biblical narrative as God's people are placed in the safety and security of the Garden (Gen 2). After their expulsion from this good place due to their disobedience, this desire for placement is expressed again with God's promise to give Abram and his descendants a new place, a land that will be their inheritance forever (Gen 12:1–7). From this point onward, Abram and his descendants embark on a journey towards placement in the Promised Land; a journey fraught with challenges and setbacks.[32] Yet, even in their precarious journeys from landlessness to land, there are many encounters with YHWH in specific locales that reinforce the placed nature of God's people in relationship with him; Abram at Moreh

28. Bouma-Prediger and Walsh, *Beyond Homelessness*, 255–61.

29. Brueggemann, *Land*, 3–4.

30. Ibid., 199–200.

31. Ibid., 3.

32. Ibid., 15–25.

(Gen 12:6-7), Mamre (Gen 18) and Moriah (Gen 22); Jacob at Bethel (Gen 28:16-17); and Moses at Horeb (Ex 3:1-5) and Sinai (Ex 19) to name but a few.[33] These encounters and others enter into the storied history of Israel as a people in covenant with their God on their way to landedness.

When they finally receive the gift of land they were promised after three generations of sojourning (Abraham, Isaac, and Jacob), four centuries of dislocation from the land as slaves in Egypt, and four decades of wandering in the wilderness, they enter into a place that meets all of their expectations, a place where they will lack nothing (Deut 8:7-9). Israel's possession of the land, of course, is contingent upon their obedience to the covenant with YHWH (Deut 11:1-17). The subsequent challenges Israel faced attempting to live up to their end of the covenant and maintain their place in the land often resulted in famine and foreign oppression,[34] and ultimately, in displacement/exile (2 Kgs 17:7-23; 25).

God remained faithful even while the people were in exile, however. God promises their eventual return to the land, contingent again on their covenant obedience (Jer 29:10-14; 30—31), all the while securing their future through the establishment of synagogues that would prove vital for the survival of the Jewish faith after the destruction of the Temple in 70 A.D.[35] Through exile, in fact, God reinforces his desire for Israel to be a placed people, and demonstrates through his prophets that even displacement from the land can be a source of real newness, assurance, and blessing.[36] This is highlighted particularly well in the prophet Jeremiah's words to the exiles in Babylon, when he tells them to settle down, give their children in marriage, and make a home for themselves among their enemies, the Babylonians. Jeremiah does not stop there, however. He also tells them to seek the welfare of those same Babylonians who were the cause of their misery! (Jer 29:5-7)

Imagine the shock and utter dismay of the exiles upon hearing these words. With these few short words, the world of the exiles was turned upside down yet again. Not only were they struggling with their new experience of being displaced from their land, the place that gave them their identity and security, they were now being told that God's plan for them during their displacement was to make a home in enemy land. Imagine their disbelief. Imagine being told that your new focus was to dwell with and "seek the

---

33. Inge, *Christian Theology of Place*, 42.
34. See the Book of Judges.
35. Inge, *Christian Theology of Place*, 43.
36. Brueggemann, *Land*, 115-18.

peace and prosperity" (Jer 29:7 NIV) of the people you hated most. . .in the
city you feared most. . .in the place you "imagined God could never be!"[37]

God had just redefined place for them in a radical new way . . . a way
that seemed scandalous and counterintuitive.[38] Yet it is in this scandalous
re-definition of what it means for Israel to experience place, that God's people would rediscover what it means to participate with God in the mission
to redeem a corrupt urban place, to fulfill their call to be a placed people
on mission (Jer 29:5–7). It is through seeking *shalom* for Babylon that they
will find their own *shalom*, a return to the land (Jer 29:14).[39] Consider the
promise that accompanied the scandal in Jeremiah 29:10–14, where God as-
sures the exiles that they will indeed possess their land again. . .that God has
in fact not deserted them. Yet the nature of this promise makes it clear that
this re-placed future depended on their willingness to be a placed people on
mission while displaced in a city not of their choosing.

The parallels to the church's current situation of displacement are startling. Craig Van Gelder reminds us that, "there are times in the life of the
church when change is quite interruptive, where it occurs in a tumultuous
manner."[40] Borrowing a phrase from organizational leadership theory, he
refers to this situation as discontinuous change, which he suggests describes
the diverse and changing urban contexts in America's cultural milieu. Discontinuous change brings "substantive disruption" into the life of local congregations and forces them to adapt to their unexpected situations in new
and counter-intuitive ways.[41] This is not unlike exile, which forced Israel to
respond to its situation in counter-intuitive ways as well. It is no wonder,
then, that Brueggemann considers exile one of the more fitting metaphors
to describe the condition of the church in our current cultural milieu.[42]

The story does not stop with exile, however, for if it did, God's people
would still primarily be a displaced people; a people without a home living
in light of an unfulfilled promise from God. But the larger biblical narrative
makes it clear that God makes good on his promise to re-place God's people
in the land (Ezra 1–2; Neh 1–2). God brings them back from exile in an act
that foreshadows the ultimate homecoming for God's people through the
coming Messiah, Jesus. This is important to note, as the homecoming God's

37. Roxburgh, *Missional*, 145.

38. Brueggemann, *Land*, 118.

39. Clendenen ("Peace," in *Holman Illustrated Bible Dictionary*, 2003) describes
shalom as experiencing wholeness, well-being, or the fullness of life resulting from
God's coming and reigning in righteousness.

40. Van Gelder, *Ministry of the Missional Church*, 49.

41. Ibid., 49–50.

42. Brueggemann, *Land*, xviii.

people experienced upon their return from Babylon was less than ideal. They would return as a nation-state under the control of the Persian Empire. They would also re-enter the land with a new perspective, however, intent on remaining obedient to the covenant in hopes of retaining their cherished land.[43] Yet because this newfound obedience did not result in freedom and complete autonomy in the land, God's people's attention turned forward with hope and expectation of a fuller placedness yet to come. Brueggemann observes that the apocalyptic imagery contained in passages like Zechariah 9:16–17 keeps God's promise of complete placedness central in Israel's hope while they are still placed in the land with unfulfilled expectations.[44]

This hope is ultimately fulfilled in the New Testament, of course, with the arrival of the city of God (Rev 21–22). Before this happens, however, an interesting shift occurs in the New Testament narratives. The authors' foci moves away from the Holy Land as fulfillment of God's promise of placement,[45] and instead emphasizes God working in and through his people in specific places, beginning with the ministry of the incarnated Christ. As Brueggemann observes, the Gospel story is very clearly located through the person of Jesus in Bethlehem, Nazareth, Jerusalem, and Galilee among other places. Further, the early church has profound encounters with God as it fulfills its mandate to take the Gospel to "Jerusalem, and in all Judea and Samaria, and to the ends of the earth" (Acts 1:8) in specific places like Antioch (Acts 11), Iconium (Acts 14), and Philippi (Acts 16). We see in the New Testament, then, a continuation from the Old Testament narratives of what Brueggemann calls "storied place;" the fact that specific places in the scriptures have powerful "meaning because of the history lodged there" through God's interaction with humanity.[46]

More importantly, however, we see an important, yet different aspect of the placedness of God's people in the New Testament through the Incarnation. For it is through the Incarnation that we truly see places as:

> the seat of relations or the place of meeting and activity in the interaction between God and the world. . . . Place is therefore a fundamental category of human and spiritual experience. In defining the locus of God's relations with humanity to be focused in one particular individual the incarnation asserts the importance of place in a way different from, but not less important than, the Old Testament. It entails a movement away from

43. Inge, *Christian Theology of Place*, 44.

44. Brueggemann, *Land*, 156.

45. Inge, *Christian Theology of Place*, 52.

46. Brueggemann, *Land*, 198.

a concentration upon the Holy Land and Jerusalem but at the same time initiates an unprecedented celebration of materiality and therefore of place in God's relations with humanity.[47]

What Inge is saying here is that the Christian faith is anchored in the One who "became flesh and made his dwelling among us" (John 1:14) in a specific place. As "the locus of God's relations with humanity," the Incarnation is an act of "God's participatory presence" with humanity; the sign of his "ultimate missional participation in human life."[48] As such, it holds profound implications for the church as a placed people on mission.

Craig Van Gelder and Dwight Zscheile expound on these implications when they suggest that,

> If God loves us in Christ, so that God identifies with us relationally in a posture of humility, then we are to share this same love with our neighbors. The corollary of God's bearing humanity in Christ is the church's bearing the burdens of its neighbors as it participates deeply in the life and struggle of the community into which it is sent and within which it lives.[49]

In other words, the fact that God chose to dwell among us, and in fact still chooses to dwell among us through his Spirit[50] as God pursues his redemptive mission to humanity, should inspire us to dwell among others in similar fashion as we participate with God in that mission. But what does it really mean to dwell as a re-placed people on mission? Does it simply mean to live among those we are trying to reach . . . to maintain physical proximity and co-exist with our unchurched neighbors? Or does it mean something more? The seemingly counterintuitive instructions Jesus gives to his disciples in Luke 10:1–12 provides some valuable insight into this question.

Like the exiles in Jeremiah 29 discussed earlier, imagine how the disciples must have felt when Jesus instructs them proclaim his arrival to those in the surrounding towns "like lambs among wolves;" without money, extra clothes, or even any shoes (Luke 10: 3–4). This must have seemed irrational to at least a few of them. After all, is not one of the first things you do before you leave on a long trip double check your bag to make sure that you have enough supplies? Yet Jesus here tells them to leave their bags behind. But Jesus was not finished. He also tells them to stay in the homes of those who receive them as long as they will have them (Luke 10:7). But wasn't their

---

47. Inge, *Christian Theology of Place*, 52.

48. Van Gelder and Zscheile, *Missional Church in Perspective*, 114.

49. Ibid., 115.

50. See John 16:7–11; Rom 8:9–11

goal to get the Good News out to as many as possible? Would it not have been more expedient to go out with all the supplies they needed so that they could preach to and heal as many people as possible? They were bringing the long awaited good news of the arrival of Messiah, after all.

Alan Roxburgh asserts that Jesus might not be as irrational as he seems to those of us reading this story through our individualistic, displaced, North American cultural lenses. He suggests instead that there is a method behind his apparent madness. Roxburgh sees Jesus here teaching his disciples what it means to go forth as strangers in need of hospitality as they proclaim the Good News of the Kingdom.[51] In other words, Jesus is teaching his disciples what it means to embody a radical call to place and Gospel *shalom* as they participate in his redemptive mission to their neighbors. Notice, for example, several of Jesus' exhortations to his followers. He tells them to leave their bags behind (Luke 10:4), which puts the disciples in a state of dependence on the hospitality of those they will be visiting. Telling them to enter and remain in the homes of people they would be visiting (10:5), called them to enter into the lives of everyday people in a way that would foster true relationship through significant bonds of affection.[52] Exhorting them to eat what was set before them (10:7–8) intimated their need to enter into the worlds of those they were dwelling with on their host's terms, rather than their own.[53] And his directive for the disciples to speak the *shalom* of God (10:5–6) would remind their hosts of God's promised future — the coming of Jubilee and the reign of God, which was the heart of Jesus' message.[54]

MISSION AS A PLACED PEOPLE IN THE NORTH AMERICAN URBAN CONTEXT

What then does this brief examination of the importance of place in the Scriptures reveal about God's intent for the relationship between his people and specific urban locales in the North American urban context? Following Roxburgh, I suggest that displacement is never the final will of God for his people.[55] Just as the exiles were called to participate in God's redemptive initiatives as a placed people in a city that was not their own, so are North American churches today called to participate in mission as placed people

51. Roxburgh, *Missional*, 137.
52. Sheldrake, *Spaces for the Sacred*, 164.
53. Roxburgh, *Missional*, 172.
54. Ibid., 157.
55. Ibid., 119.

in urban locales not their own. From the account of the exiles in Jeremiah 29, we see that this necessarily involves displaying radical hospitality to the other. As Van Gelder suggests, "God is a God of hospitality who is always inviting his people to welcome the stranger or the foreigner that comes into their midst;"[56] or in this case, when God's people have been brought into their midst. Through Jeremiah, God calls on churches located in America's urban locales to dwell radically with our neighbors — the foreigners in our midst — who need the *shalom* of God just as much as the church. But what exactly does seeking *shalom* on behalf of our neighbor entail?

If biblical *shalom* involves experiencing wholeness, welfare, or the fullness of life the way God intended,[57] then seeking the *shalom* of people in the city is necessarily multifaceted. It will involve seeking the restoration of relationships that are broken and divided between individuals and groups. It will involve the pursuit of justice and equity in the midst of unjust and oppressive socio-political structures. It will involve ecological care and earth keeping. And it will certainly involve the pursuit of restoration of right relationships with God. Radical hospitality for the other entails all of these things because hospitality carries with it the connotation of making the other feel welcome—like he or she is at home. And where there is injustice, inequity, or division, there can be no real sense of home in God's Kingdom.

But pursuing *shalom* involves more than showing hospitality to our neighbor. Reflecting on Luke's account of Jesus' interactions with his disciples, we must also acknowledge that experiencing the fullness of life as God intended means an even more radical departure from church as usual. Instead of simply providing hospitality to our neighbor, or providing religious goods and services that will attract people to us, Jesus instead seems to be calling the church into a radical posture of dwelling with our neighbors as strangers in need of hospitality ourselves.[58] The church in this passage, after all, seems to be occurring in the public spaces and homes of people who are largely outside of the walls of the synagogue (Luke 10:5, 8-10). Instead of figuring out how we can meet the needs of those around us that we believe need of our help, Jesus instead seems to be calling us toward a posture of interdependence and relationship with the very people we are trying to "fix." This can only happen, however, if we learn to recognize and shed the prevailing cultural values of mobility and individual autonomy that have led to our current state of displacement in our urban contexts. It can only occur as we re-engage those living in North America's urban contexts

56. Van Gelder, *Ministry of the Missional Church*, 51.

57. Clendenen, "Peace," in *Holman Illustrated Bible Dictionary*.

58. Roxburgh, *Missional*, 169–70.

in the public spaces and in their homes; "sitting at their tables, listening to their stories, breaking bread with them, and entering into a human dialogue that is not a well-rehearsed sales pitch."[59] It can only occur as we learn to dwell among others authentically in specific places as a re-placed people on mission.

What I am talking about here is akin to Sheldrake's notion of what it means to live in a "humanizing city." Sheldrake suggests that in a humanized city, dwelling together is characterized by a sense of belonging; and to truly belong together means that people need to be connected in bonds of "affection and fulfillment," not simple co-existence.[60] What this means practically is that we need to stop seeing our neighbors as objects of our mission efforts, and instead see them as human beings that we are called to love, laugh with, and cry with. We need to see them as people made in God's image who have as much to offer us, as we have to offer them. It is not about what we bring to the table, but what we bring to the table together. In taking this posture we begin to live out what it means to be a truly placed people, sent by God to radically dwell with our neighbors as we seek to embody *shalom* together in the cities God has placed us in.

59. Roxburgh, *Missional*, 146.
60. Sheldrake, *Spaces for the Sacred*, 164.

9

Migrancy, Exile, Mission

Missional Readings of Exilic Texts in Francophone Migrant Churches in Pretoria

—Philemon G. Beghela

TELLING SOME STORIES

I am an immigrant living in Pretoria since February 2005 for reasons of insecurity in my home country. To introduce the topic of this survey, I briefly mention three stories as a testimony of migrant ministry in Pretoria.

Story One: From Layman to Church Leader in a Foreign Land

A young man, 26 years old, from the Democratic Republic of Congo (DRC) was dreaming of furthering his postgraduate studies in Europe but could not get a visa because the Mobutu regime was being embargoed by the International Community. He was told by his uncle (a business man) that South Africa has good universities. So, he decided to come to South Africa in January 1991 to study. From DRC, he had a degree in development sciences and he was coming from a Baptist Church congregation in Kinshasa.

He was a layman and did not receive a mandate from his church to minister in South Africa as he was not yet qualified to do mission work.

To keep with his traditional church faith, he became a member of another Baptist Church in Johannesburg. A year later, in 1992, the Baptist Church decided to minister to poor people in the area of Hammanskraal at a place called "Stink Water" about 45 kilometers from Pretoria. The church wanted to establish a holistic ministry including rural development, and this young man was the right person for the job. Twice in prayer meetings, including a retreat, a church elder approached the young man and told him that God wanted to use him to work in Hammanskraal. After being interviewed, the church appointed him to minister to the community at "Stink Water."

Ten years later, a comprehensive ministry focused on proclamation, church planting and community ministries, was established under the banner of *Lethabile* (which means, "the sun has risen") Baptist Church. Currently, the *Lethabile* Church plays a key role as a mission center with programs reaching out to people, including orphans with HIV/AIDS, food security, economic development, small businesses, adult education programs, advocacy and lobbying. Around 150 members are worshipping together in this newly planted church, and the young man was ordained as pastor after the necessary training. Eventually he was joined by his family and is now doing his doctoral studies in missiology at the University of South Africa (UNISA).

Story Two: A Visitor Ministering to an International Church of Refugees

An elder from a Pentecostal Church in the Democratic Republic of Congo (DRC) became sick and in 2003 was transferred to South Africa for medical care. He requested that God should lead him to the only church that would warmly welcome him and receive him as a member. On arriving in Pretoria, he visited a Pentecostal church in town for Sunday worship. At this first Sunday Service, he was not sure that this church was the place to which God had called him. After fellowship with this church for a couple of Sundays, he began to realize that this was truly the right place God needed him to be. To his surprise, he found that many members were refugees originating from various African countries, including Burundi, Democratic Republic of Congo, Malawi, Mozambique, Rwanda, Uganda, and Zimbabwe. At that time, the church was looking for a way to develop ministry among refugees.

During 2004, while the visitor was recovering, and as his treatment required time, the church approached him as it had discerned that their guest was spiritually gifted. After serving ten months as a volunteer, he was appointed to establish an African Service Ministry for Refugees. He served the church as a pastor for eight years until he retired. A letter of recognition by the United Nations High Commissioner for Refugees (UNHCR) was sent to the pastor for helping to integrate refugees and asylum seekers into local communities. About a hundred refugees, including South Africans, still faithfully worship there as church members. Some families, who left Pretoria for overseas, have greatly benefited from his ministry and they are witnessing where they now reside.

Story Three: God Providing for Mission

Without friends or contacts in South Africa he decided to leave his country, Ivory Coast, and travel with a group of friends to South Africa. On their way they passed through Gabon, and he had a vision during the night. He was holding mud in his hands in which was a flame of fire, and behind him a crowd of people followed. But then he realized that the crowd was behind him because of the flame, which provided light for the path they followed. He came to the point where he concluded that God was going to establish him as a minister of several nations. On a Sunday service in Gabon, the preacher approached and asked them: "Who are you and where are you going?" He replied that they were a team of missionaries traveling to South Africa. The preacher was concerned and said: "Why are you taking the long way to South Africa? Come and see me after the service and I will provide you with air tickets." The next day they got the necessary funds and they flew to South Africa. That was in 1996.

He came to Pretoria where a friend who welcomed him in Laudium, an area predominated by a community of Indians, and he became part of a church there. One year later, in 1997, the church lost its founder and he was the first black African to be nominated as senior pastor for the Indian congregation.

He procured a large tent with a capacity for 1500 people. Through interpreters, he ministered for eleven years and renamed the church a "Pentecostal Revival Center." He spent his time in prayer, fasting, Bible study, organizing Gospel crusades and having seminar sessions. He married there, while continuing to be in touch with his home church in the Ivory Cost. His church has now grown to more than 250 members. He has built a 500-seat chapel and planted an additional five churches in the city and the provinces.

The church has sent missionaries to Italy (where a church of 50 members has been planted) and is in the process of sending others to Brazil.

Clearly, when God calls, God is able to provide support for this calling. What a Providing God we have for mission! Francophone migrants are active in mission, even in foreign lands. The following sections provide more detail. We need to keep in mind the following questions that can bring clarity to this study: How do francophone migrants, in the context of Pretoria, South Africa, read exilic texts of the Bible? Are there any missiological contributions that francophone migrants living in Pretoria can make? What is God's vision for francophone migrants living in Pretoria? To give answers to these questions, I shall depict briefly the political context of South Africa indicating how the winds of democracy are opening the country to the world, including French speaking countries.

FACTORS THAT BROUGHT DEMOCRACY TO SOUTH AFRICA

Pull Factors

Since the 1980s many events have occurred which triggered socio-economic and political changes around the world. One can mention the falling of the Berlin Wall in 1989, the end of the cold war, and the winds of democracy which swept through Central and Eastern Europe. A similar wind is profoundly affecting Africa as well. The beginning of the 1990s introduced a new era. The whole of Africa has been moving and we witnessed the fall of certain dictatorial regimes in Central and Southern Africa. It is important to mention Nelson Mandela's release from prison on February 11th 1990, after 27 years behind bars. After his liberation, Mandela worked for the reconciliation of the country and negotiated with the government of Frederik de Klerk to bring the apartheid political system to an end. The end of the regime in 1994 laid the foundation for a new democratic South Africa (ILT 2012).[1] Notwithstanding a transition period of high conflict, Nelson Mandela was elected as the first black president in 1994.

After Mandela took power, a period of liberation began as several diplomatic missions came to open embassies in Pretoria among which were diplomats of the French-speaking world. University institutions such as University of South Africa (UNISA), Tshwane University of Technology

---

1. In this and subsequent interviews, the letter "I" stands for "interview," the letter "L" stands for "Leader," and the third letter refers to the family name of the interviewed person.

(TUT), University of Pretoria (UP) and University of Limpopo, Medunsa, began to register international students in large numbers, and postgraduates were often accompanied by their families. Many doctors and engineers from French speaking countries came to South Africa as they were attracted by the prospects of employment, such as in Gauteng Province (containing Johannesburg and Pretoria) and its neighborhoods (ILT 2012).

Push Factors

Another factor that triggered migration to South Africa is that most French speaking countries were experiencing political instability—there was genocide in the Democratic Republic of Congo (about five million dead) and Rwanda (about 800 thousand). In addition there was war and repeated rebellions in Burundi, Republic of Congo, Central African Republic, Ivory Coast, Chad, and Mali.[2] Many who fled from their countries for political or economic reasons became asylum seekers in South Africa, primarily in the cities of Johannesburg and Pretoria where many of the newcomers now live.

Most of these newcomers do not have the opportunity to master the primary means of communication, namely English. They face difficulties in becoming integrated; some were unable to communicate, others were even rejected and despised when they approached local churches. In general, most of the French speaking migrants were not readily accepted and so it was necessary to respond by creating structures of encounter and places for socialization, each centered on Jesus Christ. There everybody could speak *la langue du Coeur*, the language of the heart, namely French. Sometimes, French speakers came for a brief stay, keeping French as their first language in an environment where many languages are dominated by English speaking citizens. Such was the case in Pretoria. What was needed was the creation of a structure to enhance acquaintance with the new environment, where French speaking people could feel at home (ILT 2012).

BRIEF PROFILE OF FRANCOPHONE CHURCHES

In speaking about francophone migrant ministry, we need first to discover what francophone churches look like. The following information is based on semi-structured interviews conducted with leaders and members of some of these churches.

---

2. Mutombo-Mukendi, *La théologie Politique Africaine*, 1.

Physical Plan

The francophone churches consist of a majority of foreign migrants. These churches are as young as one year old; others were founded some 20 years ago. It is not easy to know the exact number of these churches in Pretoria because they are not all well organized. Archives supplied by *Portique de Salomon*, a pastoral meeting network, reports around 30 churches in Pretoria. They are not big; most members gather according to the country, province and ethnic group of the leader or the minister. Church membership ranges between 20 to 250 persons, with a combined total of more than 3000 members. Places of worship are apartments, garages, cellars, or basements. Most are tenants and do not own their own buildings. Only one or two congregations hold services in a building belonging to a local church.

Language and Culture

French is used to communicate and celebrate the religious services. To integrate local Christians, certain French-speaking churches adopted simultaneous translation of French to English during their worship and at the other public gatherings. Most of the leaders are unqualified ministers who have completed brief training in biblical and theological studies. Some of these leaders are looking for a way to further their study. However, church members are very active and give a lot of time to the activities of their church. These churches are competitive, fragile and often split.

Spiritual Plan

The liturgical programs are elastic and give a large space to praise and dance. Often, the main theme of the preaching is the prosperity Gospel; tithing is taught and required as a sort of compulsory tax paid to the church. Prophecy plays a major role among the members as it builds up hope for a better future. These churches spend a lot time in prayer and praise. The worship is energetic and noisy, and the leader or minister is venerated and exercises the power of a traditional village chief. For the members, the church is their real family.

Social Plan

These churches develop a social character somewhat like a club or powerful association for mutual assistance and insurance. Most members are without jobs and live a life of great poverty. Spiritually active, the church compensates for hard social realities. Members show solidarity toward one another and during times of enjoyment or sadness the members of the church unite as a caring community. This description supports what was expressed by one of the leaders who said that creating a French-speaking ministry in Pretoria was a way to offer the migrants a place where they could feel at home (ILT 2012).

The next section focuses on how migrants living in Pretoria read some exilic texts of the Bible. This will not be an exegetical reading of the texts. The reason for the Babylonian exile in the Bible was conquest and subsequent captivity. The Judean leaders were taken by force. They had little peace of mind and could not sing joyfully "the Lord's song" in their predicament of torture and enslavement. In a real way, francophone migrants in Pretoria are prisoners of political, social and economic wars which forced them to flee their countries. To return home would be more dangerous than staying in South Africa. Most francophone countries are facing chronic instability.

EXPRESSING FAITH IN A FOREIGN LAND

The interpretation of certain biblical texts as given in this presentation received favorable responses among francophone migrants. The interpretation is spiritual and contextual. Here are some of the comments based on the readings of the texts:

Joseph: Potential Instrument in a Foreign Land (Gen 39:1)

The narrative of Genesis on Joseph's stay in Egypt is one of the most important passages which demonstrate how migrants can be carriers of great potential to transform a host country. Someone might reflect on what a country like South Africa would be without the presence of migrants from Asia and Europe. Does not the most powerful country of the world, the United States of America owe its glory to immigrants? To ignore immigrants in the history of the United States of America would be to announce its disappearance (ILT 2012). The Democratic Republic of the Congo, one of the biggest countries of the French-speaking world, has poured a large number of its educated citizens—doctors, engineers, and professors—into South Africa.

In the narrative of Genesis 39, Joseph is an anointed man, a bearer of God's vision in exile who received God's call to carry out a mission. Circumstances forced him into slavery and to be sold into the house of an Egyptian officer. Potiphar was captain of the guard for Pharaoh, the king of Egypt (ILK 2012).

When God sends, God always confirms with signs which accompany the chosen instrument. Joseph succeeds and flourishes in everything he does (39:2–15). The Eternal God was behind the difficult situations Joseph underwent. Through the entire narrative, Joseph was filled with the spirit of God, with wisdom and intelligence. Joseph's suggestions were well received by the Pharaoh and his officials. So Pharaoh asked his officials, "Can we find anyone else like this man so obviously filled with the spirit of God?" Then the Pharaoh said to Joseph, "Since God has revealed the meaning of the dreams to you, clearly no one else is as intelligent or wise as you are. You will be in charge of my court, and all my people will take orders from you. Only I, sitting on my throne, will have a rank higher than yours" (Gen 41:37–40). The role Joseph played in this text reveals to us a person who remains faithful to God until the end of his life. This motivates francophone migrants living in Pretoria and all Christian refugees, who are encouraged "to stand firm." At the end of the day, God will reward the one who remains faithful (ILK 2012).

I contend that it is possible to prosper although one is in a foreign country as long as God is on one's side and one becomes a blessing for others. This is one way to value the migrant phenomenon.

Foundation for Political Strategies for Migrant Integration (Jer 29)

As stated previously, migrants are not losing their time debating the context of each individual text. Their interest is focused on the spiritual dimension of each text. The text of Jeremiah 29 is powerfully used to build up a strong hope among francophone migrants who are living in Pretoria and in the rest of the country. It is seen as a kind of a *tour de force* of political strategies for migrant integration. Four strategic dimensions emerge from the pericope of Jeremiah 29:1, 4–9.

"Build homes. . ."

Here is the starting point for every political strategy that Jeremiah develops in the letter he claimed that he received from the Lord of Heaven's Armies, the God of Israel. The letter is sent to all the people exiled in Babylon by King Nebuchadnezzar. To send an order to the elders, priests, prophets and everyone exiled, Jeremiah is engaging high politics in a foreign land. To "build homes and plan to stay" is both serious and risky in addressing the situation of "land and Home Affairs" (Jer 29:5) (ILTu 2012). The exiles are not to dream of a quick return. It is not clearly indicated how the message was delivered to the exiles in Babylon. It is a sensitive matter that could easily annihilate the Judeans in Babylon. The prophet was telling the exiles to create in Babylon an environment which will allow them to feel at home. The exiles should settle down and build their homes, leave Jerusalem behind and enjoy staying in Babylon despite the deportation. They are told to identify with the inhabitants of the country and make Babylon their new homeland (ILTu 2012).

"Sustainability"

The exiles need food security, and so develop a food bank. Instead of becoming indolent and waiting for God to provide "manna" as in the desert, the exiles are forbidden to become beggars and should sustain themselves through farming (ILTu 2012). The laborious planting of gardens and waiting for the harvest requires a long period of time; they will need permanent residences. As one leader argued, one practical way for francophone migrants to understand Jeremiah 29 is to give one's full support to the "Transforming Tshwane Project' which sustains the welfare of migrants in Pretoria and the rest of South Africa (ILT 2012).

"Re-settlement"

The exiles need to consider a new perspective for settling in a foreign land. Instead of maintaining the purity of the race and immortalizing its culture (ghettoization), which could delay the resettlement dynamic, the Judeans were asked to engage with a new marriage concept. One can surmise that Jeremiah's sayings went beyond the ordinary practice of marriage. There should be mixed marriages, even interracial marriages. The exiles should marry while they were in Babylon, have children, then the parents should find spouses for their children and so have many grandchildren. Keep multiplying, do not decrease, says the prophet (ILTu 2012). Eventually if the law was favorable to the exiles, the new generations of children and grand-children born in Babylon would obtain citizenship. Thus, in the coming years, nobody among the exiles would be considered a foreigner; resettlement would have been successfully achieved.

To return again to the context of Pretoria, francophone migrants are still facing xenophobic attitudes which are delaying integration. Most foreign youth, even those qualified, are forced to survive in temporary security jobs nick named "car watch"; the lucky ones are employed as security guards (ILT 2012).

"Welfare Building"

To live in peace in Babylon, the exiles need to work effectively in order to promote the wellbeing of the country where they reside. The more the country becomes prosperous and peaceful, the more the exiles will benefit and enjoy the happiness of their new homeland. Here the prophet raised an important spiritual concern. It is the duty of exiles not only to concern themselves with a better life for the inhabitants; they must also intercede on behalf of the country so that God can send them peace (ILMP 2012). Even as exiles, migrants are valuable resources to generate happiness for all. All this is put into a positive context in the next verse, which states: "For I know the plans I have for you," says the Lord. "They are plans for good and not for disaster, to give you a future and a hope" (Jeremiah 29:11)

The narrative of Daniel and his companions (2:46–49) in Babylon is a powerful illustration whereby God elevated four foreigners as the highest spiritual leaders in a foreign nation (ILMP 2012). From this same perspective, one can endorse what was said by one francophone leader: it is possible to prosper even in a foreign country, as long as God is on your side and you become a blessing for others (ILMP 2012).

From tearful people to conquerors: Psalm 137

A most frequent comment from francophone migrants was to read the text of Psalm 137 as a strong reason to keep complaining as long as one lives away from their homeland. Seemingly, not all francophone migrants have a positive attitude and seize every circumstance as an opportunity to do mission. This psalm releases a general feeling in migrants who plan to return to their home country. They can identify with Psalm 137 (ILK 2012). The situation of violence these days brings this passage close to the heart of the displaced migrant. One will never be totally satisfied in a foreign country. In November 2011, when challenging Kabila's election in Democratic Republic of Congo, some francophone people were arrested by the police. These arrests reinforce feelings which foreigners experience here in a foreign land in relation to the psalm. It is better to possess little at home than to live in agony abroad. We heard people say that "You will never become a president of South Africa even if you hold an important diploma." The American situation, which allowed for the election of Barack Hussein Obama as president of the USA, is not the same in South Africa (ILT 2012).

If migrants keep weeping in a foreign land, it leads to a devastating position, for lamentation and weeping are echoes of failure (ILA 2012). In an argument, one of the leaders read Psalm 137 positively. According to him, this text should not be applied to the Christian Community, which has received a missionary vocation. The Church of Jesus Christ was called to existence for mission; if it does not fulfill its duty, which is not an option, it can disappear. The Master of Mission, our Lord, expects the Church to stand firmly and work actively to defeat the devil and the devil's realm. Whatever the circumstance, God's children must take up the cause of mission.

The Earth, a Strange Place for Everyone (Heb 13:11–14)

This passage applies not only to francophone migrants; it addresses all foreigners, as well as the citizens of every country. There is no permanent city for anyone here on the earth. This illustrates the reality of refugees, who are constantly confronted with diverse situations such as: monthly rent, daily food, and schooling—in other words, looking for ways to survive (ILKa 2012).

Our personal story as migrants in South Africa is one such testimony. I arrived in South Africa in 2005 with my family due to insecurity in my home country, and had the opportunity to study. We were accommodated in a center run by a missionary society. At the beginning everything went well because I had a scholarship with which I could see to the first year's rent. But during the second year the grant ended and I returned to my home country to sell goods and property to finance my studies. Nevertheless towards the end of the second year, in 2006, our resources were totally exhausted. During winter, we were chased away from the house, threatened with expulsion and then ordered to leave the country. A francophone church accommodated us in a hall, which served as an office. Our family scattered; two of our children were taken care of by the family of a francophone church elder. During 25 days, we lived in a very difficult situation. There was neither a bed to sleep in nor a room for bathing. My wife fell ill and she underwent a surgical intervention at the local hospital. The progress of my thesis was interrupted following the resignation of my promoter. In spite of these difficult circumstances, God touched an old missionary couple who had lived for a long time in Francophone Africa to help us financially and spiritually during this trying period. Then, with the aid of my professors, two organizations gave us some resources to continue for the final two years. By the grace of God, my studies continued until I obtained my doctorate in November 2010. It is necessary to note that, even at this level of education, integration into social life can still be problematic as long as you are a migrant without citizenship.

However, such circumstances do not prevent one from playing an active role to re-establish the Kingdom of God. Once more, by the grace of God, my wife and I founded the Bread for Peace Foundation's (BPF) project among homeless people in Pretoria. BPF's mission is the transformation of the community and environment through education in non-violence and through the empowerment of homeless people for their reinsertion into society.

FRANCOPHONE MIGRANTS' CONTRIBUTION TO MISSION IN PRETORIA

Despite experiencing rejection in Pretoria, francophone migrants contribute in many ways to the wellbeing of South Africa. The most important area where the francophone community still contributes is the spiritual and ethical dimension. Most leaders and church members think they can do better in other aspects only after they are fully integrated; they still have a feeling of not being well regarded in South African society (ILKa 2012).

Some contributions of the francophone community can be listed as follows. There are more than thirty churches planted in Pretoria by migrants. Most migrant churches are located in downtown areas like Sunnyside, Arcadia and Pretoria North. These churches have trained missionaries and sent them back to the francophone world. Francophone migrants, along with their fellow West African Anglophones, have brought the wind of revival to Pretoria. Houses and flats have been purchased, rented and managed as places for praising and worshipping God. Due to the spiritual impact, migrants are happy to help in fighting against crime, abortion, sexual immorality, divorce and HIV/AIDS. Some leaders are part of the "Forum of Pastors." Francophone migrants have successfully contributed to the increase of the Christian Community in Pretoria, and they constitute an army of intercessors on behalf of the country. They are fighting against racial discrimination by supporting and celebrating mixed marriage. To survive, francophone migrants started small businesses around many street corners and in saloons and as security guards. Today, a number of Christian francophone laypeople are serving as engineers, doctors, professors and managers of companies and the best is still to come in the years ahead.

GOD'S VISION FOR MIGRANTS LIVING IN PRETORIA

The francophone Christian Community in Pretoria can count on the presence of God as a key for comfort, strength, and wisdom. Hebrews 13:5 states: "For He himself has said, I will never leave you nor forsake you." God promised to be present with us no matter where we are or what we are doing. The circumstances of life may change, but it will never alter the nature of God and God's promise to the chosen people is unshakable. Furthermore, one would like to build hope from the statement of Jeremiah 29:11, "For I know the plans I have for you," says the Lord. "They are plans for good and not for disaster, to give you a future and a hope." If it can be said that, "Even a tree has more hope! If it is cut down it will sprout again and grow new branches" (Job 14:7). Should not there be more hope in nurturing francophone migrants in Pretoria than in cutting a tree?

God has the power to value migrants for the purpose of using them for mission. It often happened that Israel was sent by God as a fugitive to other nations in order to become an instrument of blessing. Most francophone migrants claim that they do not consider their presence in Pretoria as an accident. In the third story above, the founder of Champions of Faith Ministry International said that he travelled to South Africa by the calling of God which was confirmed through the vision he had on his way in Gabon: "Arise, Jerusalem! Let your light shine for all to see. For the glory of the Lord rises to shine on you" (Isa 60:1). Some francophone migrants had been told to go back and minister in their home country before coming to South Africa. They replied by saying that they received an unlimited calling from God, which sends them wherever in the world. They refer to the saying in the Gospel of John, "But I say, wake up and look around. The fields are already ripe for harvest" (4:35).

One could argue and say that "as the world becomes like a global village," South Africans should adopt a positive attitude towards non-South Africans. Migrants have the right to be treated as other human beings. However, everyone should respect laws relating to migrants in each country, and welcome asylum seekers according to positive and constructive laws, while denouncing those laws that are discriminatory.

CONCLUSION

According to my research, everywhere across the world, the image of the migrant has to be reformed and re-humanized in the hosting countries. Migrants should no longer be perceived as a threat to the local inhabitants.

The phenomenon of francophone migrants shows how God is breathing the wind of missionary revival in Pretoria. The analysis of this paper shows how, despite harsh, everyday experience, francophone migrants in Pretoria are playing a constructive missional role showing their capacity of singing the Lord's song in the strange land of Pretoria. For some francophone migrants, their current circumstances are perceived positively as a God-given opportunity for effective witness. The contexts of Genesis 39 and Jeremiah 29 are similar to contemporary migrant conditions. And so these two passages have been used as a powerful source of renewing Christian mission in Pretoria.

QUESTIONNAIRE

The interviews were undertaken by Philemon G. Beghela in 2012 with francophone church leaders and members in Pretoria, South Africa, who are part of the Portique de Salomon network. In the six interviews referred to in the text, the first letter "I" stands for "interview," the second letter "L" stands for "Leader," the third to the family name of the interviewed person.

Interview with Leader of Church/Congregation

1. When and why did you start this church/congregation in Pretoria?

2. What is the main purpose and role that you envisaged for this church/ congregation when it was established?

3. How do you see the Church in South Africa?

4. Were there any key Bible verses or passages that guided you in establishing the church/congregation?

5. What are the main problems (challenges) that the church *as an institution* is facing?

6. What are the main problems (challenges) that the church *members* are facing?

7. Did the members belong to different churches in their home countries? Does this cause tension in the church? Does it enrich your church? How do you deal with these issues?

8. Is there much mobility in the church (members joining and leaving again)? What are the reasons for this? How do you address this?

9. Do you collaborate with other churches in Pretoria? Immigrant churches? Local churches? What are the issues arising in those contacts?

10. Are there any South African members in your church?

11. Please read the following passages and explain how you understand the message of each: Genesis 39:1–6; Psalm 137; Jeremiah 29:1, 4–9; Hebrews 13:11–14.

Interview with Members of Church/Congregation

1. When and why did you come to South Africa?

2. What is your legal status in South Africa? Or: Do you see yourself staying in South Africa for a long time (or permanently)? Why (not)?

3. What kind of problems are you facing in the country and how do you address them? Do you get help/support from the church/congregation on these issues?

4. Did you belong to another denomination in your home country? Do you find it difficult to get along with members from other church backgrounds? Do you find this situation enriching or troublesome?

5. What do you miss of your home country? Do you feel at home in South Africa? Do you have regular contact (visits and otherwise) with your home country?

6. What do you miss of church life in your home country? What do you enjoy about church life in South Africa?

7. Has your life changed since coming to South Africa? In what ways?

8. Are there some passages in the Bible that have gained a special meaning for you during your stay in South Africa? Give examples and explain what they mean to you.

9. Does your church/congregation make a contribution to Christian mission in South Africa? In other African countries?

10. Do you play an active role in the life of your church/congregation? Give details.

11. Please read the following passages and explain how you understand the message of each: Genesis 39:1–6; Psalm 137; Jeremiah 29:1, 4–9; Hebrews 13:11–14.

10

"Failed" Migrants Return
A Transforming Word from the Book of Ruth

—John Mansford Prior

> "How come rejection is so deeply rooted? Why is it so difficult to accept people living with HIV (PLHIV) who, yes, may have a sullied background? Honestly, I am disillusioned with the attitude of clergy, sisters and seminarians who judge us without bothering to listen to how we arrived at this situation. They condemn us without looking at the root of the problem. Discarded by family, friends and clergy, I, like many other PLHIVs, have often given way to despair. What's happened to Christian doctrine? Is our Church only for the righteous? I am very disturbed. . ."

I hear such outpourings all too often. This one came from Ibu Magda, the founder-chair of an *HIV/AIDS Support Group*. This group of mainly Catholic HIV/AIDS carriers is based in the town of Maumere on the island of Flores in eastern Indonesia. At monthly meetings we open the Bible. As they are mostly returned migrants, we once read through the Book of Ruth. The following is a reflection on this particular Bible sharing among these "failures" who have discovered a transforming Word in the story of Naomi and Ruth, and a renewed personal faith, while being largely ostracized by family, parish and the wider society.

THE READERS

Flores Island, eighty-seven percent Catholic, is part of the most Christian Province (NTT) in majority Muslim Indonesia. The two million Florenese population, to a significant extent, depends on money sent back to families by its tens of thousands of economic migrants.[1] This migrant people can be found all over Indonesia and beyond, the majority migrating to the logging camps and palm-oil plantations of Kalimantan and the plantations and factories of Malaysia, while others go to the economic zone of Batam that nestles alongside Singapore. A large majority is men, over half are single, some twenty-two percent under eighteen years of age. Most have little formal education; some sixty-nine percent are primary school drop-outs. The majority stays for life, while many wives and children remain in Flores.[2] In the relative anonymity of city and migrant settlement, freed from traditional village norms, beliefs, mores and values, loosened from social-religious control mechanisms embedded in family and village life, the practice of sexual abstinence among the young bachelors and of fidelity among the married men are not universally observed.

Returned Migrants

Increasingly, some of these Christian migrants have been returning home early with the HIV/AIDS virus, which they then pass on to their wives, and subsequently the mother to her newborn infant. To date the single cause of infection is casual or commercial sex by male migrants abroad and subsequent contact with their wives at home.[3] Migrants depart Flores full of hope and vigor, but return empty, an embarrassing failure, having lost not just their health, but their social location and their financial independence. Above all they find themselves shunned and ostracized by their family network and, often enough condemned by Church authorities, enduring a "social death" more painful than the virus itself. Unsurprisingly, early returnees tend to lose their self worth becoming suspicious of others, convinced that everyone knows of their pariah health condition. Lacking trust and self-

1. Bank records in each of the nine district capitals in Flores show substantial sums being transferred from migrants each month. Most is spent on school fees and improved housing.

2. See the preliminary survey of Huberto Hasulie of the Candraditya Research Centre, "Ke Malaysia Mengadu Nasib. Laporan Awal tentang Perantauan dari Flores."

3. Commercial sex in Maumere by the military and the police, bus, truck and motor-cycle taxi drivers may well be spreading the virus locally beginning with these most-at-risk populations (MARP).

respect, many become depressed. Alienated and rejected, having lost their defining economic, socio-cultural and religious supports, PLHIVs have had to fall back onto their own inner resources. And it is precisely here where they can reignite hope and renew faith in the unconditional and compassionate love of God.

Local Support Group

One such young widow, Ibu Magda, negotiated with health authorities and opened a consultation clinic, *Voluntary Counselling and Testing (VCT) Sehati* for peer counseling and medical advice, at the local general hospital in Maumere town. Later she formed the *Kelompok Dukungan Sebaya (KDS) Flores Plus Support Group*. KDS is a faith-based network run entirely by PLHIVs, which accepts members where they happen to be emotionally, spiritually and socially. Apart from practical advice on medication, diet and lifestyle, they give priority to psychosocial support. This is proving to be the key feature that decides whether HIV morphs into a fatal virus (AIDS) or remains a chronic lifelong condition.[4] For while HIV/AIDS is caused by a virus, its spread among migrants is fuelled by stigma, fear, misinformation and indifference. Medication can control the disease, but only compassion, love, respect and understanding brings healing. As a safe space, KDS Flores Plus Support Group works at improving health, while organizing for the mutual psychosocial support and self-empowerment of its members.[5]

Key metaphors associated with HIV/AIDS globally also fit the local situation: the virus is *alien* (originates overseas), *invasive* (attacks local cultural and religious norms), *shameful* (exposes the carrier's prior sexual practice), and *accusatory* (the carrier is presumed guilty). In short the virus, the carrier, and in some cases the care-takers, are stigmatized.[6]

And so while medication is essential it is not sufficient. PLHIVs need to come to accept themselves in all their fragility, regain self-respect and rekindle the courage to be loved and cherished again. In a trusting, nonjudgmental atmosphere they can learn to become human again.

4. In the West the expected lifespan of PLHIVs is now similar to the national average; in Indonesia (2011) it was improving but still seven years shorter. Thus the virus is no longer fatal but still chronic.

5. KDS Flores Plus Support Group is a community-based, low cost, low tech and culturally grounded faith-based network. On culturally grounded ways to discourage sexual (and drug-using) behaviors that drive the spread of HIV, see Green and Ruark, *AIDS, Behavior, and Culture*. A broader range of theological reflections is found in Paterson, *HIV Prevention*.

6. Sontag, *Illness as Metaphor and Aids and its Metaphors*.

In such a safe unmonitored site, Bible Sharing can break through fear and so break the shield of silence. Wherever the Word of God is "read with soul"[7] the Word proves sharper than any two-edged sword, cutting open any encapsulating or enervating mask, dispelling fear and uncertainty, while conferring affirmative meaning by opening up the person to a greater fidelity, purity and sincerity, embraced by the unconditional and compassionate love of a vulnerable, crucified God. Only when carriers are willing to be honest with themselves can this contagious virus, caught and transmitted by behavior, be halted. In certain circumstances Bible reading can prompt this breakthrough as readers confront the reality of their own lives and opt for change.

THE READING

Some 20 members of KDS Flores Support Group read the *Book of Ruth* in four sessions over as many months.[8] No reading strategy was announced in advance; members were free to react to the text in any way they wished, each from their individual or group context, in what, *post factum*, can be termed "an hermeneutics of compassion in detachment."[9] Here I report the story of Magda and her fellow PLHIVs as the text opened up their wounded selves. Their transparency in the face of the Word and in the presence of the others, pried open those members who were still imprisoned in numbing indecision, fear and self doubt. The non-judgmental atmosphere engendered trust, and trust gave birth to new hope. Undeniably the story of Naomi and Ruth has rekindled the self esteem of the PLHIV readers who had been rejected and excluded by family and society in general; they now realize that they are accepted by God, by their fellow PLHIVs, and by themselves.

A Merging of Horizons

The facilitator's role was limited to brief explanations of some cultural aspects of the text and to answering questions of biblical exegesis, while silently monitoring the sharing, ready to raise questions if the reading seemed to "contradict" professional exegetes' studies of the text.[10] However, this latter monitoring role proved to be superfluous.

7. Martin Buber, "The Man of Today and the Jewish Bible," 242–43.

8. Other passages studied recently, Mark 10:46–52 and John 5:1–18.

9. Bae, "Dancing around Life: An Asian Woman's Perspective," 390–91.

10. Commentaries read on Ruth include Amy-Jill Levine, "Ruth"; Jack Miles,

A single word, a short phrase, or a simple verse from the *Book of Ruth* echoing personal traumas, broke through the silence of persons suppressed by stigmatization and rejection. They were surprised to find their story retold in the Bible, a story that cut through their fear and uncertainty. Each PLHIV quickly identified with one or more of the characters in the narrative. Almost immediately the biblical account and the individual stories intertwined becoming a single, colorful, coherent tale.

Samples with Commentary

". . . . there was a famine in the land" (Ruth 1:1). "Ah that's me!" Between many tears, and for the very first time, Magda told her story. "I am Ruth [Hebrew meaning "friendship"], my husband was Mahlon [Hebrew meaning "sickness"]. After junior high school I had to find a way to support my mother and younger siblings. I learned to sew and then opened a tailoring stall at the local market, but only earned enough to feed myself a day at a time. Eight years later my brother migrated to Batam.[11] When he planned to marry a fellow migrant I was sent to Batam as the family's representative at the wedding. It was there that I met my future husband. I didn't know he was HIV positive. He was a good man. He respected me. He respected my brother. I accompanied my sister-in-law to Java to her mother's house where she was to give birth to her first born, and then returned to Flores to marry my fiancé. We cohabited. My family insisted that we should marry before living together, but in those days I was naive, I didn't know how strong-willed men can be. As a woman I had little choice. Nevertheless, we separated a week before our marriage. Then he fell sick, very sick indeed." Comment by facilitator: as elsewhere, HIV/AIDS thrives among conformist populations marred by poverty and lack of education, gender inequality and low social status. In the haunting words of Paul Farmer, "HIV/AIDS has a 'preferential option for the poor.'"[12]

"Where you go I will go, and where you lodge I will lodge; your people shall be my people, and your God my God" (Ruth 1:16). The loneliness, invisibility and social isolation of Naomi and Ruth sparked this outpouring from the heart: "My family demanded I separate, but how could I? I loved him, loved him very much. If I left him he would die, and if he died alone

---

"Bystander: 'Returned to Her People and Her Gods.' Ruth"; Madipoane Masenya, "Ruth"; and Isabel Apawo Phiri, "Ruth."

11. Batam Island is an economic zone close to Singapore, some two thousand kilometers from Flores Island.

12. Overberg, *Ethics and AIDS*, 11.

my heart would die also. And so I cared for him in the intensive care unit of Maumere hospital. My family was adamant and I had to choose between my elder brother and my husband. My family cut me off. They accused my husband of beating me, but he was fierce only with words, never physically. He fell into a coma and for three months he never recognized anyone, including his wife who tended him daily. Then he recognized who I was and advised me to return to my family. 'If I leave you, you will die, and I will die also.' I lay beside him every night in the hospital. I bore this burden alone for, as yet, his mother knew nothing."

"Do not call me Naòmi [pleasant], call me Mara [bitter], for the Almighty has dealt very bitterly with me" (Ruth 1:20). "I cared for him calmly, but cried bitterly when alone. And so he died and together with his family I attended his funeral, but not a single member of my family came. Then my brother came to me weeping. 'Why are you crying,' I asked, 'my husband is dead. He cannot hear you. It's too late for sympathy, too late to make peace. Truly, "'I departed full, and the Lord has brought me home empty'" (Ruth 1:21).

"And when they came to Bethlehem, the whole town was stirred . . . ." (Ruth 1:19). "Village society is very conformist; the nonconformist must migrate or be excluded. Rapid social change is shaking village life, our families feel threatened; traditional ethical norms no longer hold. I feel that we PLHIV returnees are a scapegoat, we 'represent' all that threatens social stability that is outside our control. We seek protection but are confronted with persecution." The facilitator notes: The returnee men take longer to accept their condition than the women. In our patriarchal society men are fairly free in their sexual encounters as long as it does not disturb social harmony. But now the virus is revealing to the public their previously private life and our patriarchal double-standards are being laid bare. Societal healing is needed and so women PLHIVs urge greater gender justice and equality. Returnee PLHIVs will be accepted only when the wider society is able to question the unequal and unjust male-female relations and question the institution-centered role of the ordained male Church officials, and the causal link between the two.

As the story of Naòmi and Ruth continued, so other verses elicited experiences long suppressed even to the bearers themselves: "Let me go to the field, and glean among the ears of grain after him in whose sight I shall find favor" (Ruth 2:2). Individuals recalled how they live from day to day, from one casual job to another. The women PLHIVs recalled their survival strategies.

"Have I not charged the young men not to molest you?" (2:9) They acknowledge their unfulfilled need to have a strong male protector in order to survive in a male-centered society. They respect Na'omi for not going straight to Bo'as [Hebrew meaning "in him is strength"] to seek protection; she would be embarrassed but, more importantly, in principle she wished to be self-reliant.

"Why have I found favor in your eyes, that you should take notice of me, when I am a foreigner?" (Ruth 2:10) The women PLHIVs discussed their status as widows, which mirror those in the Bible. The facilitator explained: *'almānâ* (Ruth 4:5, 10), a widow, is a woman without any male to support her socially and financially, neither father, husband, nor adult male sibling. Like Na'omi and Ruth, the PLHIVs are not just widows but also migrants (Hebrew *gēr*), that is, resident aliens, forced to leave family and live among strangers, outside the geographical area of their own kin.[13]

"When he lies down, observe the place where he lies; then, go and uncover his feet [genitals] and lie down; and he will tell you what to do" (Ruth 3:4). At this verse a cacophony of voices erupted, "Yes, like Na'omi and Ruth we must devise cunning tricks with much deceit. There is no other way for a stigmatized woman with no male support in this male-centered society." The facilitator notes: to date none of the PLHIVs had encountered a Bo'as [in whom is strength]. People are infected with fear, with a fear stronger than faith. The stigma of HIV/AIDS is contagious and tends to infect anyone in the vicinity, caretakers and helpers alike, as the virus is associated with sexual contact outside accepted religious and cultural norms. Just two generations ago leprosy and the leper were stigmatized in Flores, today it is HIV/AIDS, its carriers and their caretakers.[14]

"The day you buy the field from the hand of Na'omi, you are also buying Ruth the Moabite, the widow of the dead . . . ." (Ruth 4:5) Unlike Na'omi and Ruth, Magda and other PLHIV women migrants have no male authority figure to grant access to family and social life in a society where a woman's economic well-being is directly related to her link with some male.

"Blessed be the Lord, who has not left you this day without next of kin . . . ." (Ruth 4:14) Cut off from family, economic support and from many clergy due to the stigma of HIV/AIDS, the PLHIVs were left with nobody but themselves and their God, the God who takes a special interest in the *'almānâ* and *gēr*), a God who sustains the widow and accompanies the stranger, supplying the providing role of the missing male kin.[15] Alienated from family and all that kinship means in an indigenous society, living with the material poverty and psychological stress that social marginalization

13. Hiebert, "'Whence Shall Help Come to Me?'" 125–41.

14. Sontag, *Illness as Metaphor and Aids and its Metaphors.*

15. Hiebert, "'Whence,'" 126–30.

and stigmatization entail, deep personal faith in a saving God has brought these women together and now they are supporting and counseling fellow male PLHIVs as they endeavour to live by faith, a faith that does justice. *Emmanuel*: the experience of "I am with you" changes everything.

Although Ruth's name has been "erased" from the royal genealogy ("Now these are the descendants of Perez . . . Salmon of Bo'az, Bo'az of Obed (sic.), Obed of Jesse, and Jesse of David"), the PLHIV readers were inspired by God's plan in placing the foreigner, the pagan Ruth, in direct line to David, and so Jesus. Buoyed up by renewed self esteem, some were inspired by the possibility that in God's plan they, too, can live once again for others. Some began to believe that, in God's grace, they too might be able to become active agents of their own future. Nevertheless, none could identify with the "happy ending" of the biblical book; more than one cried out: "I have suffered more than I can bare, will rejection never come to an end?" They have regained fidelity, yet are aware of their fragility as they face an unknown and unknowable future; they fumble towards the necessary courage to choose uncertainty rather than succumb to certain death.

Further Observations

Key names drew the PLHIVs into the heart of the biblical story: "Moab" is enemy territory yet fertile, just as Flores migrants are drawn to economically advantageous sites among unwelcoming local inhabitants. They easily identified with "Chilion" [Hebrew meaning "failure"] and Orpah [Hebrew meaning "returnee"] while appreciating Ruth [Hebrew meaning "friendship"] who, as a Moabitess would have been stigmatized in Bethlehem as an aggressive temptress who worshiped false gods, and yet she loved Na'omi unconditionally without any guarantee for the future, for both were without child or husband and had lost everything and, as such, were icons of The Other who loves us faithfully and unreservedly from the "failure" of the Cross. Na'omi and Ruth, two widow returnee failures, also image the KDS Flores Support group itself in virtually every way: as economic failures, as socially stigmatized and rejected, as women and men under great psychosocial stress, with an unknown and unknowable future. The reader and the read, the outcaste and the Christ coalesced. Na'omi and Ruth's "unfathomable" bonding mirrored their own "illogical" friendships that they had struck up among fellow PLHIVs, relationships outside ethnic ties, unthinkable to family, a tight bonding among "failures" without any apparent economic advantage or gain in future security.

THE REDACTION

"If [you] keep quiet, the stones themselves will cry out" (Luke 19:40).

Patterning Fractured Stories

What was happening when the PLHIVs read the text? Were they simply reading into the text what they liked, instrumentalizing the text as an occasion to expound their personal word? I think precisely the opposite was happening. The PLHIVs were "seduced" by the Word (Jer 20:7). The narrative of Naomi (pleasant yet bitter) and Ruth (faithful yet alien) became each one's personal story, each discovered his or her own story in the text. In the biblical account broken and scattered lives take on a narrative structure, make sense; they are transformed and transfigured and given a graced meaning.

One can transpose Rowan Williams' understanding of Augustine of Hippo's spiritual reading of the psalms to the PLHIV migrants' reading of the *Book of Ruth*. The PLHIV readers could again "imagine a wholeness of experienced history in our life as if life itself were a text, as if the remembered story of our conversation with God represented part of an intelligible narrative or a single song."[16] In reading the text, fractured lives become whole. Hence, the story of Naomi and Ruth "unseal[ed] deep places, emotions otherwise buried, and provid[ed] an analogy for the unity or intelligibility of a human life lived in faith. Here is a conversation with God . . . [a]nd in the course of that conversation, the human speaker is radically changed and enabled to express what is otherwise hidden from him or her."[17]

As with Augustine in praying the psalms, so with the returned migrants in reading the *Book of Ruth*: the biblical narrative proposed a structure that gave a unified story and a graced meaning to their thereto inarticulate, fearfully scattered lives. In reading the text the PLHIVs found themselves reading their own story and for the first time found meaning and purpose within it. They discovered a pattern in their traumatic lives that redeemed, liberated, and gave new hope. In the biblical account they heard "a language of doubt, near-despair, repentance, and lonely suffering, as well as praise and thanksgiving, [namely] the acceptance of that human condition that Christ embraced in his incarnation."[18]

---

16. Williams, "Augustine and the Psalms," 18.

17. Ibid.

18. Ibid., 21.

This spiritual reading of the story of Na'omi and Ruth does not evade or relativize the historical sense of the biblical narrative, which has rooted the readers in their own contemporary history. The reading does not simply link them with a scriptural past; what occurred in the past is happening today in the lives of the readers. This open, intuitive way of reading the scriptures reopened the possibility for growth and wholeness. As Rowan Williams concludes, "there is a paradoxical dimension to [Augustine's] hermeneutics: what most locates us in our earthly experience in all its reality is what most opens up the fuller sense because it most prompts desire."[19]

The story of Na'omi and Ruth offered a way for members of the PL-HIV group to appreciate their personal narrative anew, acknowledging their incomplete, sinful and depressing present moment, while experiencing renewed hope in the embrace of the unconditional and passionate love of God. The Book of Ruth provides a script for a conversation between the failed and rejected migrant and the newly rediscovered faithful and life-affirming Companion of the stranger, the God who willingly suffered with us on Calvary and so was raised from the dead.

The biblical Word thus transforms the personal narrative, from a story of a migrant's failure with her/his limited economic goals, to become a record of radical hopefulness that looks forward to the future, albeit to a future that cannot be determined or described from where she/he now stands. In reading the Word, the Word has read, interpreted and converted the reader who is now exposed to the Word as the Way, the Truth and the Life (John 14:6), the Jesus of the Beatitudes (Matt 5:1–12), the nonconformist Jesus who touched lepers, becoming defiled himself, in order to heal (Mark 1:40–45; Matt 8:1–4; Luke 5:12–16).

Furthermore, these readers are reminding all of us that authentic human life cannot be found in striving for success, power or pleasure. Once again in the words of Rowan Williams, "What holds the two stories together is our reproduction of Christ's acceptance of the fallen and struggling condition to which we are, without exception, destined. And in that identification of narratives, the narrated human life of the believer becomes a sign of God.[20]

19. Ibid., 23.

20. Ibid., 26.

A Committed, Compassionate Reading

"Failed" migrants returning with HIV/AIDS are teaching us how to read the Bible anew, in discovering a "surplus of meaning"[21] hitherto hidden in the text and suppressed in our lives. In their compassionate readings from their fragmented site, "failed" migrants engage the written Word as promoting the good and the beautiful, however tragic the situation in which they find themselves. Such readings work only when we displace any assumption that might tend to compromise the unconditional love of God. Only then can the evocative phrase *"and the Lord has brought me home empty"* be experienced as part of God's plan, as *kenosis*, the necessary condition for each one of us before the Spirit can take over and new life is born. This biblical understanding by PLHIV migrants invites us to place compassion ("willingly suffer with") at the heart of our exegesis, as an essential hermeneutical key, and place it even more so, at the core of our faith and culture (cf. Luke 6:36).

So it is becoming apparent that these "failed" migrants, those most rejected by society and most embarrassing to the Church, precisely these "lepers" are breaking down barriers by challenging key alienating customs and laws embedded in our patriarchal society. They are challenging us to read the Bible compassionately, readings that are transparently transformative of personal and inter-personal relationships. Patriarchal, indigenous societies like that on Flores need the challenge of such a hermeneutic, and not just the clan-based, "male-stream," judgmental society of honor and shame, but also, and more specifically, the clerical Church locked into the power structures of the surrounding society.

Compassionate Readers

When Church leaders position themselves primarily as officials and representatives of the ecclesial institution, they will always be tempted to defend the institution, insisting on following the law that promises clarity and certainty, insist on obedience to its ethical norms, and so tend to be intolerant of those who cross them.[22] This is a particular danger in indigenous societies where clergy enjoy high status. We clergy need, in all humility, to listen, to repent, and to re-imagine our role charismatically and prophetically

21. Paul Ricoeur, *Interpretation Theory: Discourse and the Surplus of Meaning.*

22. Rödlach, "Reflections of a Missionary-Anthropologist," 298–300. Surveys of the attitudes of Evangelical and Pentecostal pastors to HIV/AIDS in neighboring Papua New Guinea are not encouraging. See Schwarz, ed., *Blessed are the Virtuous?* See also the special issue of *Catalyst.*

rather than act as enforcement officials of institutional norms. The returned migrants challenge us clergy to face the *Abba* of the crucified and risen One. For the God ever-present in a conformist, patriarchal culture and clerical Church, is the God who punishes illicit sex with the scourge of HIV. As for the PLHIVs so it must be with Church leaders, the Revengeful Judge must give way to the God who lives in solidarity with the sufferer, the orphan and widow, the vulnerable God of solidarity in suffering and hope. And not just in the rhetoric of homilies or in the fruit of abstract, uncommitted exegesis, but in supportive relationships with the fragile outcastes of society. The "failed" migrants are inviting us to look deeply into ourselves and to test against the Scriptures some of our intensely held beliefs and practices.[23]

Towards a More Compassionate Society

The "failed" migrants are challenging us to widen the scope of their reading to embrace the wider society. The transformative reading of the stigmatized must lead to societal repentance, the renewal of the society that stigmatizes and excludes. Their reading urges us to rewrite relationships so that they transparently embody the inclusive values of the Reign of God. Once again a missional hermeneutics is arising from the periphery, from faith reflection by marginal groups. God is choosing "What is weak in the world to shame the strong, what is low and despised in the world . . . . to bring to nothing things that are . . . ." (1 Cor 1:27–28) Inter-textual readings, that weave the scriptural text and the personal text into a single pattern, are one way of accompanying today's "lepers." Their reading is sorely needed by an institutional church locked into a patriarchal culture of power and success. If we but listen to the faith-readings of these returned migrants, we can experience again the Christ who dwells in our hearts in faith, "That being rooted and grounded in love, [we] may have power to comprehend with all the saints what is the breadth and length and height and depth, and to know the love of Christ which surpasses knowledge, that [we] may be filled with all the fullness of God" (Eph 3:17–19).

---

23. Overberg, *Ethics and AIDS*, 29

11

Reading Acts Missionally in a City of Migrants

—*George M. Wieland*

Auckland is New Zealand's largest city, home to a third of the country's inhabitants. A census in 2006 found that 37 percent of the city's residents had been born overseas,[1] and many others are the children of recent immigrants. According to its Mayor, Len Brown:

> Auckland is a city of migrants, from people whose ancestors have been here for generations to our most recent arrivals. Together Auckland is home to more than 180 different ethnicities, and we embrace the vibrancy this cultural mix brings to our region and our lifestyle.[2]

The city center teems with international students and migrant workers and various suburbs have acquired distinctive Polynesian, Asian, South African, or other characteristics as they have become destinations of choice for immigrants from particular source countries.

For Auckland's churches this represents a changed—and still changing—mission context. How are they to live faithfully in relation to the

1. Statistics New Zealand. Online: http://www.stats.govt.nz/Census/2006CensusHomePage/

2. Len Brown, *LINKZ* 51 (2012), 6. Online: http://www.ssnz.govt.nz/publications/LINKZ_Issue51.pdf.

realities of immigration and increasing cultural diversity?[3] Read in this location, the book of Acts, with its stories of multiple journeys and people in motion, representing a dazzling range of participations in the mission of God, resounds with "deep resonances, authentic parallels, and legitimate implications."[4] A missional reading of Acts has the potential to shape Auckland's Christian communities for their participation in that continuing mission today.

READING THE BIBLE MISSIONALLY

James Brownson is credited with being the first to use the term "missional hermeneutic" to describe an approach to interpreting the Bible that takes seriously its missionary character.[5] His contention was that where it was recognized that a particular document had been produced in the context of mission by people engaged in mission, that should be the starting point in its interpretation and appropriation:

> I call the model I am developing a *missional* hermeneutic, because it springs from a basic observation about the New Testament: the early Christian movement that produced and canonized the New Testament was a movement with a specifically *missionary* character. One of the most obvious phenomena of early Christianity is the way in which the movement crossed cultural boundaries and planted itself in new places. More than half of the New Testament was in fact written by people engaged in and celebrating this sort of missionary enterprise in the early church. This tendency of early Christianity to cross cultural boundaries is a fertile starting point for developing a model of biblical interpretation. It is fertile, especially for our purposes, because it places the question of the relationship between Christianity and diverse cultures at the very top of the interpretative agenda. This focus may be of great help to us in grappling with plurality in interpretation today.[6]

3. For a brief description of migration in the story of New Zealand and initial proposals for response from New Zealand churches see Butcher and Wieland, "Go from your country."

4. Goheen, "Continuing Steps," 99.

5. Hunsberger ("Proposals," 316) refers to Brownson's contributions to The Gospel and Our Culture Network gatherings in 1992 and 1994 and his published article, "Speaking the Truth."

6. Brownson, "Speaking the Truth," 482.

George Hunsberger describes the scholarly conversation that has ensued, specifically the exploration of a missional hermeneutic that has been conducted through meetings of the Society of Biblical Literature and the American Academy of Religion, in association with the Gospel and Our Culture Network.[7] He identifies "four streams of emphasis" among the contributions, namely a focus on mission as the theme of the Bible,[8] an appreciation of the purpose of the Bible to shape and resource communities for mission,[9] an insistence that a genuinely missional reading of the Bible must emerge out of the readers' own missional locatedness,[10] and attention to the ways in which the New Testament writers brought their biblical tradition into engagement with their various cultural contexts, guided by the gospel as interpretive matrix.[11] Dean Flemming synthesizes these perspectives into two broad orientations: "A *missional hermeneutic* . . . attempts to read Scripture in light of God's mission and from the vantage point of a people engaged in God's mission."[12] Mission explains the production, content and purpose of the Bible and it is as participants in mission that contemporary readers are able to receive and appropriate the biblical texts.

Michael Barram and others have lamented the disciplinary divide between biblical scholars and missiologists, evident in the relative lack of engagement of each guild with the work of the other, and expressed the hope that aspects of newer missional approaches to the Bible might make closer collaboration possible.[13] It might well be the case that missiologists, attuned to the mission dynamics of contexts in which many of the New Testament documents were produced, could have observations to offer to biblical scholars seeking to explain features of those texts in relation to their social locations.[14] While there may be a degree of overlap in relation

7. Hunsberger, "Proposals," 309–310. It should be acknowledged of course that it is possible to discuss Biblical interpretation in relation to mission without using the expression "missional hermeneutic." David Hesselgrave, for example, speaks of a "missionary hermeneutic" (Hesselgrave, "A Missionary Hermeneutic"), while Ross Wagner prefers "apostolic hermeneutic" (Wagner, "Missio Dei").

8. Hunsberger, "Proposals," 310–13 refers particularly to Christopher J. Wright.

9. Ibid., 313–14, citing Darrell Guder.

10. Ibid., 314–16, reporting the work of Michael Barram.

11. Ibid., 316–18, discussing the contributions of James Brownson and Ross Wagner.

12. Flemming, "Exploring," 5.

13. Barram, "The Bible, Mission, and Social Location," 47–48; cf. Goheen, "Continuing Steps," 50–51.

14. I have tried to offer such observations on the letter to Titus in an article published in *New Testament Studies* ("Roman Crete"). Titus is one of the "disputed" Pauline Letters that Barram suggests missiologists should avoid if they want to be taken seriously by New Testament scholars ("Bible, Mission and Social Location," 54n30),

to Flemming's first orientation, through shared interest in mission contexts and an acknowledgement of the significance of mission considerations in explaining the origins of at least some biblical texts, a gulf remains. A recognition of the mission content and character of certain texts does not in itself constitute a missional hermeneutic. For that, Flemming's second orientation is crucial. It is as participants in the mission of God that missional readers open themselves to hearing the texts speak in their own mission contexts and to being shaped and energized by them for their participation in the mission. This orientation cannot be required of all students of biblical texts and the guild of biblical scholars will continue to represent a wide range of perspectives and motivations.[15]

More serious for the life of the people of God in mission than disciplinary divisions within the academy is the gulf between the academy and the church, scholars and practitioners, and more generally "the yawning chasm that has opened up between critical readings of Scripture and religiously committed readings."[16] Here a missional hermeneutic has the potential to make a very constructive contribution. It presupposes the purposeful activity of God in the world, the call of God to people to share in that purpose, and the instrumentality of Scripture in enabling that participation. These are faith commitments. Furthermore, a missional hermeneutic necessarily assumes a posture of receptivity and engagement. The scholar who adopts a missional hermeneutic may utilize the tools of critical study in the exploration of that faith and in the service of that engagement but will also recognize and learn from the illuminating and empowering effects of Scripture as it operates beyond the academically trained to effect the mission of God and shape God's people in every part of God's world for participation in that mission. Readers outside the academy, who have experienced that effect, will welcome contributions to their appreciation and appropriation of the biblical witness from students of the Bible who are sharers with them in the life and mission of God and are themselves taught and energized by the Scriptures whose missional character and power they seek to grasp.

A missional hermeneutic is properly a communal hermeneutic. It is operative as the missional community (in both local and global aspects)

---

though to be fair Barram's objection is to uncritical assumptions and failure to engage in Biblical scholarship.

15. The Society of Biblical Literature, for example, describes itself as "devoted to the critical investigation of the Bible from a variety of academic disciplines." SBL Strategic Vision Statement (revised October 23, 2011). Online: http://www.sbl-site.org/aboutus.aspx.

16. Goheen, "Continuing Steps," 50, following Wolters, "Confessional Criticism and the Night Visions of Zechariah," 90–117.

receives Scripture as an instrument of the mission of God towards them, in them and through them. A particular implication of this observation is that from the perspective of Scripture's missional instrumentality it is not essential that the process of interpretation should begin with an attempt to recover the "original meaning" of a text. This starting point, and the historical-critical method as a means of proceeding, are so widely held in seminaries and Bible colleges that it is often assumed to be self-evident that, "biblical interpretation begins with the process of (1) understanding the biblical writer's original meaning within that writer's particular context, and (2) translating that meaning to today's setting."[17]

For all its merits in terms of respect for the text and discipline in its interpretation, this insistence is missionally—and pneumatologically—deficient. It drastically underestimates the continuing communicative and effective power of Scripture as an instrument of God's mission in diverse people and contexts. It also undervalues the direct, untrained or vernacular reader as a partner in the hermeneutical task.[18] Conversely, it has the lamentable effect of claiming control of the text and its message for individuals trained in a certain way and, within the global Christian church, for those parts of the church that are heir to the western intellectual tradition in its modern form. Werner Kahl particularly poses the challenge:

> Thus the historical-critical method is an expression of the extremely aggressive and exclusive European ideology of superiority—and that in different respects: it not only denies the right to existence of *other* analyses, whether popular or academic, but also reserves, as a sort of secret science, the one acceptable access to the scriptures to an authoritarian priestly caste which has long dominated the study and interpretation of the Bible.[19]

Even if historical-critical exegesis is viewed more positively as a useful tool of biblical study, to claim for this method (and those trained in it) exclusive power to determine the significance of biblical texts is

17. Gallagher and Hertig, *Mission in Acts*, 14; cf. Ben Witherington's note in the introduction to his excellent commentary on Acts, that "The real hermeneutical task cannot be undertaken without first having a detailed engagement with the text itself, resulting in sound exegesis" (*Acts*, 97n287).

18. It is easier to find a term for academic, trained or professional readers of the Bible than to agree on a satisfactory way of referring to the great majority of readers of the Bible who are not trained in academic Biblical scholarship. Gerald West, pioneer of contextual Bible reading, often refers to "ordinary" and sometimes "non-scholarly" readers. For example, see West, "Contextual Bible Reading." Jason Upkong uses the expression, "untrained readers" in "Inculturation hermeneutics."

19. Kahl, "Intercultural Hermeneutics," 422.

pneumatologically—and missionally—deficient. A missional hermeneutic assumes the continuing presence of the Spirit of God as the agent of God's mission in the world, cultivates attentiveness to the Spirit's activity in the realization of that mission, and listens for the Spirit's enlivening of the text in each mission context. As well as the missional orientation to the character and content of the text that results from framing the Bible's witness within the *missio Dei*, the missional reader approaches the text with the intentionality of a participant in mission, in self-conscious locatedness within a context of mission, and in an attitude of receptivity to the text as an agent of mission towards its readers.

Is there, then, no place in a missional hermeneutic for historical and literary study? Indeed there is. These and related scholarly enterprises can contribute to sharpening and enriching the reading of the text, enabling connection across chronological and cultural distance between contemporary readers and the text's authors, subjects and first readers, and opening up the potential for conversation between the worlds of the text and the worlds in which it is being heard today. The text's missional significance is however not restricted to mission-related applications developed in the movement from historical study of the text to the reader's contemporary context; it is discovered also in turning to the text in that contemporary context and hearing resonances in the biblical text of the same mission that the Spirit is accomplishing today. The coherence between that which is being experienced by the contemporary reading community in the context of mission and elements of the mission of God to which the text bears witness sets a trajectory that orients the practice of mission in the readers' context. It is such a reading that we shall begin to sketch here as we read Acts in Auckland.

READING ACTS: RESONANCES AND IMPLICATIONS

The narrative of Acts begins in Jerusalem, at the heart of Jewish faith and expectation, moves through Judea, Samaria and several regions around the western end of the Mediterranean, and finally concludes in Rome, the capital of the empire that dominated the world of the New Testament authors. This movement is more than simply geographical. As Luke Johnson observes,

> [T]he sense of spatial expansion is closely connected to the portrayal of the Gentile mission . . . . [Luke] has wonderfully joined a spatial progression to a demographic phenomenon (conversion of Gentiles more than Jews), and has joined this to a

cultural transformation (an ever-increasing sense of the 'Greek world' as the narrative progresses).[20]

Structurally, this geographical movement provides the narrative framework for the unfolding of the significance of the witness to the risen Jesus in and for the world. The faith and life into which believers in Jesus are incorporated is itself designated "the road" (*hē hodos*, 9:2; 18:25, 26; 19:9, 23; 24:14, 22). From start to finish the story related in Acts concerns people on the move, whether they are purposely fulfilling missionary roles, travelling for quite different reasons or indeed bent on opposing the new faith. Time and again a journey turns out to be significant in this book's story of mission.

How might a missional hermeneutic operate in relation to this narrative of journeys? In the light of our earlier discussion we might suggest three of several possible dimensions of a missional reading. First, by adopting an orientation to the text that interprets it within the larger story of the mission of God, missional readers ask in what ways those journeys contribute to the realization of that mission. Second, by attending to the location in which the text is being read and recognizing it to be a context of the continuing mission of God, readers are attuned to resonances in their own context of the mission story in Acts. The resulting sense of coherence in the story of mission that is being played out in both contexts awakens them to the missional potential of elements of that story, including the journeys of migrants and others. Third, by approaching the text in the posture of participants in the same mission that is discovered in the text, readers are drawn into the narrative as fellow actors with its *dramatis personae*. As they find themselves in the story they are engaged by it more directly and open themselves to being called, challenged and instructed together with those earlier participants in the mission of God who are represented in the text and the audience(s) that it originally envisaged.

In the remainder of this chapter we shall note some examples of ways in which features of the story of mission in Acts have resonated with the experiences of participants in mission in the city of Auckland, and indicate ways in which missional attitudes and practice are being shaped by the reading of Acts in this mission context. The examples that follow have arisen in reading and discussing Acts in Auckland with a wide range of partners. These include immigrant churches, one and a half and second generation migrant groups, older local congregations, migrant and indigenous pastors and church leaders of various denominations, mission practitioners, and students (many of them migrants), particularly in the Carey Baptist College

20. Johnson, *Acts*, 11.

course, "Acts: A Missional Reading." It has been in these diverse communities of readers that the resonances reported here have been heard.

Leaders with Limited Imagination (Acts 1:6–11)

In the opening paragraphs of Acts we encounter mission leaders whose vision of the mission of God is too small. The question the apostles ask the risen Jesus is, "Lord, is this the time when you will restore the kingdom to Israel?" (1:6) Although they have heard Jesus teaching about the kingdom of God their imagination does not reach beyond their own place and people, and what they hope for is a restoration of what they look back on as a glorious past. They do not seem to envisage any movement on their part: the question assumes that the hoped for kingdom will come to them where they are. Jesus' reply stretches their horizons and orients them towards movement outwards as witnesses to the ascended Lord: "But you will receive power when the Holy Spirit has come upon you; and you will be my witnesses in Jerusalem, in all Judea and Samaria, and to the ends of the earth" (1:8). Both the hope for the kingdom and their mission in relation to it turned out to be bigger and much different than what they had anticipated. This text resonated with an Auckland congregation that was planning to launch a "season of mission." Appropriately, they turned to the book of Acts for guidance. It raised questions about the hopes with which they were embarking upon their mission project. These seemed to focus largely on attracting more people into their church building and increasing the number of church members (perhaps even restoring the congregation to numerical levels from which they had declined in recent years). This congregation and its leaders were challenged to set aside their own agendas for mission and to have their mission horizons stretched to include not only "the ends of the earth" but people from the ends of the earth who through migration were now living in their own locality.

The same text disturbed a group of ministerial students at the end of their training. In a context of demographic, social and cultural change in what will be their ministry and mission settings, Jesus' reorientation of the apostles challenged small expectations of the kingdom of God and preoccupation with inward-looking measures of success in their congregations. Locating themselves in continuity with the mission to which Jesus called those first disciples they determined to look to the wider horizon of God's mission and discern their own participation in it.

Foreign-born Residents (Acts 2:5–6)

"Now there were devout Jews from every nation under heaven living in Jerusalem" (2:5). When the Pentecost narrative is read in Auckland congregations, this statement often evokes wry smiles of recognition, particularly from longer-term residents who have experienced in their life-times a dramatic increase in the diversity of the population around them. There seem to be "people from every nation under heaven" in their city as well! That entry point has led to consideration of the circumstances of diaspora people, the experience of dislocation and only partial belonging whether in their place of birth or in the place that their family looks back to as their emotional and spiritual home. Where such an appreciation begins to shift attitudes from fear or even resentment of those who "don't fit in" to a greater empathy, that is already a missional shaping, and several Auckland churches have initiated such ministries as friendship groups or assistance for new immigrants. From a missional perspective the Pentecost account highlights the significance of diaspora people and their transnational networks, as the witness to the risen Jesus was unleashed on the world. Awakened to the missional potential in the diaspora people in their own contexts, some groups are engaging with Japanese, Chinese and other diasporas in the city and, through them, with families and communities in the migrants' source countries.

More generally, a missional reading of the familiar Pentecost text in Acts chapter 2 has energized some for participation in mission in a fresh way. Whereas formerly their main interest in the passage might have been in the particular type of spiritual experience that it describes, a missional orientation throws into relief the function of the Spirit's activity in enabling the whole community of believers to bear witness. Taking note of the coming of the Spirit upon all (2:3–4), regardless of gender, age or socio-economic status (2:17–18), has challenged some churches to see the potential for participation in mission of people or groups that they had traditionally expected little of or even excluded from participation. People who had not considered themselves competent for the work of mission, believing it to be the task of leaders and preachers, have been encouraged to discern those whose "language" they might be uniquely equipped to speak as agents of God's mission to them.

International Student (Acts 7:58; 22:3)

Although he lived in a prominent university city, the eager young man and his family knew that there was only one place he could go to receive the education he wanted for his chosen career path. Determined to make the most of the opportunity to study with the leading scholar in his field, Saul made the journey from Tarsus to Jerusalem and enrolled with Gamaliel. Unknown to him, this relocation had put him in the place where he was to encounter the Jesus movement. At first, sharing the stance of the guild in which he aspired to excel and eager to be faithful to what he understood to be the pure religion that honored and pleased God, he was appalled by this new sect. Apparently impatient with his mentor's caution (5:33–39), he supported the execution of one of the movement's leaders and set about opposing it with all the force he could muster (8:1–3; 9:1–2). The persecutor, however, was stopped in his tracks by a traumatic, disorienting encounter, and reoriented towards a life of astonishing and costly dedication to spreading the faith he had formerly tried to destroy. This pivotal change is described no less than three times in Acts (9:3–22; 22:3–20; 26:4–23) indicating how significant it is for the larger story of mission that Acts recounts.

For those who read Acts as participants in mission in the context of contemporary Auckland, the story of Saul opens up the missional potential represented by the thousands of international students that the city receives every year. Of a total of 92,995 international students who studied in New Zealand in 2012, some 58,255 (62.6%) were in the schools, colleges, and universities of Auckland.[21] A city center church that has built extensive relationships with international students has found that some arrive with absolutely no prior knowledge of Jesus, churches or Christian faith. They are surprised and often intrigued to encounter people for whom this faith, of which they had been completely unaware, is evidently so important. A campus chaplain finds that some international students may at first be suspicious or hostile, but Saul's story shapes his response to them, confident that the mission in which he is engaged is a continuation of the mission represented in Acts, in which initial opposition may be the prelude to dedicated allegiance to Jesus.

Spiritual Seekers (Acts 8:26–40)

The cameo account of the interaction between the evangelist Philip and the royal treasurer of Queen Candace of Ethiopia, a court eunuch, is vividly narrated in Acts. Those who read it with the intention to participate in mission note Philip's qualities of attentiveness to God's prompting, obedience

21. Statistics provided by the New Zealand government Ministry of Education. Online: http://www.educationcounts.govt.nz/__data/assets/pdf_file/0012/115050/ Enrolments-of-international-students-2006–2012.pdf.

and courage, and the relational, dialogical mode of his engagement with the traveler. A missional reading in the context of a city at the nexus of considerable transnational movement is also alert to the role journeys play in this mission episode. This sensitizes them to the possibility that some of those who pass through their city are actually on a spiritual quest, and are people in whom the mission of God is already operative. The visit to Jerusalem of a senior official of a foreign monarch might be expected to be a matter of state business. Perhaps it was, but what the narrator notes is that "he had come to Jerusalem to worship" (8:27) and as he returned home he carried with him a biblical scroll whose content he was anxious to understand (8:28–34). It is at the traveler's request, not the evangelist's urging, that he is baptized (8:36–38). In mysterious ways God's mission is being realized in those who are coming to faith by means prior to and beyond the activity of human agents of mission.

In one of Auckland's Baptist churches the congregation recently arrived one Sunday morning to be told that the service would include a baptism. Normally baptismal services are planned some weeks in advance, giving time for preparation of those who are to be baptized, who are usually well known to the congregation. On this occasion it was different. No one knew the woman who stood up to tell her story. She was in Auckland as a member of a business delegation from a country where Christian faith is not encouraged. Well educated and in a senior role, she had nonetheless been troubled by existential questions which her training did not equip her to answer. Finally she had acquired a Bible and, through reading it, had come to believe in Jesus as the source of meaning and hope. Reading the Bible, she learned that her new faith and commitment should be expressed in baptism, but she did not know how that might be accomplished in her home environment. She had therefore seized the opportunity to join the delegation to New Zealand because she knew it to be a "Christian country" where she could find a church and be baptized.

When she had made contact with the church a few days before that Sunday to make her unusual request, a missional hermeneutic was called for to guide the response. Although there were potential obstacles in the church's normal processes and requirements, resonances of the Ethiopian official's appeal to Philip, "What is to prevent me being baptized?" (8:36) helped to orient the pastors to recognize the same mission of God in operation and respond accordingly. In contemporary Auckland, as in first century Jerusalem, a business trip may carry missional significance beyond its official purpose.[22]

22. In the course of the mission of Paul and Silas they come across Lydia, an Asian

Refugees (Acts 11:19)

As the narrative of Acts unfolds attention shifts from Jerusalem to the prominent city of Antioch, capital of the Roman province of Syria.[23] The church established there was notable in several respects. It was more ethnically and culturally diverse than the church in Jerusalem, moving for the first time beyond the community's overwhelmingly Jewish base to include large numbers of "Greeks" (11:20–21).[24] It became the context for Saul's first (at least in the narrative of Acts) sustained period of teaching the faith (11:25–26). Appropriately for a church so diverse in its composition, its principal ministers themselves represented a range of backgrounds: Barnabas, a wealthy Cypriot Jew prominent in the Jerusalem church; Simeon Niger, presumably black and if so probably of African origin; Lucius of Cyrene, in North Africa; Manaen, evidently a member of a social and political elite judging by his close association with the court of Herod Antipas, ruler of Galilee and Perea until 39 CE; and Saul, who had been brought up in Tarsus, around the coast from Antioch in the Roman province of Asia Minor (13:1). This church was the first to organize an international relief effort (11:27–30), and it was from here that Barnabas and Saul were sent out on mission (13:1–3).

It is not always noticed that those who founded this remarkable church were refugees. It was "those who were scattered because of the persecution that took place over Stephen" who arrived in Antioch, carrying with them their witness to Jesus (11:19–20).[25] A missional hermeneutic, attentive to ways in which the mission of God is being played out, finds in this observation a fresh orientation to a particular aspect of Auckland as a current context of that mission, namely the presence of refugees. As a signatory to the

---

business woman apparently looking after the export end of the family business in the Roman colony of Philippi in Macedonia (16:13–15, 40). Her commercially motivated migration had taken her to the place where she first received and then became a participant in mission.

23. Witherington entitles the section of his commentary dealing with Acts 11:19–15:35 "The Antioch Chronicles" (*Acts*, 366–470).

24. There is a textual issue over whether those evangelized were *hellēnas* (Greeks) or *hellēnistas* (Hellenists). If it is the former, gentiles are clearly in view; if the latter, the reference might still be to (non-Jewish) people of the prevailing Greek culture, but the term might also be taken to designate Hellenistic Jews (cf. Acts 6:1). If that were the intention, however, it would be difficult to see the point of contrasting that category with "Jews." See Bock, *Acts* 419–20.

25. The Jewish couple, Aquila and Priscilla, became refugees from Rome when the Emperor Claudius moved against the city's Jewish population (18:1–3). In their case also this unplanned and most likely unwanted circumstance eventuated in very significant mission participation. See in this book (62–75), vanThanh Nguyen, "Migrants as Missionaries: The Case of Priscilla and Aquila."

United Nations Convention on the Status of Refugees, New Zealand receives a quota of 750 refugees annually, all of whom spend their initial period of induction in Auckland, and many remain here.[26] In addition to those who come with official refugee status there are others whose decision to embark upon migration has been compelled by circumstances beyond their control. The plight of such displaced people can evoke a compassionate response from Auckland's Christian community in terms of participation in resettlement support programs, gifts of household goods and clothes, etc. A missional reading of Acts, however, suggests a new question: who among those refugees are bearers of the mission of God, through whom that mission may be realized in fresh ways both here in Auckland and beyond?

The service was underway at a small church in Auckland when a visitor slipped in. A Middle Eastern man, he spoke very little English but managed to communicate that he had just arrived in the country and was staying at the Refugee Center which was just a short distance away. As the congregation got to know him over the following few weeks they learned his story. He had become a believer in Jesus through the care and witness of a friend, but there had been severe consequences, and finally it had been necessary for him to flee for his life and seek asylum elsewhere. He rapidly became an integral part of the church and expressed the desire to be baptized. At his baptismal service the church members were outnumbered by immigrants from his country of origin, the great majority of them adherents of that country's majority religion. Like those refugees in Acts whose witness wherever they travelled was so significant in the story of mission, this asylum seeking refugee was less an object of the mission of the Auckland church than an agent of that mission through whom the church's participation in mission was greatly enhanced.

Bicultural People (Acts 2:5–11; 6:1–6; 11:20; 16:1–3)

The narrative of mission in Acts is heavily populated with characters of complex cultural identity. There are the diaspora returnees at the Pentecost festival whose faith and heritage are focused on Jerusalem but whose heart languages are those of the places where they had grown up, scattered over the Mediterranean world (2:5–11). When the strain on the apostles of caring for the burgeoning community of believers in Jerusalem got too great and it was necessary to share the load, it was, judging by their Greek names, people comfortable in Hellenistic environments who were brought into

26. Online: http://www.refugeeservices.org.nz/refugees_and_new_zealand/quota_programme (accessed 20.9.2013)

ministerial roles (6:1–6). Two of their members become the pioneers of the next stage of mission, to Hellenistic Jews in Jerusalem (6:8–10), across the barriers of religious difference and historical hurt to Samaria (8:4–13), and to a foreign visitor (8:26–39). It was bicultural people, brought up as members of minority Jewish communities in North Africa and the Greek islands, who precipitated the paradigm shift in the missionary practice of the Jesus movement by taking the witness to Jesus beyond the Jewish diaspora to the majority culture of the Roman world (11:20–21).[27] Even greater identity confusion is intimated in the case of Timothy, the young man whom Paul and Silas met in the Galatian town of Lystra (16:1–3). The author explains that his mother was both Jewish and a believer in Jesus but his father was a gentile. The child had not been circumcised, which indicates that he had not been fully accepted into the local Jewish community.[28] Among the believers, however, he had received both acceptance and recognition, and he became a member of Paul's missionary team. Interestingly, Paul requires him to undergo circumcision, a move that would enable freer relating to the Jewish communities to whom they would go in the course of their mission.

Among 1.5 and 2nd generation immigrants in Auckland's churches a missional reading of Acts that detects the significance of bicultural people in the mission of God can be energizing. A few churches in Auckland were planted by immigrants from Hong Kong and Taiwan in the 1980's. They now typically include young people struggling with conflicted identities, trying to be "Kiwi" (i.e. New Zealanders in culture, attitudes and behavior) at school or work and Chinese at home. In common with "Third Culture Kids" everywhere they feel that they do not quite belong in either context. The figure of Timothy has resonated with some of them, encouraging them to be open to what might be their distinctive contribution to the mission of God. A young theological student, of Tongan heritage but brought up and living within New Zealand's majority culture, reflected on Timothy from the perspective of his own participation in mission, with a particular concern for Tongan young men, some of whom seem alienated from wider society. Timothy's circumcision has prompted him to consider what aspects of his Tongan identity he might be able to embrace more fully in order to relate more effectively with a Tongan community from which he had felt disconnected.

27. It could be argued that in the structure of the book this shift takes place with the episode of Peter and the gentile Cornelius (10:1—11:18). The principle is certainly established there but it is in the Antioch episode that the departure from what seems to have been standard practice ("they spoke the word to no-one except Jews") is underlined (11:20).

28. See brief discussion by Johnson, *Acts* 283–84.

Among a group of pastors of immigrant churches in Auckland con-sideration of the extensive contribution of bicultural people as agents of mission in the Acts' narrative yielded some fresh inspiration and direction for their mission engagement. A Korean missionary who has lived in New Zealand for several years working almost entirely among other Korean immigrants exclaimed, "For the first time I see that we can be partners in mission!" That multi-ethnic group began to move their conversation past the needs of their particular congregations to the distinctive contributions that they could bring in partnership together and with the wider Christian community to the mission of God both in Auckland and along the channels of the transnational networks that link Auckland to much of the world.

CONCLUSION

The examples offered above illustrate some outcomes of reading Acts with various groups in Auckland, New Zealand, utilizing aspects of a missional hermeneutic. Interpreting the narrative of Acts within the larger story of the mission of God, understanding the readers' location to be a context in which that mission is being realized, and assuming the posture of partici-pants in that mission, readers have entered the narrative of Acts, heard reso-nances that have alerted them to coherence with their own mission realities in Auckland, "a city of migrants," and been oriented towards attitudes and action in continuity with the mission of God that the book of Acts both witnesses to and effects.

12

Current Trends of Migration in Asia
Prospects and Challenges*

—vanThanh Nguyen

On the highways and byways of every continent, millions of people are constantly on the move. In the last two and a half decades, the number of people on the move has doubled from 100 million to nearly 200 million people. It is estimated that approximately three percent of the world's 6.5 billion people are displaced. That is one out of every thirty-five people on the planet now living away from his or her homeland. Because of the growing inequalities of wealth caused by globalization, political and ethnic conflicts, environmental disasters, implementation of free trade, and viable means of transportation, more and more people are migrating than ever before, causing some to call our era "the age of migration."[1]

Crossing international borders is a major characteristic of our present epoch. No countries or regions are immune from this phenomenon, certainly not Asia. In 2005 it was estimated that there were 53 million Asian immigrants scattered across the globe. Facing the complexities and concerns of this current worldwide phenomenon, this chapter seeks to develop

* This chapter was previously published in the *Asian Christian Review* 4.2 (Winter 2010) 18–31 entitled, "Asian in Motion: A Biblical Reflection on Migration." The author is grateful for the journal allowing it to be republished in this collection.

1. See Castles and Miller, *The Age of Migration*.

an appropriate Christian response to the issue of international migration particularly for the people of Asia. Since the Bible is the word of God and the ultimate authority for faith and practice, I will turn to the Christian Scriptures to search for guidance. The aim is to provide groundwork for a biblical spirituality for immigrants and a biblical theology of migration from the vantage point of the immigrants themselves. But first let us examine the current situation in Asia.

ASIA IN MOTION

International migration from Asia increased significantly in the 1970s and 1980s. There were basically three major political events that triggered the massive movement of people within and from Asia. In the early 1970s, the West-East Pakistan conflict forced approximately ten million people to flee from East Pakistan to India.[2] With the fall of Saigon to the communist regime in 1975, millions of refugees—initially from Viet Nam and subsequently from Laos and Cambodia—fled by land and by sea to escape the violence of post-war retribution. It is estimated that between 1975 and 1995 some three million people fled the region. While most Asian countries pushed backed the rickety boats from their shorelines, the United States, Canada, Australia, and a few other European countries rescued these refugees and helped settle them in a foreign land. The third major exodus of people began in 1979 during the successive occupations of Afghanistan. The political conflicts that triggered the massive Afghan refugee crises were first set off by the former USSR, followed by the Taliban, and have been drawn out till even today. These events are believed to have caused millions of people being displaced in 71 different countries.[3]

Since the 1990s, especially with the rapid economic growth of several Asian countries, migration in Asia has changed remarkably in character and landscape. While emigration continues, primarily for family reunification outside of the Asian region, for example to North America, Europe, and Australia, recent data show that new trends of migration are happening within Asia itself.[4] The most noticeable trend is the migration of temporary labor

---

2. Maruja M. B. Asis, *Understanding International Migration in Asia*, 12. See also http://www.onwar.com/aced/data/bravo/bangladesh1971.htm (accessed September 22, 2010).

3. For a good synopsis of the situation up until 1993, see Silvano M. Tomasi, "The World-wide Context of Migration: The Example of Asia," 3–10.

4. Castles and Miller, *The Age of Migration*, 125; see also Asis, *Understanding International Migration in Asia*, 17.

from less developed countries to the increasingly industrializing countries. It is estimated that in the last decade alone there were about 6.1 million Asian economic migrants working outside of their own native places but within East and Southeast Asia (such as Japan, South Korea, Taiwan, China, Hong Kong, Malaysia, and Singapore).[5] In the Middle East alone, there are some 8.7 million Asian contract workers employed in the Gulf oil countries like Kuwait, Saudi Arabia, Dubai, and United Arab Emirates. While some migrant workers are highly skilled workers, many are hired to do the 3D jobs (dirty, difficult, and dangerous).[6] Castles and Miller noted that China alone has a "floating population" of 100–150 million people moving from rural areas to the new industrial areas. India too experiences large-scale internal migration and urbanization. India's "diaspora" population alone is estimated at around 20 million people.[7] It is well noted that many of the "Tiger economy countries" (Japan, South Korea, Hong Kong, Thailand, Taiwan and more recently Malaysia) have huge numbers of migrant workers. Malaysia alone has a foreign work force estimated at 2.6 million, while Japan and Thailand each have around 2 million.[8] It is really impossible to know exactly how many Asian migrant workers there are in the Asian region because many are clandestine (undocumented), overstaying their visa permit, or running away from an employer. However, statistics show that emigration for employment within Asia has grown exponentially, "with about 2.6 million people leaving their homes in search of work each year."[9]

The participation of women in international labor migration is another key recent development in the Asian region. Before the late 1970s labor migration was predominantly male; by 1985 however, with the demand for domestic workers, nurses, sales clerks and other female services in the Gulf States, 3.2 million female Asians were working in the Middle East.[10] In the late 1980s and the early 1990s the demand for foreign domestic workers also increased tremendously in the newly industrialized countries in East and Southeast Asia (e.g. Japan, Taiwan, South Korea, Hong Kong, Singa-

---

5. Castles and Miller, *The Age of Migration*, 127.

6. Asis, *Understanding International Migration in Asia*, 17.

7. Castles and Miller, *The Age of Migration*, 125 and 139.

8. Ibid., 136–41.

9. Castles and Miller, *The Age of Migration*, 127. For a very comprehensive picture and statistics of the situation of migration in the Asia-Pacific region until 2005, see Graeme Hugo, "Migration in the Asia-Pacific Region," A paper prepared for the Policy Analysis and Research Programme of the Global Commission on International Migration, September 2005. For the online version, see http://www.gcim.org/mm/File/Regional%20Study%202.pdf (accessed on September 20, 2010).

10. Castles and Miller, *The Age of Migration*, 130.

pore, and Malaysia). In Taiwan, for example, migrant domestic workers and caretakers comprised of 41.5 percent of the foreign workforce by 2004.[11] In Indonesia, 81 percent of those who registered to work abroad, mainly to Malaysia and Saudi Arabia, were women. Women's labor migration also increased in the Philippines to 72 percent in 2006.[12]

Another growing phenomenon related to female migration since the 1990s is international marriages in the Asian region. Foreign brides who come from the Southeast Asian countries of Viet Nam, Indonesia, Thailand, and the Philippines, have been sought especially by men from Taiwan, Japan, China, and South Korea. It is estimated that as of 2004, foreign spouses in Taiwan alone reached around 300,000, and most of the women came from China and Southeast Asia. Notably, between 1995 and 2005, the number of Vietnamese women married to Taiwanese men skyrocketed from 1,476 to about 100,000.[13] In 2004 there were 57,000 international marriages registered in South Korea.[14] It is estimated that since 2006 at least 5,000 Vietnamese brides emigrate to South Korea every year.

Current trends suggest that labor migration in the Asian region will persist and continue to increase as newly industrialized countries demand more foreign migrants to work in 3D jobs as well as more foreign domestic workers.[15] Since most migrant workers in Asia are not protected by labor laws, men and, more so women (particularly "professional entertainers," a euphemism for prostitutes) are vulnerable to abuse, exploitation, and violence. Many women and girls run the risk of becoming trafficked or forced

---

11. Asis, *Understanding International Migration in Asia*, 21.

12. Castles and Miller, *The Age of Migration*, 133; see also Gemma Tulud Cruz, "Migration in the Asia Region: Retrospect and Prospects," 21–30; for the online version, see http://www.sedos.org/english/cruz_2.htm (accessed on September 1, 2010).

13. See Quang Hanh, "VN-Taiwan discuss brides' rights in illegally-made matches," *Vietnam Net Bridge*, http://english.vietnamnet.vn/features/2005/08/482081/ (accessed on September 15, 2010). In the article, Hanh states that "According to Professor Chyong-fang Ko from the Taiwanese Central Research Institute, Vietnamese brides account for 35% of 338,000 foreign brides in Taiwan, or around 118,300 women, mainly from the south of Vietnam." See also Hsia, http://cc.shu.edu.tw/~e62/NewSiteData/Teacher/Hsia/Hsia_file/imaged%20and%20imagined%20national%20anxiety.pdf (accessed on September 15, 2010).

14. Asis, *Understanding International Migration in Asia*, 28.

15. While Asian migration has been of low-skilled workers, emerging trends indicate that the mobility of the highly skilled professionals, such as technicians, engineers, nurses and medical doctors, is growing. Student mobility which is part of the skilled migration is also steadily increasing in numbers. The number is large enough to alarm some countries of the "brain drain" that has been caused by these professionals leaving their countries of origin. See Castles and Miller, *The Age of Migration*, 141; Asis, *Understanding International Migration in Asia*, 30.

into prostitution.[16] While the contemporary trends of labor migration have brought "a breath of fresh air"[17] to the region's economic landscape, the situation raises serious concerns about the inhumane treatment of the vulnerable migrant workers and their psychological marginalization and alienation while living away from home. It is even more heartbreaking to see the many host countries in Asia treating their very own Asian brothers and sisters as aliens and strangers without much dignity or rights.[18] How should Christians therefore respond more appropriately to the migration issue today? We now turn to the Bible for guidance and inspiration.

A CHRISTIAN RESPONSE TO MIGRATION TODAY

Migration is by no means a new phenomenon. Since the dawn of human history, wave upon wave of people have been on the move for a variety of reasons, including trade, war, persecution, natural disasters, economic opportunities, asylum, and even adventure. Interestingly, the Bible is loaded with stories written by, for, and about strangers, migrants and refugees. It begins with the first human parents being exiled from Paradise and ends with the prophet John in exile on the island of Patmos. Encapsulated between these two bookends, namely Genesis and Revelation, are stories of God's people constantly being purified and transformed as they struggled to find their way home to be with their creator. Thus, one scholar correctly noted that the Bible is essentially "a literary tapestry woven from the stories of migrants."[19] Since these sacred texts are written by, for, and about migrants, it is worthwhile to examine some of its key figures and events in order to draw out appropriate responses to one of the most challenging phenomena of our time.

---

16. According to UNIFEM (United Nations Development Fund for Women), women and children being trafficked in Southeast Asia could be around 225,000 out of a global figure of over 700,000 annually. For concrete scenarios of abuses of female migration in Asia, see Cruz's article. For an excellent resource and powerful reflection on the current "terrible scourge" of human trafficking, see the latest document published by the Society of the Divine Word, entitled, *Human Trafficking: Present Day Slavery*.

17. Asis, *Understanding International Migration in Asia*, 21.

18. Stephen Castles notices three dominant policies or attitudes that host countries in Asia have toward immigrants: 1) immigrants should not be allowed to settle; 2) foreign residents should not be offered citizenship apart from exceptional cases; and 3) national culture and identity should not be modified in response to external influences. See Stephen Castles, "The Myth of the Controllability of Difference."

19. Hoppe, "Israel and Egypt," 209.

Biblical Ancestors as Immigrants and Refugees

The first eleven chapters of the book of Genesis are filled with stories of forced migration. Due to pride and selfishness, namely wanting to be like God, Adam and Eve disobeyed God's commands and consequently were expelled from the Garden of Eden (Gen 3:16–24). They barely had time to enjoy the fruits and sanctuary of Paradise provided by God. Interestingly however, before the first parents were exiled to earth to secure their own shelter and till the land for food, God showed deep affection and concern for the earliest sojourners by sewing skins together to clothe them and protect them from the elements (3:21). The theme of alienation and displacement continues with Cain who kills his brother Abel out of jealousy (3:8–16). As a punishment, he became a fugitive and wanderer on the earth. Despite Cain's hideous act of cruelty, God still cares for the criminal vagrant by placing a mark of protection on him so that no one will kill him. As the inhabitants of the earth increase, wickedness, violence, and degradation of the earth sickened God to the point of regret for having created humanity. Thus, God purged the earth and all its inhabitants. Noah and his family, who were righteous before God and chosen to continue the human race, were forced to flee their land because of the great flood. Like many victims of natural disaster, they became immigrants without a known destination. Nevertheless, trusting in the covenant promised by God (6:18) Noah sailed over the waves of fear and chaos to find a new home on a distant shore. But that is not the end! The Tower of Babel presents another tale about forced migration. In this story, the whole of humanity decided to challenge God by constructing a tower that would reach heaven. For their sin of pride God confused the language of all the inhabitants and scattered them throughout the face of the earth (11:1–9). In short, the first eleven chapters of the book of Genesis recount tales of the earliest human families as migrants and refugees moving about the earth seeking a land to settle and a home in which to dwell. What is most noticeable in these accounts is that God cares for and protects these fugitives, vagrants or immigrants despite their frailty and sin.

Israel's ancestral history really begins with Abraham and Sarah when they responded to God's uncertain promises and invitation to leave their familiar surroundings in Mesopotamia (literally "between the two rivers" of Tigris and Euphrates) and to sojourn to the land of Canaan (Gen 12:9). While they were still wandering about searching for a dwelling, a famine broke out in the land forcing them to flee to Egypt and reside there as "aliens" (12:10).[20] After finding refuge in Egypt, they continued to wander

---

20. All scriptural references come from the New Revised Standard Version, unless otherwise indicated.

about aimlessly in the Negeb (a semi-desert area located in the southern part of today's Israel-Palestine) to Bethel and then to Ai (13:1–3). Eventually Abraham and his clan pitched their tents at Mamre near Hebron as their principal place of residence but only for a time because their journey did not end there. As nomads, Abraham and his kinsfolk continued to move about in Canaan searching for food and pasture for their livestock. They seemed to have finally settled in Beer-sheba (21:33), but it is interesting to note that at the death of Sarah, Abraham had to purchase a burial place for her and for himself in the cave of the field of Machpelah (23:19). This is a clear indication that even until the very end of their earthly existence Abraham and Sarah never ceased being strangers in the land of promise. The same is true with Isaac and Rebekah, as well as with Jacob and his two wives Leah and Rachel. While Isaac's primary domicile was at Beer-sheba and Jacob's at Shechem, each also moved about with his flocks and herds, not attached to any particular place. Eventually, one of Jacob's twelve sons, Joseph, was sold into slavery in Egypt because of sibling rivalry. The dramatic epic of Joseph's displacement and rise to power in Egypt sets the stage for Israel's massive migration to the land of the Pharaohs where they will be saved from a terrible famine in Palestine and eventually became permanent resident aliens.[21]

Israel's memory of their founding ancestors is fundamentally as "*gerim,*" a Hebrew designation that can loosely be translated as "resident aliens, strangers, sojourners, or (more appropriately) immigrants."[22] We learn from these ancestral stories that God encounters and calls people who are less than perfect and frequently on the run. They are often not the best of characters. Some are not even honest. Jacob, for example, was a deceiver and schemer; yet God chose him and placed him in the line of promise. Even though these *gerim* are vulnerable, frail and even sinful, they are not nameless and faceless but rather created in the image and likeness of God. They are real human beings and should be treated with the dignity that has been divinely bestowed upon them. Frequently, those who show kindness to

21. Timothy A. Lenchak, "Israel's Refugee Ancestors," 11–15.

22. Abraham (Gen 12:10; 17:8; 20:1; 21:23, 34; 23:4), Lot (19:9), Isaac (26:3; 35:27; 37:1), Jacob (28:4; 32:5), Esau and Jacob (36:7), and Joseph (47:4, 9) are designated as *gerim* (cf. also Exo 6:4). Abraham even described himself as a *ger* (Gen 23:4). In Exod 6:4 the patriarchs are referred to collectively as *gerim* when YHWH declares to Moses that he had promised to give the fathers the land in which they were dwelling as outsiders. Even the psalmist refers to Abraham, Isaac and Jacob as *gerim* who wandered about Canaan before their descendants took possession of the land at a later time (Ps 105:8–13). And in two other instances, Ps 39:13 and 1 Chr 29:15, Israel's fathers are called *gerim*. While in Egypt, the Israelites were also identified as *gerim* (Exod 22:20; 23:9; Deut 10:19; 23:8). See Feldmeier, "The 'Nation' of Strangers," 241–70.

these folks do not go unnoticed but are rewarded abundantly. Consequently, biblical writers continue to remind their readers to treat the strangers and immigrants in their midst with respect and dignity (Exod 22:20; 23:9; Lev 19:33–34; Deut 5:15; 10:19) for to neglect the needs of these vulnerable migrants makes one liable to punishment (Deut 24:14–15).

An interesting feature found in the Hebrew Scriptures' legal code, which is completely absent from other law codes of the Ancient Near East, is the inclusion of numerous laws favoring the *gerim* or foreigners.[23] Authors of the Hebrew Scriptures aim to protect the vulnerable *gerim* in their midst through various concrete legislations. There are laws that safeguard them from mistreatment or injustice (Exod 22:21; Deut 24:17) and provide them gleaning rights during harvest time (Deut 24:19–21). Other laws allow them to receive a portion of the special tithe that was collected every three years for the poor (Deut 14:28–29; 26:12–13) and granting them fair treatment in legal cases (Deut 1:16–17). The foreigners are even permitted to rest on the Sabbath (Exod 20:10; 23:12; Deut 5:14) and to assimilate into Israel's cultic life: Day of Atonement (Lev 16:29–30), Passover (Exod 12:48–49), Feast of Weeks (Deut 16:11), and Feast of Tabernacles (Deut 16:14). Amazingly, Israel's laws demand everyone—literally at all levels of society—to assist and care for the immigrants: community (gleaning rights), workplaces (payment of wages), religious centers (collecting the tithe and distributing it justly), city gate where the elders meet for judicial matters (fairness in legal cases), and family (giving the immigrant rest on the Sabbath and including them in the religious festivals).[24]

The *gerim* however must act responsibly in the host countries. They are required to be present at the periodic reading of the law (Deut 31:10–13), which assumed that the immigrants must learn to speak and understand the local language of the people, namely, Hebrew. Furthermore, the *gerim* are expected to avoid sexual taboos (Lev 18:26) and are subject to the penalties of criminal law (Lev 24:22). They are also obligated to obey the purity laws (Num 19:10) and other dietary restrictions (Exod 12:19; Lev 17:10–15), and most importantly prohibited from worship of other gods and blaspheming against the LORD (Lev 20:1–2; 24:10–16; Num 15:30–31).

Jesus as Border Crosser and Guest-Host

The closest equivalent to the Hebrew Scriptures' concept of *ger* (singular) or *gerim* (plural) for New Testament writers is *paroikos*, which can be

23. Rendtorff, "The *Ger* in the Priestly Laws of the Pentateuch," 77–87.
24. Carroll R., *Christians at the Border*, 91–112.

translated in different ways in English: "stranger," "resident alien," "sojourner," or "immigrant."[25] Interestingly, all the Gospel writers depict Jesus in one way or another as *paroikos*. According to the Gospel of Luke, the birth of Jesus is situated at the time when Joseph and Mary had to return from Nazareth to their ancestral home—namely Bethlehem—to enroll in a census imposed by Emperor Augustus (2:1–7). Thus, Jesus is literally born on the road, sheltered in a stable and surrounded by animals and shepherds from the field. In the Gospel of Matthew Jesus' origins are told even more dramatically within the context of migration. First, Jesus comes from a genealogy that includes female foreigners: Tamar, Rahab, and Ruth. Secondly, shortly after his birth, Joseph and Mary have to take the newborn infant into Egypt to flee the death threat of a despotic ruler and the mass killing of infants in Bethlehem (2:13–23). Interestingly, the one who seeks to end the life of an innocent child ends up dead prematurely. Thus, after having heard the news of Herod's death, the Holy Family returns to Bethlehem only to discover that Archaelaus, the heir to the territory of Judea, is just as cruel, if not worse, than his father. Once again, Joseph and Mary take the child Jesus and migrate to the north, to Nazareth, to start a new life in a completely new place and among new kinfolk. In depicting Jesus as a refugee and immigrant, the evangelist Matthew evokes Israel's experience of migration from Canaan to Egypt and from Egypt back to the promised land, which fulfills the prophecy of Hosea, "Out of Egypt I have called my son" (Hosea 11:1; cf. Matt 2:15). Although Son of God and Messiah, Jesus is driven into exile, estranged from his own country, and returned to his homeland only to be displaced once again.[26] But it does not end there!

Jesus' entire adult life is portrayed as an itinerant who is often viewed by others as an outsider and a vagabond.[27] Jesus leaves behind family and possessions and calls his followers to do the same (Mark 10:28–31). He constantly moves about from one town to another without even a place to lay his head: "Foxes have holes, and the birds of the air have nests; but the Son of Man has no place to lay his head" (Luke 9:58; Matt 8:20). His whole life is actually portrayed as a "journey" to Jerusalem (Luke 9:51–19:28).[28] Finally, Jesus dies as a crucified criminal, hanging between heaven and earth and is

25. The Hebrew *ger* (singular) or *gerim* (plural) is translated into Greek in basically four ways: *xenos, parepidemos, proselyte,* and *paroikos*. For a concise study of the word *paroikos* and its LXX counterparts, see Chin, "A Heavenly Home for the Homeless," 96–112. See also Maurizio Pettena, *Migration in the Bible*, 10–15.

26. Nguyen, "In Solidarity with the Strangers," 219–24

27. Senior, "'Beloved Aliens and Exiles," 26–27.

28. Interestingly the early Christian movement was originally called the "Way" (Acts 9:2).

buried alone outside the city wall in a stranger's tomb.[29] Thus, the evangelist Luke correctly calls him a *paroikos*.[30] In the Emmaus story, when asked what they were discussing along the way, the two despairing disciples respond to Jesus, "Are you the only stranger (*paroikos*) in Jerusalem who does not know the things that have taken place in these days?" (Luke 24:18).

It is not surprising therefore for Jesus to feel like a stranger in this world. This view is artfully developed in the Gospel of John. Jesus is portrayed like a temporary resident alien who is constantly crossing borders. He is the divine Word (logos) that became flesh and dwelt (or literally pitched his tent)[31] among us (John 1:14); yet the world does not know or accept him (v. 10–11). In John, Jesus often says that his home is not of this world (18:36) but from above (19:11), and therefore he will return to his Father in heaven (16:28). Jesus' first words to Mary Magdalene after having been raised from the dead reiterate his intention to return from whence he had come, "Go to my brothers and sisters and say to them, I am ascending to my Father and your Father, to my God and your God" (20:7).

Consequently, Jesus knows and feels what it is like to be a marginal *paroikos*—stranger, foreigner, or immigrant—in this world. He often travels with those in need and associates with those on the margin of society, namely women, the poor, the sick, and Gentiles. He even breaks Sabbath regulations and social customs to accommodate their needs. He knows exactly what it is like to depend on the hospitality of others since he too has been both a guest and a host on numerous occasions. In the Gospel of Luke especially, Jesus dines with all sorts of people: a Pharisee (7:36–50), women (10:38–42), tax collectors (5:27–32; 19:1–10), and strangers (24:13–35). It is frequently noted by Lucan scholars that in this Gospel Jesus is either going to or coming from a dinner party. Although a teacher with no place to lay his head, Jesus graciously welcomes the lost and generously feeds huge crowds (Luke 9:10–17). At the hour of his passion and death, Jesus breaks bread and shares a cup of wine with his disciples as a last remembrance of his covenant of love. After his resurrection, he prepares a breakfast of fish and bread for Peter and the other disciples on the shore of Lake Galilee (John 21:9–14). Furthermore, in his teachings, he urges human hosts to invite those who

29. Ancient burial practices gathered from archaeological remains show that family members are buried together in one tomb. It is an anomaly for a person to be buried alone.

30. While the NAB translates *paroikos* as "visitor," the NRSV and KJV more appropriately translate it as "stranger."

31. Noticeably, in using the Greek verb *eskenosen*, which is literally translated as "tabernacle" or "tented," John evokes the Hebrew Scriptures' image of God's presence travelling about with his people through the tent of meeting.

could not return the favor to come to their banquets (14:12–14). He uses parables to highlight the virtue of hospitality in the kingdom of God: the Friend at Midnight (Luke 8:5–8), the Wedding Banquet (Luke 14:15–24); the Lost Sheep, Lost Coin and Prodigal Son (15:1–32); and the Rich Man and Lazarus (16:19–31).

The portrayal of Jesus as stranger, guest, host, and food makes hospitality a central motif in the New Testament and constitutes the greatest challenge concerning issues surrounding migration today.[32] Jesus teaches that "whoever welcomes this child in my name welcomes me" (Luke 9:48). Similarly, in the last judgment story where the sheep and goats are separated, Jesus even identifies himself with the hungry and thirsty, with strangers and prisoners, with the naked and the sick. Those who welcome any of these welcome Him, and those who neglect the least of these neglect the Son of Man. Jesus says, "Truly I tell you, just as you did it to one of the least of these who are members of my family, you did it to me" (Matt 25:40). In a similar vein, the author of the letter to the Hebrews reminds us of the moral obligation to offer hospitality to strangers for, like Abraham and Sarah, they might be entertaining angels (Heb 13:2). Hospitality to strangers is a fundamental expression of the Christian faith and its mandate of charity. Refusal to extend hospitality can have greater consequences than those endured by the people of Sodom (Luke 10:12; cf. 9:54). Thus, hospitality to the stranger is not only a moral or Christian duty but an esteemed virtue, and the reward for those who practice it is priceless (Ps 41:1).

HOSPITALITY TO STRANGERS AS RELIGIOUS VIRTUE

Hospitality to strangers was a highly regarded virtue worldwide and by many religions in antiquity.[33] For the ancient Greeks, hospitable treatment of strangers was a mark of civility and piety.[34] In Homeric literature, just as in the Jewish biblical tradition (Gen 18:2–8; cf. Heb 11:13), the divine frequently took on the appearance of a stranger.[35] For the Romans hospi-

---

32. Koenig, *New Testament Hospitality*; see also Byrne, *The Hospitality of God*. For a concise survey of the texts in Luke-Acts which deal with hospitality, see Denaux, "The Theme of Divine Visits and Human (In)Hospitality in Luke-Acts," 255–79.

33. See Nguyen, "An Asian View of Biblical Hospitality," 445–59.

34. Roth, "The Theme of Corrupted Xenia," 1–17, here 2; Bolchazy, *Hospitality in Early Rome*, 2 and 14.

35. In the *Odyssey*, for example, Athena frequently appeared in various disguises to assist Odysseus, since she was Odysseus' special patroness. Three examples are worth mentioning. Athena, who is the goddess of victory and wisdom, appeared in various disguises to assist Odysseus: as a young maiden carrying a pitcher (*Od.* 7.19), as an

tality was divinely sanctioned, because receiving a stranger was obedience to divine will and therefore *ius Dei or* divine law.[36] According to Cicero, hospitality to a guest had become something sacred, even more lofty than receiving a friend: ". . .I will not say that you were bound to him by friendship, which is the most glorious thing in the world, nor by hospitality, which is the most sacred (*hospitem, quod sanctissimum est*). . ."[37]

For Asians, hospitality to strangers is considered an important religious virtue. In the Buddhist tradition, the teaching of "Dana" (generosity or hospitality) is a basic virtue that every Buddhist must practice from the beginning stages of the spiritual life.[38] Without Dana, Enlightenment can never be achieved. Taoism too teaches much about compassion and hospitality: "Relieve people in distress as speedily as you must release a fish from a dry rill [lest he die]. Deliver people from danger as quickly as you must free a sparrow from a tight noose. Be compassionate to orphans and relieve widows. Respect the old and help the poor."[39]

The Prophet Muhammad also teaches the importance of hospitality to the stranger. The Qur'an states:

> Be kind to parents, and the near kinsman, and to orphans, and to the needy, and to the neighbor who is of kin, and to the neighbor who is a stranger, and to the companion at your side, and to the traveler, and to [slaves] that your right hands own. Surely God loves not the proud and boastful such as are niggardly, and bid other men to be niggardly, and themselves conceal the bounty that God has given them. (*Qur'an* 4.36–37)

The world's great religious traditions have long affirmed the connection between religion and hospitality to strangers. The Judeo-Christian traditions especially highlight this motif, not only as a moral responsibility but as a spiritual practice, a way of life or a *habitus*. Since hospitality is love

---

ordinary man (*Od.* 8.193), and as a beautiful skilled woman (*Od.* 16.156).

36. Bolchazy, 25. For a complete text of Livy's *History of Rome* (also known as *Ab Urbe Condita*), see http://etext.lib.virginia.edu/etcbin/browse-mixed-new?id=Liv1H is&tag=public&images=images/modeng&data=/texts/english/modeng/parsed (accessed on March 1, 2009).

37. Cicero, *Orationes Verrinae* 2.2.110, quoted from Bolchazy, 26. Bolchazy correctly noted that hospitality to a stranger is a lofty virtue because offering to friends comes naturally, but to a guest it requires more motivation and altruism (91n44).

38. http://ratnaghosa.fwbo.net/danatwo.html (accessed on September 20, 2010).

39. Taoism, *The Tract of the Quiet Way*; see http://www.sacred-texts.com/tao/ycw/ ycw03.htm (accessed on September 25, 2010).

in action, it is the most appropriate response to the immigration and migration issue today.[40]

CONCLUSION

It is said that migration is as old as history. While migration is certainly not a new phenomenon, it is however a major crisis of our epoch. Every day millions of people are relentlessly on the move. Some travel for the purpose of tourism. Others do it for business. Many however migrate because of political, economic, and ecological reasons. While international migration from Asia has slowed down significantly, migration within the Asian region has increased in the last two decades and will continue to grow as newly industrialized countries in Asia demand more male and female foreign workers. The contemporary trends of labor migration in Asia, particularly of feminization in migration, have caused serious issues and raised many concerns about the treatment of the vulnerable migrants.

The brief survey of Israel's ancestors as sojourners and of the Hebrew Scriptures' legal codes concerning the immigrants serves as a "paradigm" for Christians and host countries in the Asian region today. First of all, God loves the vulnerable immigrants and therefore demands that we do the same: "For the LORD your God is God of gods and the Lord of lords, the great God, mighty and awesome, who is not partial and takes no bribe, who executes justice for the orphan and the widow, and who loves the strangers, providing them food and clothing. You shall also love the stranger, for you were strangers in the land of Egypt" (Deut 10:17–19). Furthermore, the Bible challenges us to love the strangers "as one of [our] native born. Love him [or her] as yourself" (Lev 19:34). Secondly, God holds everyone responsible—from individual to society—to assist and care for the immigrants because to neglect their cry is a sin (Deut 24:14–15; 27:19).

In the New Testament, Jesus is consistently portrayed as a stranger, guest, host, and even as food. Such depictions of Jesus highlight the virtue of hospitality. Jesus teaches that when someone feeds the hungry, gives water to the thirsty, clothes the naked, cares for the sick, and visits the prisoner, in other words, welcomes a stranger, he or she does it for Christ himself (Matt 25:31–46). Furthermore, since hospitality is an esteemed religious virtue in many religious traditions, especially those that are being practiced in Asia,

---

40. See Pohl, "Responding to Strangers," 81–101. This article provides moral, theological and practical insights for contemporary responses to the needs of refugees, asylum seekers and immigrants. For further helpful reflection on the issue of immigration today, see Soerens and Hwang, *Welcoming the Stranger*.

welcoming the strangers is the most appropriate response to the worldwide phenomenon of migration today. There are many ways to practice hospitality. We can begin by being generous with and practicing charity to our friends and neighbors. But we cannot and must not end there! The religious practice of hospitality must go beyond family, acquaintances, and even fellow citizens. Genuine hospitality reaches out to those we do not yet know, particularly to the immigrants who are in our midst. By extending ourselves to these vulnerable ones we might not only entertain angels but actually meet God face to face.

Bibliography

Abogunrin, Samuel Oyin. "Luke." In *The International Bible Commentary: A Catholic and Ecumenical Commentary for the Twenty-First Century*, edited by William R. Farmer, 1368–1437. Collegeville, MN: Liturgical, 1998.

Ackroyd, Peter. *The First Book of Samuel*. Cambridge, England: The University Press, 1971.

Albright, William F. "From the Patriarchs to Moses." *The Biblical Archaeologist* 36 (1973) 7–15.

Anderson, Arnold A. *2 Samuel*. Word Biblical Commentary 11. Dallas, TX: Word, 1989.

Anderson, Gerald H. *Witness to World Christianity: The International Association for Mission Studies, 1972–2012*, with John Roxborough, John M. Prior, SVD, and Christoffer H. Grundmann. New Haven, CT: OMSC Publications, 2012.

Arnold, Bill T. *Genesis*. The New Cambridge Bible Commentary. Cambridge, England: Cambridge University Press, 2009.

———. *1 & 2 Samuel*. The NIV Application Commentary. Grand Rapids, MI: Zondervan, 2003.

Arnold, Clinton E. *Powers of Darkness: Principalities and Powers in Paul's Letters*. Downers Grove, IL: InterVarsity, 1992.

Asamoah-Gyadu, J. Kwabena. "'To the Ends of the Earth:' Mission, Migration and the Impact of African-led Pentecostal Churches in the European Diaspora." *Mission Studies* 29.1 (2012) 23–44.

Asis, Maruja M. B. *Understanding International Migration in Asia*. Exodus Series 2; Quezon City, Philippines: Scalabrini Migration Center, 2005.

Auge, Mark. *Non-Places: Introduction to an Anthropology of Supermodernity*. London: Verso, 1997.

Bae, Hyunju. "Dancing around Life: An Asian Woman's Perspective." *The Ecumenical Review* 56 (2004) 390–403.

Baggio, Fabio. "The Migrant Ministry: Concern of the Catholic Church." *Asian Christian Review* 4 (2010) 47–69.

Bakke, Raymond. *The Urban Christian*. Downers Grove: InterVarsity, 1987.

Baldwin, Joyce G. *1 & 2 Samuel*. Tyndale Old Testament Commentaries. Downers Grove, IL: InterVarsity, 1988.

Barclay, John M. G. *Jews in the Mediterranean Diaspora: From Alexander to Trajan (323 BCE—117 CE)*. Edinburgh: T. & T. Clark, 1996.

Barnes, Albert. *Acts of the Apostles*. Notes on the New Testament Series. Grand Rapids, MI: Baker, 1953.

Barram, Michael. "The Bible, Mission, and Social Location: Toward a Missional Hermeneutic." *Interpretation* 43 (2007) 42–58.

Battistella, Graziano. "The Poor in Motion: Reflections on Unauthorized Migration." *Asian Christian Review* 4 (2010) 70–81.

Bauer, Walter and Frederick William Danker, ed. *A Greek-English Lexicon of the New Testament and Other Early Christian Literature*, 3rd ed. (BDAG). Chicago: University of Chicago Press, 2000.

Benedict XVI. *92nd World Day for Refugees and Migrants Message*, 2006.

Berkhof, Hendricus, and Philip Potter. *Key Words of the Gospel*. London: SCM, 1964.

Biddle, Mark E. *Deuteronomy*. Macon, GA: Smyth & Helwys, 2003.

Bock, Darrell L. *Acts*. Grand Rapids, MI: Baker Academic, 2007.

Boff, Leonardo. *Faith on the Edge: Religion and Marginalized Existence*. Trans. Robert R. Barr. San Francisco: Harper & Row, 1989.

Boice, James Montgomery. *Acts: An Expositional Commentary*. Grand Rapids, MI: Baker, 1997.

Bolchazy, Ladislaus. *Hospitality in Early Rome: Livy's Concept of Its Humanizing Force*. Chicago: Ares, 1997.

Bonora, Antonio. "Lo 'Straniero' in Deuteronomio," *Parola Spirito e Vita* 27 (1993) 25–36.

Boring, M. Eugene. "The Gospel of Matthew." In *The New Interpreter's Bible*, vol. viii, edited by Leander E. Keck et al., 89–505. Nashville: Abingdon, 1995.

Bosch, David. *Transforming Mission: Paradigm Shifts in Theology of Mission*. Maryknoll, NY: Orbis, 1991.

Bouma-Prediger, Steven, and Brian J. Walsh. *Beyond Homelessness: Christian Faith in a Culture of Displacement*. Grand Rapids, MI: Eerdmans, 2008.

Brand, Chad, Charles Draper, and Archie England, eds. *Holman Illustrated Bible Dictionary*. Nashville, TN: Holman Bible Publishers, 2003.

Brändle, Rudolf, and Ekkehard W. Stegemann. "The Formation of the First 'Christian Congregations' in Rome in the Context of the Jewish Congregations." In *Judaism and Christianity in First-Century Rome*, edited by Karl P. Donfried and Peter Richardson, 117–27. Grand Rapids, MI: Eerdmans, 1998.

Branson, Mark Lau, and Juan F. Martinez. *Churches, Cultures and Leadership: A Practical Theology of Congregations and Ethnicities*. Downers Grove, IL: IVP Academic, 2011.

Brown, Len. "Mayor's Message." *LINKZ* 51 (2012) 6. Online: http://www.ssnz.govt.nz/publications/LINKZ_Issue51.pdf.

Brownson, James V. "Speaking the Truth in Love: Elements of a Missional Hermeneutic." *International Review of Mission* 83 (1994) 479–504.

Bruce, F. F. *The Book of the Acts*. The New International Commentary on the New Testament Series. Grand Rapids, MI: Eerdmans, 1988.

Brueggemann, Walter. *David's Truth in Israel's Imagination and Memory*. 2nd ed. Minneapolis, MN: Fortress, 2002.

———. *First and Second Samuel*. Interpretation: A Bible Commentary for Teaching and Preaching. Louisville, KY: John Knox, 1990.

———. *Genesis*. Atlanta: John Knox, 1982.

———. *The Land: Place as Gift, Promise, and Challenge in Biblical Faith*. 2nd ed. Minneapolis, MN: Fortress, 2002.

Buber, Martin. "The Man of Today and the Jewish Bible." In *The Writings of Martin Buber*, edited and introduced by Will Herberg, 242–43. New York: World, 1957.

Burnett, David. *God's Mission: Healing the Nations*. Kent, England: Sending the Light, 1986.

Butcher, Andrew and George M. Wieland. "'Go From Your Country': Missiological Reflections on Asian Christians in New Zealand." *Stimulus* 18.1 (2010) 2–8.

Butler, Trent C. *Luke*. Holman New Testament Commentary 3. Nashville: Broadman & Holman, 2000.

Byrne, Brendan. *The Hospitality of God: A Reading of Luke's Gospel*. Collegeville, Minnesota: Liturgical, 2000.

Caldeira, Theresa P. R. "Fortified Enclaves: The New Urban Segregation." In *Theorizing the City: The New Urban Sociology Reader*, edited by Setha M. Low, 83–107. New Brunswick, NJ: Rutgers University Press, 2005.

Camarota, Stephen A., and Karen Zeigler. "A Shifting Tide: Recent Trends in the Illegal Immigrant Population." Center for Immigration Studies July 2009. No pages. Online: http://cis.org/IllegalImmigration-ShiftingTide.

Campese, Gioacchino. "¿CuantosMás?: The Crucified Peoples at the U.S.-Mexico Border." In *A Promised Land, A Perilous Journey: Theological Perspectives on Migration*, edited by Daniel G. Goody and Gioacchino Campese, 271–98. Notre Dame, IN: University of Notre Dame Press, 2008.

Cardellini, Innocenzo. "Stranieri ed 'emigrati-residenti' in una sintesi de teologia storico biblica." *Rivista biblica* 40 (1992) 129–81.

Carroll R., M. Daniel. "Biblical Perspectives on Migration and Mission: Contributions from the Old Testament." *Mission Studies* 30.1 (2013) 9–26.

———. *Christians at the Border: Immigration, the Church, and the Bible*. Grand Rapids, MI: Baker Academic, 2008.

Carter, Warren. *Matthew and the Margins*. Maryknoll, NY: Orbis, 2000.

Casey, Edward S. *The Fate of Place*. Berkeley, CA: University of California Press, 1997.

Castles, Stephen. "The Myth of the Controllability of Difference: Labour Migration, Transnational Communities and State Strategies in East Asia." No pages. Online: http://www.unesco.org/most/apmrcast.htm#attitudes.

Castles, Stephen, and Mark J. Miller. *The Age of Migration: International Population Movements in the Modern World*. Fourth Edition. Revised and Updated. New York: Palgrave Macmillan, 2009.

Catalyst: Social Pastoral Journal for Melanesia. "AIDS Belief and Culture in PNG." 39.2 (2009) special issue.

Chin, Moses. "A Heavenly Home for the Homeless: Aliens and Strangers in 1 Peter." *Tyndale Bulletin* 42 (May 1991) 96–112.

Clendenen, E. Ray. "Peace." In *Holman Illustrated Bible Dictionary*, edited by Chad Brand, Charles Draper, Archie England, et al. Logos Bible Software. Nashville, TN: Holman Bible Publishers, 2003.

Cornelius, Wayne A. "Controlling 'Unwanted' Immigration: Lessons from the United States, 1993–2004." Working paper 92, The Center for Comparative Immigration Studies, University of California, San Diego (2004). No pages. Online: http://www.ccis-ucsd.org/publications/wrkg92.pdf.

Craigie, Peter C. *The Book of Deuteronomy*. New International Commentary on the Old Testament. Grand Rapids, MI: Eerdmans, 1976.

Cruz, Gemma Tulud. "Migration in the Asia Region: Retrospect and Prospects." In *Migration and Interculturality: Theological and Philosophical Challenges*, edited by Raul Fornet-Betancourt, 21–30. Aachen: Institute of Missiology, 2004. No pages. Online: http://www.sedos.org/english/cruz_2.htm.

Culpepper, R. Alan. "Luke." In *The New Interpreter's Bible*, vol. IX, 1–490. Nashville, TN: Abingdon, 1995.

Cotter, David W. *Genesis*. Berit Olam Series. Collegeville, MN: Liturgical Press, 2003.

De Ridder, Richard. "Old Testament Roots of Mission." In *Exploring Church Growth*, edited by Wilbert R. Shenk, 171–80. Grand Rapids, MI: Eerdmans, 1983.

———. *Discipling the Nations*. Grand Rapids, MI: Baker, 1975.

Denaux, Adelbert. "The Theme of Divine Visits and Human (In)Hospitality in Luke-Acts." In *The Unity of Luke-Acts*, edited by J. Verheyden, 255–79. Leuven: University Press, 1999.

Doran, Robert. *Birth of a Worldview: Early Christianity in Its Jewish and Pagan Context*. Boulder, CO: Westview, 1995.

Effa, Alan L. "Releasing the Trigger: The Nigerian Factor in Global Christianity." *International Bulletin of Missionary Research* 37.4 (2013) 214–17.

Escobar, J. Samuel. "Mission Fields on the Move." *Christianity Today* 54.3 (2010) 28–31.

Evans, Mary. *1 and 2 Samuel*. New International Biblical Commentary. Peabody, MA: Hendrickson Publishers, 2000.

Feld, Steven and Keith H. Basso. *Senses of Place*. Santa Fe, NM: School of American Research Press, 1996.

Feldmeier, Reinhard. "The 'Nation' of Strangers: Social Contempt and Its Theological Interpretation in Ancient Judaism and Early Christianity." In *Ethnicity and the Bible*, edited by Mark G. Brett, 241–70. Leiden: Brill, 1996.

Ferguson, Everett. *Backgrounds of Early Christianity*. Third Edition. Grand Rapids, MI: Eerdmans, 2003.

Fernando, Ajith. *Jesus Driven Ministry*. Wheaton, IL: Crossway. 2002.

Finegan, Jack. *Light from the Ancient Past: The Archeological Background of Judaism and Christianity*, volume I. Princeton, NJ: Princeton University Press, 1959.

Finn, Thomas M. *From Death to Rebirth: Ritual and Conversion in Antiquity*. New York: Paulist, 1997.

Flemming, Dean. "Exploring a Missional Reading of Scripture: Philippians as a Case Study." *Evangelical Quarterly* 83.1 (2011) 3–18.

Foucault, Michel. "Of Other Spaces." *Diacritics* 16.1 (Spring 1986) 22–27.

France, R.T. *The Gospel of Matthew*. Grand Rapids: Eerdmans, 2007.

Francis I. *Apostolic Exhortation Evangelii Gaudium*. Rome, Italy: Vatican Press, 2013.

Gallagher, Robert L., and Paul Hertig, eds. *Mission in Acts: Ancient Narratives in Contemporary Context*. Maryknoll, NY: Orbis, 2004.

Gallagher, Sarita D. "Blessing on the Move: The Outpouring of God's Blessing through the Migrant Abraham." *Mission Studies* 30.2 (2013) 147–61.

Gerhard Hoffmann. "Solidarity with Strangers as Part of the Mission of the Church." *International Review of Mission* 78 (1989) 53–61.

Giddens, Anthony. *The Consequences of Modernity*. Cambridge: Polity, 1990.

Glasser, Arthur F., with Charles E. Van Engen, Dean S. Gilliland, and Shawn B. Redford. *Announcing the Kingdom: The Story of God's Mission in the Bible*. Grand Rapids, MI: Baker Academic, 2003.

Goheen, Michael W. "Continuing Steps Towards a Missional Hermeneutic." *Fideles* 3 (2008) 49–99.

Goleman, Daniel. *Emotional Intelligence: Why It Can Matter More Than IQ.* New York: Bantam, 1995.

Gornik, Mark R., and Maria Liu Wong. "Christ in the Capital of the World: How Global Christians are Revitalizing NYC Far Beyond Manhattan." *Christianity Today* 57.7 (2013) 38–43.

Gottdiener, Mark, and Ray Hutchison. *The New Urban Sociology.* Fourth ed. Boulder, CO: Westview, 2011.

Gottwald, Norman K. *The Tribes of Yahweh: A Sociology of the Religion of Liberated Israel, 1250–1050 B.C.E.* Maryknoll, NY: Orbis, 1979.

Green, Edward C., and Allison Herling Ruark. *AIDS, Behavior, and Culture. Understanding Evidence-based Prevention.* Walnut Creek: Left Coast, 2011.

Groody, Daniel G. "Fruit of the Vine and Work of Human Hands: Immigration and the Eucharist." In *A Promised Land, A Perilous Journey: Theological Perspectives on Migration,* edited by Daniel G. Goody and Gioacchino Campese, 299–315. Notre Dame, IN: University of Notre Dame Press, 2008.

Gunkel, Hermann. *Genesis.* Translated by Mark E. Biddle. Macon, GA: Mercer University Press, 1997.

Gushee, David P. "Our Missing Moral Compass." *Christianity Today* 49.11 (2005) 88. Online: http://www.christianitytoday.com/ct/2005/november/27.88.html.

Halpern, Baruch. *David's Secret Demons: Messiah, Murderer, Traitor, King.* Grand Rapids, MI: Eerdmans, 2001.

Hamilton, Victor P. "Genesis." In *The Baker Illustrated Bible Commentary,* edited by Gary M. Burge and Andrew E. Hill, 5–49. Grand Rapids: Baker, 2012.

Hanciles, Jehu J. *Beyond Christendom: Globalization, African Migration, and the Transformation of the West.* Maryknoll, NY: Orbis, 2008.

———. "Migrants as Missionaries, Missionaries as Outsiders: Reflections on African Christian Presence in Western Societies." *Mission Studies* 30.1 (2013) 64–85.

———. "Migration and Mission: Some Implications for the Twenty-first-Century Church." *Missiology: An International Review* 27.4 (2003) 146–53.

Harrison, Ronald K. "Madness." In *The Interpreter's Dictionary of the Bible an Illustrated Encyclopedia,* vol. 3, edited by George Arthur Buttrick, 220–21. Nashville, TN: Abingdon, 1962.

Hartley, John E. *Leviticus.* Word Biblical Commentary 4. Dallas, TX: Word, 1992.

Hasulie, Huberto. "Ke Malaysia Mengadu Nasib. Laporan Awal tentang Perantauandari Flores." Maumere: Candraditya Research Centre, 2012. Unpublished electronic manuscript.

Heidegger, Martin. "Building Dwelling Thinking." In *Martin Heidegger: Basic Writings,* edited by D. Krell, 319–39. New York: Harper & Row, 1977.

Heifetz, Ronald A., and Marty Linsky. *Leadership On The Line: Staying Alive through the Dangers of Leading.* Boston, MA: Harvard Business School Press, 2002.

Herzog II, William R. *Jesus, Justice, and the Reign of God: A Ministry of Liberation.* Louisville: Westminster John Knox, 2000.

Hesselgrave, David J. "A Missionary Hermeneutic: Understanding Scripture in the Light of World Mission." *International Journal of Frontier Missions* 10 (1998) 17–20.

Hiebert, Paul G., R. Daniel Shaw, and Tite Tiénou. *Understanding Folk Religion: A Christian Response to Popular Beliefs and Practices.* Grand Rapids, MI: Baker, 1999.

Hiebert, Paula S., "'Whence Shall Help Come to Me?': The Biblical Widow." In *Gender and Difference in Ancient Israel*, edited by Peggy L. Day, 125–41. Minneapolis: Fortress, 1989.

Hoffmaier, James K. *The Immigration Crisis: Immigrants, Aliens, and the Bible*. Wheaton, IL: Crossway, 2009.

Holmgren, Fredrick C. "Looking Back on Abraham's Encounter with a Canaanite King: A Reversal of Expectations (Genesis 20:1–18)." *Currents in Theology and Mission* 37.5 (2010) 366–77.

Hondagneu-Sotelo, Pierrette, Genelle Gaudinez, Hector Lara, and Billie C. Ortiz. "*There's a Spirit that Transcends the Border*: Faith, Ritual and Postnational Protest at the U.S.-Mexico Border." *Sociological Perspectives* 47 (2, 2004) 133–59.

Hoover, Robin. "The Story of Humane Borders." In *A Promised Land, A Perilous Journey: Theological Perspectives on Migration*, edited by Daniel G. Goody and Gioacchino Campese, 160–73. Notre Dame, IN: University of Notre Dame Press, 2008.

Hoppe, Leslie J. "Israel and Egypt: Relationships and Memory." *The Bible Today* 45 (July/August 2007) 209–13.

Horsley, Richard A. *Galilee: History, Politics, People*. Valley Forge: Trinity Press International, 1995.

Hugo, Graeme. "Migration in the Asia-Pacific Region," A paper prepared for the Policy Analysis and Research Programme of the Global Commission on International Migration, September 2005. No pages. Online: http://www.gcim.org/mm/File/Regional%20Study%202.pdf.

Hunsberger, George R. "Proposals for a Missional Hermeneutic: Mapping a Conversation." *Missiology* 39.3 (2011) 309–21.

Inge, John. *A Christian Theology of Place*. Burlington, VT: Ashgate, 2003.

Jeffers, James S. *The Greco-Roman World of the New Testament Era: Exploring the Background of Early Christianity*. Downers Grove, IL: InterVarsity, 1999.

John Paul II. "Message for the 1995 World Migration Day."

Johnson, Luke Timothy. *The Acts of the Apostles*. Collegeville, MN: Liturgical, 1992.

Johnson, Todd M., and Gina A. Bellofatto. "Key Findings of Christianity in Its Global Context, 1970–2020." *International Bulletin of Missionary Research* 37.3 (2013) 157–64.

———. "Migration, Religious Diasporas, and Religious Diversity: A Global Survey." *Mission Studies* 29.1 (2012) 3–22.

Johnstone, Patrick. *The Future of the Global Church: History, Trends and Possibilities*. Downers Grove, IL: InterVarsity, 2011.

Kahl, Werner. "Intercultural Hermeneutics—Contextual Exegesis: A Model for 21st Century Exegesis." *International Review of Mission* 89 (2000) 421–33.

Kahn, Miriam, "Your Place and Mine: Sharing Emotional Landscapes in Wamira, Papua New Guinea." In *Senses of Place*, edited by Steven Feld and Keith H. Basso 167–96. Santa Fe: School of American Research Press, 1996.

Kaiser, Walter C. *Mission in the Old Testament: Israel as a Light to the Nations*. Grand Rapids, MI: Baker Academic, 2000.

Karris, Robert J. "The Gospel according to Luke." In *The New Jerome Biblical Commentary*, edited by Raymond E. Brown, Joseph A. Fitzmyer, and Roland E. Murphy, 675–721. Englewood Cliffs, NJ: Prentice Hall, 1990.

Keller, Marie Noël. *Priscilla and Aquila: Paul's Coworkers in Christ Jesus.* Collegeville, MN: Liturgical, 2010.

Kerwin, Donald. "The Natural Rights of Migrants and Newcomers: A Challenge to U.S. Law and Policy." In *A Promised Land, A Perilous Journey: Theological Perspectives on Migration,* edited by Daniel G. Goody and Gioacchino Campese, 192–209. Notre Dame, IN: University of Notre Dame Press, 2008.

Kidner, Derek. *Genesis: An Introduction and Commentary.* Tyndale Old Testament Commentaries. London: Tyndale, 1967.

Klein, Ralph W. *1 Samuel.* Word Biblical Commentary. Dallas, TX: Word, 1983.

Koenig, J. *New Testament Hospitality: Partnership with Strangers as Promise and Mission.* Philadelphia: Fortress, 1985.

Koser, Khalid. *International Migration: A Very Short Introduction.* Oxford, England: Oxford University Press, 2007.

Kupp, David D. *Matthew's Emmanuel: Divine Presence and God's People in the First Gospel.* Cambridge: Cambridge University Press, 1996.

Lee, Sang Hyun. *From A Liminal Space: An Asian American Theology.* Minneapolis: Augsburg Fortress, 2010.

Lemche, Niels Peter. "Habiru, Hapiru." In *ABD* 3:6–10.

Lenchak, Timothy A. "Israel's Refugee Ancestors." *The Bible Today* 35 (1997) 11–15.

Levine, Amy-Jill. "Matthew's Advice to a Divided Readership." In *The Gospel of Matthew in Current Study,* edited by David E. Aune, 22–41. Grand Rapids, MI: Eerdmans, 2001.

———. "Ruth." In *The Women's Bible Commentary,* edited by Carol A. Newson and Sharon H. Ringe, 78–84. London: SPCK, 1992.

———. *The Social and Ethnic Dimensions of Matthean Salvation History.* Lewiston: Edwin Mellen Press, 1988.

Lingenfelter, Sherwood G. *Agents of Transformation: A Guide for Effective Cross-Cultural Ministry.* Grand Rapids, MI: Baker, 1996.

———. *Transforming Culture: A Challenge for Christian Mission.* Second edition. Grand Rapids, MI: Baker, 1998.

Longenecker, Richard N. "Acts." In *John and Acts,* vol. 9 of *The Expositor's Bible Commentary with the New International Version,* edited by Frank E. Gæbelein, 205–573. Grand Rapids, MI: Zondervan, 1981.

Low, Setha M., and Denise Lawrence-Zuniga. *The Anthropology of Space and Place: Locating Culture.* Malden, MA: Blackwell, 2003.

Magonet, Jonathan. "Abraham and God." *Judaism* 33.2 (1984) 160–70.

Malherbe, Abraham J., ed. *The World of the New Testament.* Austin, TX: R. B. Sweet, 1967.

Malina, Bruce. *The Social World of Jesus and the Gospels.* London/New York: Routledge, 1996.

Maloney, Robert P. "Priscilla and Aquila Set Out Again: A Profile of the Lay Catholic in the 21st Century." *America Magazine* 188 (August 2003) 7–9.

Malony, H. N. "Mad." In *The International Standard Bible Encyclopedia,* vol. 3, edited by James Orr, 1960–61. Vol. 3. Grand Rapids, MI: Eerdmans, 1947.

Maruskin, Joan M. *Immigration and the Bible: A Guide to Radical Welcome.* New York: United Methodist Women's Schools of Missions, 2012.

Masenya, Madipoane. "Ruth." In *Global Bible Commentary,* edited by Daniel Patte, 86–91. Nashville: Abingdon, 2004.

McCarter, P. Kyle. *1 Samuel*. The Anchor Bible. Garden City, NY: Doubleday, 1980.

⸻. *II Samuel*. The Anchor Bible. Garden City, NY: Doubleday, 1984.

Miles, Jack. *God: A Biography*. New York: Alfred A. Knopf, 1995.

Miller, Patrick D. *Deuteronomy*. Interpretation: A Bible Commentary for Teaching and Preaching. Louisville, KY: John Knox, 1990.

Mowinckel, Sigmund. *Religion und Kultus*. Göttingen, Germany: Vandenboeck & Ruprecht, 1953.

Murphy-O'Connor, Jerome. "Prisca and Aquila: Traveling Tentmakers and Church Builders." *Bible Review* 8 (1992) 40–51, 62.

Murphy, Patrick. "The Ninety-Nine Sheep and the Mission of the Church: The Pastoral Care of Hispanic Immigrants." In *A Promised Land, A Perilous Journey: Theological Perspectives on Migration*, edited by Daniel G. Goody and Gioacchino Campese, 141–59. Notre Dame, IN: University of Notre Dame Press, 2008.

Mutombo-Mukendi, Felix. *La théologie Politique Africaine: Exégèse et Histoire*. Paris: L'Harmattan, 2011.

Myers, Ched and Matthew Colwell. *Our God is Undocumented: Biblical Faith and Immigrant Justice*. Maryknoll: Orbis, 2012.

Nelson, Richard. *First and Second Kings*. Interpretation: A Bible Commentary for Teaching and Preaching. Louisville, KY: John Knox, 1987.

Nguyen, vanThanh, SVD. "Asian in Motion: A Biblical Reflection on Migration." *Asian Christian Review* 4.2 (2010) 18–31.

⸻. "An Asian View of Biblical Hospitality." *Vidyajyoti Journal of Theological Reflection* 74 (2010) 445–59.

⸻. "In Solidarity with the Strangers: The Flight into Egypt." *The Bible Today* 45.4 (2007) 219–24.

⸻. "Migrants as Missionaries: The Case of Priscilla and Aquila." *Mission Studies* 30.2 (2013) 194–207.

Noordtzij, Arie. *Leviticus*. Bible Students Commentary. Translated by Raymond Togtman. Grand Rapids, MI: Zondervan, 1982.

O'Kane, Martin. "The Flight Into Egypt: Icon of Refuge for the H(a)unted. In *Borders, Boundaries and the Bible*, edited by Martin O'Kane, 15–60. Sheffield: Continuum, 2002.

Okoye, James Chukwuma. *Israel and the Nations: A Mission Theology of the Old Testament*. American Society of Missiology Series 39. Maryknoll, NY: Orbis, 2006.

Overberg, Kenneth R. *Ethics and AIDS: Compassion and Justice in Global Crisis*. Oxford: Rowman & Littlefield, 2006.

Palmer, Parker J. *The Company of Strangers: Christians and the Renewal of America's Public Life*. New York, NY: Crossroad, 1994.

Passel, Jeffrey S., and D'Vera Cohn. "Unauthorized Immigrant Population: National and State Trends, 2010." Pew Hispanic Center (February 1, 2011). No pages. Online: http://www.pewhispanic.org/2011/02/01/unauthorized-immigrant-population-brnational-and-state-trends-2010/.

Paterson, Gillian, ed. *HIV Prevention: A Global Theological Conversation*. Geneva: Ecumenical Advocacy Alliance, 2009.

Peterson, Eugene H. *First and Second Samuel*. Westminster Bible Companion. Louisville, KY: Westminster John Knox, 1999.

Pettena, Maurizio. *Migration in the Bible*. Exodus Series 2. Quezon City, Philippines: Salabrini Migration Center, 2005.

Phiri, Isabel Apawo. "Ruth." In *Africa Bible Commentary*, edited by Tokunboh Adeyemo, 319–24. Grand Rapids: Zondervan, 2006.

Plaskow, Judith. "Contemporary Reflection." In *The Torah: A Woman's Commentary*, edited by Tamara Cohn Eskenazi and Andrea L. Weiss, 107–8. California: Women of Reform Judaism, 2008.

Pohl, Christine D. "Responding to Strangers: Insights from the Christian Tradition." *Studies in Christian Ethics* 19.1 (2009) 81–101.

Pope Benedict XVI. Address at the general audience on February 7, 2007. No pages. Online: http://www.ewtn.com/library/papaldoc/b16ChrstChrch29.htm.

Provan, Iain. *1 and 2 Kings*. New International Biblical Commentary. Peabody, MA: Hendrickson, 1995.

Reed, W. L. "Beard." In *The Interpreter's Dictionary of the Bible an Illustrated Encyclopedia*, vol. 1, edited by George Arthur Buttrick, 368. Nashville, TN: Abingdon, 1962.

Rendtorff, Rolf. "The *Ger* in the Priestly Laws of the Pentateuch." In *Ethnicity and the Bible*, edited by Mark G. Brett, 77–87. Leiden: Brill, 1996.

Ricoeur, Paul. *Interpretation Theory: Discourse and the Surplus of Meaning*. Fort Worth: Texas Christian University Press, 1976.

Robinson, Bob. *Jesus and the Religions: Retrieving a Neglected Example for a Multicultural World*. Eugene, OR: Cascade, 2012.

Rödlach, Alexander, "Reflections of a Missionary-Anthropologist on the Response of the Society of the Divine Word to HIV/AIDS." *Verbum SVD* 52 (2011) 287–305.

Rodman, Margaret. "Empowering Place: Multilocality and Multivocality." In *The Anthropology of Space and Place: Locating Culture*, edited by Setha M. Low and Denise Lawrence-Zuniga, 204–223. Malden, MA: Blackwell, 2003.

Rodman, Margaret. *Masters of Tradition: Consequences of Customary Land Tenure in Longana, Vanuatu*. Vancouver: University of British Columbia Press, 1987.

Rogers Jr., Cleon L., and Cleon L. Rogers III. *The New Lingustic and Exegetical Key to the Greek New Testament*. Grand Rapids, MI: Zondervan, 1998.

Roth, Paul. "The Theme of Corrupted Xenia." *Mnemosyne* 46 (Feb 1993) 1–17.

Roxburgh, Alan J. *Missional: Joining God in the Neighborhood*. Grand Rapids, MI: Baker, 2011.

———. *The Missionary Congregation, Leadership, and Liminality*. Harrisburg: Trinity, 1997.

Rutgers, Leonard V. "Roman Policy toward the Jews: Expulsions from the City of Rome during the First Century C.E." In *Judaism and Christianity in First-Century Rome*, edited by Karl P. Donfried and Peter Richardson, 93–116. Grand Rapids, MI: Eerdmans, 1998.

Sanders, Cheryl J. *Ministry at the Margins: The Prophetic Mission of Women, Youth and the Poor*. Downers Grove: InterVarsity, 1997.

Savage, Mike, Alan Warde, and Kevin Ward. *Urban Sociology, Capitalism and Modernity*. Second ed. New York: Palgrave MacMillan, 2003.

Schwarz, Nick, ed. *Blessed are the Virtuous? Evangelicals and Pentecostals in Papua New Guinea Speak about HIV/AIDS*. Point No.35. Goroka: Melanesian Institute, 2012.

Selman, M. J. "Hospitality." In *New Bible Dictionary*. 3rd ed. Downers Grove, IL: InterVarsity, 1996.

Senior, Donald, and Carroll Stuhlmueller. *The Biblical Foundations for Mission*. Maryknoll, NY: Orbis, 1983.

Senior, Donald. "'Beloved Aliens and Exiles': New Testament Perspectives on Migration." In *A Promised Land, A perilous Journey: Theological Perspective on Migration*, edited by Daniel G. Groody and Gioacchino Campese, 20–33. Notre Dame, IN: University of Notre Dame Press, 2008.

Sheldrake, Philip. *Spaces for the Sacred: Place, Memory, and Identity*. Baltimore: The Johns Hopkins University Press, 2001.

Smillie, Gene R. "'Even the Dogs': Gentiles in the Gospel of Matthew." *Journal of the Evangelical Theogical Society* 45 (2002) 73–97.

Smith, David I., and Barbara Carvill. *The Gift of the Stranger: Faith, Hospitality, and Foreign Language*. Grand Rapids, MI: Eerdmans, 2000.

Soerens, Matthew, and Jenny Hwang. *Welcoming the Stranger: Justice, Compassion and Truth in the Immigration Debate*. Downers Grove, IL: InterVarsity, 2009.

Soja, Edward W. *Postmodern Geographies: The Reassertion of Space in Critical Social Theory*. New York: Verso, 1989.

Sontag, Susan. *Illness as Metaphor and Aids and its Metaphors*. London: Penguin, 1991.

Spina, Frank. "Israelites as *gērîm*, 'Sojourners,' in Social and Historical Context." In *The Word of the Lord Shall Go Forth*, edited by Carol Meyers and M. O'Connor, 321–35. Winona Lake, IN: Eisenbrauns, 1983.

Stott, John R.W. *The Message of Acts: The Spirit, the Church and the World*. The Bible Speaks Today Series. Downers Grove, IL: InterVarsity, 1990.

Tomasi, Silvano M. "The World-wide Context of Migration: The Example of Asia." In *Migrants and Refugees*, edited by Dietmar Mieth and Lisa Sowle Cahill, 3–10. Concilium 1993/4; Maryknoll, NY: Orbis, 1993.

Trumbull, Mark. "Illegal Immigrants: Which States Have Lost the Most?" *Christian Science Monitor* (Sept. 2, 2010). No pages. Online: http://www.csmonitor.com/.

Tuan, Yi-Fu. "Language and the Making of Place: A Narrative-Descriptive Approach." *Annals of the Association of American Geographers* 81.4 (1991) 684–96.

———. *Space and Place: The Perspective of Experience*. Minneapolis: University of Minnesota Press, 1977.

Turner, Victor Witter. *Dramas, Fields, and Metaphors: Symbolic Action in Human Society*. London: Cornell University Press, 1974.

———. *The Ritual Process: Structure and Anti-structure*. Chicago: Aldine, 1969.

Upkong, Jason. "Inculturation Hermeneutics: An African Approach to Biblical Interpretation." In *The Bible in a World Context: An Experiment in Contextual Hermeneutics*, edited by W. Dietrich and U. Luz, 17–32. Grand Rapids, MI: Eerdmans, 2002.

Van Engen, Charles. "Biblical Perspectives on the Role of Immigrants in God's Mission." *Evangelical Review of Theology* 34.1 (2010) 29–43.

———. *The Growth of the True Church*. Amsterdam: Rodopi, 1981.

Van Gelder, Craig, *The Ministry of the Missional Church: A Community Led by the Spirit*. Grand Rapids, MI: Baker, 2007.

Van Gelder, Craig, and Dwight J. Zscheile. *The Missional Church in Perspective: Mapping Trends and Shaping the Conversation*. Grand Rapids, MI: Baker Academic, 2011.

Van Gennep, Arnold. *Rites of Passage*. Chicago, IL: The University of Chicago Press, 1960.

Vawter, Bruce. *On Genesis: A New Reading*. Garden City, NY: Doubleday, 1977.

Von Rad, Gerhard. *Genesis*. London: W. L. Jenkins, 1961.

Wagner, Ross. "*Missio Dei*: Envisaging an Apostolic Reading of Scripture." *Missiology* 37.1 (2009) 19–32.

Walker, William O. "The Portrayal of Aquila and Priscilla in Acts: The Question of Sources." *New Testament Studies* 54 (2008) 479–95.

Walls, Andrew F. "Mission and Migration: The Diaspora Factor in Christian History." *Journal of African Christian Thought* 5.2 (2002) 3–11.

————. *The Missionary Movement in Christian History: Studies in the Transmission of Faith.* Maryknoll, NY: Orbis, 1996.

Weber, Max. "The Three Types of Legitimate Rule." *Society and Institutions* 4 (1958) 1–11.

Wenham, Gordon J. *Genesis 1–15.* Word Biblical Commentary 1. Waco, TX: Word, 1987.

West, G. O. "Contextual Bible Reading: A South African Case Study." *Analecta Bruxellensia* 11 (2006) 131–48.

Westermann, Claus. *Blessing in the Bible and the Life of the Church.* Philadelphia: Fortress, 1978.

————. *Genesis 12–36.* Minneapolis: Augsburg, 1985.

Wieland, George M. "Roman Crete and the Letter to Titus." *New Testament Studies* 55 (2009) 338–54.

Williams, Rowan. "Augustine and the Psalms." *Interpretation: A Journal of Bible and Theology.* 58 (2004) 17–27.

Witherington, Ben, III. *The Acts of the Apostles: A Socio-Rhetorical Commentary.* Grand Rapids, MI: Eerdmans, 1998.

Wolters, Albert M. "Confessional Criticism and the Night Visions of Zechariah." In *Renewing Biblical Interpretation,* vol. 1 of The Scripture and Hermeneutics Series, edited by Craig Bartholomew, Colin Greene, and Karl Möller, 90–117. Grand Rapids: Zondervan, 2000.

Wright, Christopher J. H. *The Mission of God: Unlocking the Bible's Grand Narrative.* Downers Grove, IL: InterVarsity, 2006.

Subject Index

www.ingramcontent.com/pod-product-compliance
Lightning Source LLC
Chambersburg PA
CBHW061734270326
41928CB00011B/2234